AEROSPACE FLOW

Gerard Leone
Richard D. Rahn

Flow Publishing Inc.
Boulder, Colorado

Aerospace Flow
By Gerard Leone, Richard Rahn

Published by:

Flow Publishing Inc.
7690 Watonga Way
Boulder, Colorado 80303
(303) 494-4693
www.flowpublishing.com
contact@flowpublishing.com

ISBN: 0-9713031-5-0

Printed in the United States of America.

Portions of this book are based on the white paper "The Fundamentals of Flow Manufacturing", a collaborative effort between Business Process Consulting Group and J.D. Edwards, and were used with the permission of the authors.

All of the case studies included in this book are for illustrative and educational purposes only. Any resemblance to an actual company is completely coincidental.

Publishers Cataloging In Publication

Leone, Gerard and Rahn, Richard D.

Aerospace Flow by Gerard Leone and Richard D. Rahn

Includes bibliographical references and index.

ISBN 0-9713031-5-0 (pbk.)

1. Industrial efficiency.
2. Value added.
3. Just-in-time systems.
4. Production management.
5. Industrial management.

TABLE OF CONTENTS

TABLE OF CONTENTS

TABLE OF CONTENTS

PREFACE

Preface to *Aerospace Flow*

When we first published *Fundamentals of Flow Manufacturing* in September 2002, the aerospace industry was only one of many possible audiences for the flow manufacturing methodology. While we had consulted with aerospace companies, and one of us worked directly for an aerospace company for seven years, we had also implemented flow manufacturing in many other industries: automotive, agricultural equipment, medical products, pharmaceuticals, air conditioning, computers and electronics, electric motors, rail cars, and others. Our feeling was, and is, that the flow manufacturing approach can be adapted to any industry with outstanding results. We never apply a dogmatic or cookie-cutter approach to flow manufacturing, and our successes have come from an intelligent application of the foundation concepts to what is always a unique company environment.

It must be admitted, however, that some industries are more conducive than others to the flow/lean manufacturing strategy. A higher volume, repetitive manufacturing environment is a natural for the tools of takt time, kanban, line balancing and single-piece flow. It's not surprising that flow and lean manufacturing methods dominate in these types of industries. The Toyota Motor Company, for example, was instrumental in introducing, formalizing and documenting many of the techniques that today we call flow or lean manufacturing. The application of flow manufacturing methods in other environments often requires more creativity, more selectivity of methods, and perhaps more of a leap of faith. So what about the aerospace industry?

The importance of the U.S. aerospace industry in undeniable. Economically the industry generates about 15% of the total U.S. GNP, and employs over 600,000 people. It is the leader in export revenue, generating $30 Billion in export sales in 2002. It is critical for the national defense. And from a flow manufacturing perspective, the aerospace industry is still just emerging from the stone age. Of course there are always exceptions, and maybe your company is one of them. In general, however, aerospace has shown little fundamental improvement over the last decade, unlike the steady improvement seen in other industries like automotive and electronics. So where do we go from here?

Michael G. Beason, who served as a Baldrige examiner in the early 1990s and the Awards Council Chair for the California awards program in the late 1990s, developed the Process Maturity Model (PMM), the structure for what we are calling the *Lean Enterprise System* (LES) documented in this book. A pilot implementation for the Process Maturity Model was

PREFACE

conducted with the help of a team of professionals at Solar Turbines in San Diego. Two years later Solar won the Baldrige Award.

As Michael describes in the following foreword, the use of the word *Enterprise* in the term *Lean Enterprise System* is deliberate and important. In too many cases flow or lean manufacturing is treated only as a set of tools and methods to achieve specific operational goals like inventory reduction, productivity or quality improvements. It is not surprising to find that initial successes often prove hard to sustain. Once the initial team involved in a flow manufacturing project or Kaizen event is disbanded, the environment can quickly return to its prior state. When the process improvement champion is promoted or transferred, momentum often stalls. For these reasons the LES places great emphasis on two additional elements: *Leadership and Culture* and *Workforce Development* in addition to *Operational Excellence.*

The literature on flow and lean manufacturing is large and growing, and in these few pages we cannot hope to address all of the challenges that will arise when attempting to implement flow in your company. However, the LES approach is not a theoretical model that ignores your environment and culture. It is grounded in common sense, time proven methods, personal implementation experience, and customer successes. Rest assured that *Aerospace Flow* will serve as an excellent reference for your journey into the world of globally competitive manufacturing.

Gerard Leone
Richard D. Rahn
September 2003

PREFACE

Preface to *Fundamentals of Flow Manufacturing*

The philosophy and methods of flow manufacturing are being introduced quickly across the globe and a manufacturing company, in any industry, cannot hope to be successful long-term without using flow methods. Many companies introduced flow in the 1990's, and entire industries today are largely converted: automotive, heating and air conditioning, electronics. Other industries are just getting started. Opportunities still abound in service and non-manufacturing environments, like financial services, software development, health care and government.

Practitioners and students of flow manufacturing are frequently disappointed to find that there is little practical, down-to-earth information available on the subject, although certainly there are many books available for the reading. Most of the publications available today are either highly philosophical, obscure, or just plain difficult to apply. General concepts and case histories are interesting, but at the end of the day most people are looking for something they can use.

Is it possible to create a cookbook of flow manufacturing formulas and techniques that can be adapted easily to any manufacturing environment? Probably not. If anything, we have found that each company, each plant, is unique in many ways: people, products, processes, culture, systems, history, markets. "One size fits all" clothing usually doesn't fit very well. Paradoxically, the best flow implementations take place when the teams, team leaders and mentors understand the basics well, and then adapt them to the specific environment with intelligence and common sense. Implementations that tend *not* to go well are those that try to apply a predefined formula. Outside mentors or consultants can help you get up the learning curve more quickly, and can help keep you on the road to success. Ultimately, however, you'll have to do it yourself.

We hope that you find this book interesting, useful, and a practical resource on your flow manufacturing journey. Let us know how you're doing.

Gerard Leone
Richard Rahn
September 2002

FOREWORD

THE SEA
LEAN
ENTERPRISE
SYSTEM

Michael G. Beason

THE SEA LEAN ENTERPRISE SYSTEM

Few people in the Aerospace and Defense industries would argue that competition on a worldwide basis is now a supply chain problem. The competitiveness of our American industries is directly related to the weakest link. The solution is no longer only a Boeing solution, or a Northrop solution, or a Lockheed solution, but rather a solution that must include the entire supply chain. It is not the elegance of the solution that matters, but rather the paradigm in which it is implemented. In other words, it is more important that we make take action now, rather than make no progress while we develop the perfect plan.

The SEA Lean Enterprise System ("SEA LES") described below was designed to be simple. Perhaps it embodies the lesser-used meaning of elegant: "neat, simple, and concise." SEA LES provides a common language. It gives us a common vocabulary, one based on the language of process maturity. It also acknowledges that long-term sustainability of improvements relies on enterprise-wide solutions and well-managed change.

The following paragraphs explain the elements of the SEA Lean Enterprise System.

PROCESS MATURITY

Process Maturity and cost are directly related. The higher the process maturity, the lower the cost of quality. Baldrige award-winning companies demonstrate this truth on a continuing basis. They are more profitable and consistently produce higher return on investment because of their intense focus on process maturity.

The PMM was developed as an aid for companies who wanted to assess themselves using the Baldrige Criteria and as a management tool to assist in the management of overall process improvement. Companies often find the Baldrige scoring guidelines difficult to use and especially when most self-assessment is conducted without training on the criteria. The PMM simplifies the process.

Because the PMM serves as the backbone for all process improvement efforts, it provides for long term integration of all improvement approaches, including lean and Six Sigma. Various levels of process maturity are applied one process at a time. In other words, the model is used to define the maturity level of a process, not a function, department, or company.

THE SEA LEAN ENTERPRISE SYSTEM

Specific tools and their use are generally available from many sources. For now, we will focus on an overview of the PMM.

Level 1: The process has been identified, defined, and has an owner.

The beginning stages of process improvement are confirmed by the identification of a process. Before this stage, the process does not have an official name. Everyone calls it something different and everyone thinks of it as containing different steps with different beginning and ending points. As the process moves into Level 1, it gains an official name to which everyone refers when speaking about the process.

Also in this stage, the scope of the process, that is, the steps that are a part of the process and where the process begins and ends, becomes defined. The most direct way to ensure that everyone agrees on the scope is to draw a high-level Value Stream Map of the process. A deployment flowchart is often a valuable tool for this step because it denotes the various departments or functions for each step in the process. It also shows the transfers from one step to another. At this stage, the map of the process is often at the "50,000 foot level," meaning that it is not very detailed and only seeks to show the major steps and their sequence along with the beginning and ending of the process.

It is hard to imagine going very far with process improvement efforts if there isn't someone who is accountable for the improvement effort. A *Process Owner* is therefore an essential starting point. A Process Owner is often a person who works in the process, or someone who manages the process, or someone who is already accountable for most of the process. Their current job position is less important than whether they are capable of leading and motivating others to make improvements.

Level 2: The process has been documented to the work instruction level.

In higher levels of maturity, a process is at its best when there is very little variation. This state is only achieved through the development of standard work procedures. Achieving standard work procedures is, in part, a matter of documentation and training.

THE SEA LEAN ENTERPRISE SYSTEM

Most companies have achieved ISO or AS9100 certification, or have developed some internal process documentation. If they haven't, they should at least be on their way. These disciplines ensure that critical processes have policies and procedures established. They don't, however, always ensure that the work instructions suitable for certification of workers are present.

In this step, the establishment of work instructions is guided by their usefulness for the workforce, and for trainers who will conduct job skills certification. Good work instructions can be turned into a training guide and used to ensure consistency in a skills certification training program.

Our modern workforce is often multi-national. Foreign-born workers for whom English is not their native language often have difficulties with written work instructions in English. To compensate for this literacy barrier, work instructions are often more effective in visual, graphical form. Instead of describing how to set up a machine in four different languages, and risk that the operator doesn't read any of them, visual instructions can be created easily by taking a series of pictures of the process and training the employee by using graphical work instructions. Pictures can be also mounted on the wall in the form of a poster as a quick reminder of how to set up the machine.

If a task is complex and prone to variation due to operator error, a job aid such as a checklist, a fixture, or a tool is often used to increase the effectiveness of the quality of the work.

Documentation is not complete without a plan for corrective action. Corrective action plans are contingency plans that must be followed by the person performing the process when something out of the ordinary occurs.

Level 3: The process has certified trainers and is standardized

The focus at this level is standardization of work processes. Someone working in a process may progress through three levels to achieve mastery.

> Level 1: Completed training in how to do something using the work instructions
> Level 2: Certified by a master trainer as capable of following the work instructions
> Level 3: Certified by a master trainer as capable of training someone else

THE SEA LEAN ENTERPRISE SYSTEM

At this level, not only are the standard procedures followed to a high degree of conformance, but the corrective actions must also be followed. Therefore all work, whether normal to the process, or abnormal, follows a standard work procedure.

This level ensures that most special causes of variation have been eliminated, leaving those causes of variation that are inherent to the process itself.

Many experts argue that until Level 3 is completely achieved, you cannot actually improve a process. Most quality systems are based on this principle, including ISO, AS9100, and CMMI for software. Management doesn't always want to hear that. It is certainly true, however, that until you understand a process fully, and that includes all of its sources of variation, you will have a hard time defining an improvement that doesn't interact with others causes. The result is often to produce a net zero benefit, or even a deterioration in process quality.

Consider a process that is defined more by company culture than by a documented standard process. The people working in the process consider it an "art" rather than a science. As we work to standardize the process, the culture rebels against changes. Small islands of resistance spawn variations of how the process should be done. As each improvement is made, aiming to further standardize the process, the resistance adapts some changes, partially adapts others, and some changes are not adapted at all. The amount of variation in the process increases, taking us further from our goal.

Until the process is verifiably standardized in every respect, we cannot be sure that other sources of variation will not interact with any changes we make, increasing the variation and at least counteracting any improvements we might desire.

However, standardization on a poorly-designed process will yield less than optimum results. Kaizen events are used continuously to "lean out" the process, to eliminate wasted time, to reduce setup time and lot sizes, to improve lead-time, and to reduce inventory. Given this constant state of change, it is important that the Process Owner understand the responsibility for bringing the process back to Level 3 at the end of each Kaizen event. Documentation and work instructions should be revised and re-issued by the end of an event. Everyone can be trained and re-certified in the new work instructions and procedures.

THE SEA LEAN ENTERPRISE SYSTEM

Level 4 – the process is under process control, is analyzed, and improved using data.

The focus of this level is the introduction of statistical methods for the analysis and improvement of processes. Statistical Control is the application of analytical methods to reduce defects. Statistical controls can help us in a number of ways:

1. They provide a scientific method for triggering corrective action. If a process being monitored using statistical controls begins to vary above or below the norm, any person within the process who has been trained can take action to correct a defect before it occurs.

    For instance, consider that the temperature in a food processing line is an important variable. If the temperature is too high or too low, the food is ruined. Temperature can be monitored and if the temperature begins to vary outside the normal range, it signals the operator to take some prescribed action to correct the problem before the food is ruined.

2. Statistical controls help us to prevent "tampering". Tampering occurs when someone implements a change without understanding the process or underlying cause of a problem. When a solution is applied without this knowledge, it often causes more variation and more defects rather than less. Tampering, although well-intentioned action by those who should know, is often the reason why a process cannot achieve lower defect rates. Tampering exists mainly in a Level 1 or 2 process where standardization has not yet been achieved.

3. Statistical controls enable us to find root causes of variation in processes that already produce very few defects. Sometimes the source of variation and defects is subtle, and to improve a process beyond a certain threshold takes a more rigorous and scientific approach.

There is some debate about when Level 4 has been achieved. The Six Sigma camp believes that Level 4 requires that a process achieve a defect rate of no more than 3.4 parts per million opportunities, while others believe that a process can be in statistical control before it achieves such a low level of defects.

THE SEA LEAN ENTERPRISE SYSTEM

The purpose of Level 4 is to achieve a state of process control. Level 5 will specify the results that accrue from a process with very low defect rates.

Level 5 – the process shows continuous positive trends and benchmarks work world-class.

The focus of this level is comparison against world-class benchmarks of performance. At one time, achieving a defect rate of no more than 3.4 parts per million might have qualified anyone as an industry leader, but today, as more and more companies pursue Six Sigma to reduce process variation, a number of industry leaders may have achieved this level of performance. In these cases we look for broader definitions for "world-class."

The Baldrige Criteria introduced the concept of industry leadership by formally assigning a scoring approach, and a definition for comparing processes to determine industry-leading performance.

The norm for examination was to look for five years of progressively better performance along with industry-leading comparisons. The key issue in achieving Level 5 process maturity is to establish what the standard for industry-leading performance is. The greatest difficulty is to separate and distinguish between industry-leading companies and industry-leading process performance.

A company with an industry-leading process may not always be an industry leader. An industry leader may have a process that is *not* industry-leading. Baldrige-winners typically fall into the scoring range of 550 to 1000 points. This means they can win the Baldridge award and still have a lot of room for improvement.

Therefore, finding Level 5 comparison metrics may not always be achieved by the most obvious comparisons. It is best to collect a range of metrics with various companies in the upper third of an industry. This can be accomplished via a benchmarking agreement or via an industry association that agrees to collect data and protect its anonymity.

THE SEA LEAN ENTERPRISE SYSTEM

Roadmap to Process Maturity

How will we implement the SEA Lean Enterprise System?

▼ Process Maturity Levels

5. The process shows continuous positive trends and benchmarks world class
4. The process is under process control, is analyzed, and improved using data
3. The process has certified trainers and is standardized
2. The process has been documented to the work instruction level
1. The process has been identified, defined, and has an owner

	▶ Level 1	▶ Level 2	▶ Level 3	▶ Level 4	▶ Level 5
Criteria	• Value-Stream Map Complete • Process Owner Assigned	• Detailed Value-Stream Map • Process Documentation • Work Instructions • Training Guide	• Workers Certified • Process Training Complete • Job Skills Certification • ISO/AS9100/CMM	• Process Control Plan • Corrective Action Plan • Improvement Cycles	• Positive Trends • World Class Benchmarks
Leadership & Culture	• Performance Improvement Team • SEA Lean Enterprise System • Strategic Planning • Balanced Scorecard • Value-Stream Mapping	• Process Maturity Goals • Change Management Plan	• Implement Change Management Plan • Leadership Development		
Workforce Development	• Basic Skills • Team Development • Value-Stream Mapping	• Process Maturity • Continuous Improvement • Value-Stream Mapping	• 5S • Standard Work • Visual Workplace • Cells • Job Skills Certification • Cross-Training • Problem-Solving • Continuous Improvement • TPM • Quick Changeover/SMED	• Measurement • Statistical Tools • Process Analysis • Decision-Making	• Specific/Advanced Development
Operational Excellence	• Improvement Initiatives • Champions • Process Owners • Process Maturity Levels	• Teams • Project Priorities & Scope • Baseline Metrics • Value-Stream Map	• Improvement Approach • Customer Requirements • Stable Workflow	• Critical to Quality Characteristics • Performance Metrics • Process Capability • Variation Sources • Action Plans • New Performance Objectives	• Sustainable Results

Roadmap to Process Maturity

The Roadmap defines the developmental steps needed to progress to Level 5 maturity. The progress is incremental, and trying to skip steps may mean that you have to go back later, when you find that you needed to complete the steps in order to make further progress.

Consider the achievement of AS9100 certification. You could argue that because you don't have an outside customer demanding certification, you might escape having to adopt this quality system. And in that respect, it might seem a logical conclusion. Later on, when trying to achieve a higher level of maturity, you might find that your workforce and management team lack the discipline of managing processes to a high level of conformance to documented standards. Achieving AS9100 turns out to be both a cultural

THE SEA LEAN ENTERPRISE SYSTEM

and a technical achievement. Both are valuable in sustaining overall performance. The lack of either can undermine all your hard work.

In just in the same way, fully accomplishing all of the elements on the Roadmap is advisable in order to sustain improvement. The Roadmap represents the minimum development required to achieve long-term sustained performance improvements. The band called "Criteria" is simply the prior discussion in this chapter turned into a few key points. These are the minimum requirements to qualify for a particular level.

The remaining bands, Leadership & Culture, Workforce Development, and Operational Excellence, contain specific items important to the development of a high level of process maturity.

LEVEL 1

Level 1 - Leadership and Culture

Performance Improvement Team
The Performance Improvement Team consists of senior managers. These are the managers who will lead the overall improvement effort.

SEA Lean Enterprise System
The Performance Improvement Team will learn the SEA Lean Enterprise System, an industry-wide system for integrating all performance improvement activities.

Strategic Planning
The Performance Improvement Team will ensure that it has a schedule for activities related to the strategic planning process and develop a mission, vision, and values to drive the performance improvement effort.

Balanced Scorecard
The Performance Improvement Team will develop a balanced scorecard of 3-5 deployable measures to be used to drive the improvement effort.

Value Stream Mapping
The Performance Improvement Team will cause a high-level Value Stream Map to be developed for all of the critical macro-level processes in the business.

THE SEA LEAN ENTERPRISE SYSTEM

Level 1 - Workforce Development

Basic Skills
The Performance Improvement Team will commission an assessment to discover the level of basic skills including English and math skills within the workforce.

Team Development
The Performance Improvement Team will cause team development activities to be scheduled and conducted in order to promote a high level of collaboration on an ongoing basis.

Value Stream Mapping
The teams for each critical process will assist in the development of a Value Stream Map for that process.

Level 1 - Operational Excellence

Improvement Initiatives
The Performance Improvement Team will prioritize improvement initiatives. Improvement initiatives are broad strategic decisions that may encompass many activities over the next few years. For instance, some companies will determine that implementing lean production is a key initiative. Others will determine that integrating a new technology to capture market share in a new market is key to the future of the enterprise.

Champions
A member of the Performance Improvement Team is made accountable for each Improvement Initiative. Champions coordinate the efforts of Process Owners.

Process Owners
Process Owners usually work in the process or are in some way a key stakeholder for the process. They are aligned with a process that often spans multiple departments, thereby cutting across functional barriers.

Process Maturity Levels
A list of critical processes is created. The list is made up of five to ten key processes from each function. Each process is assigned a maturity level based on the PMM and its criteria.

THE SEA LEAN ENTERPRISE SYSTEM

LEVEL 2

Level 2 – Leadership and Culture

Process Maturity Goals
The Performance Improvement Team approves goals and action plans for all critical processes. These goals have been developed by Process Owners and Champions.

Change Management Plan
The Performance Improvement Team develops a Change Management Plan that defines how change will be managed throughout the organization. A Change Management Plan usually addresses communication, planning, reward, recognition, decision-making, and performance management at a minimum. The change management plan defines how these activities will change to support the LES. The change management plan helps to build a change-ready organization.

Level 2 – Workforce Development

Process Maturity
An inventory of critical processes yields a critical process list with initial process maturity levels assigned to each. This is the starting point for goals and priority-setting in the continuous improvement process.

Continuous Improvement
The continuous improvement process can be supported by providing problem-solving, decision-making, and continuous improvement training to the workforce. When continuous improvement is only located among managers and engineers, the pace of improvement is slow and "great ideas" are rarely adopted by the workforce.

Value Stream Mapping
A clear understanding of a process can be developed by having a team develop a Value Stream Map. Two types of maps are usually developed. The first is a "Current-State" map, showing the process as it is today. The second is a "Future-State" map, showing how the process will work after improvements are made.

THE SEA LEAN ENTERPRISE SYSTEM

LEVEL 3

Level 3 – Operational Excellence

Teams
Teams align resources to critical process improvement efforts. Team improvement projects ensure buy-in and faster implementation of change. Most improvements are made as a result of a Kaizen Event involving a team in making rapid improvements.

Project Priorities and Scope
It's important that improvement projects be prioritized and staged according to how they align with primary initiatives for improvement. For instance, if customer satisfaction is a primary initiative across the organization, then projects that can improve customer service should take priority.

Just as important is the scoping of an improvement project. A Kaizen Event is a controlled experiment. An hypothesis is formed as an objective. For instance, it might be that setup time on a machine can be reduced by 50%. The methods for reducing the setup time are known in advance. The team will be trained to understand and implement those methods. In this manner, the scope of the project is set not as an investigation, but rather as a series of steps that can definitely be accomplished by the team within the timeframe allowed for the event. Scoping early projects correctly is extremely important because if projects are too large and don't get completed with measurable results, the improvement effort loses momentum.

Baseline Metrics
Measures of current and past performance are used to establish a baseline before improvements are made. It's important to be able to quantify results from improvement efforts so that return-on-investment is always foremost in everyone's mind.

Value Stream Map
The Value Stream Map can be annotated with baseline metrics, times, and distances to describe the performance of the current process.

THE SEA LEAN ENTERPRISE SYSTEM

LEVEL 4

Level 4 – Leadership and Culture

Implement Change Management Plan
The entire senior management team implements the change management plan. Senior management has to look for visible ways to signal that things have changed and will continue to change.

Leadership Development
Leadership development activities should always be ongoing. There are many drivers for leadership development including ensuring a viable succession plan, and continually challenging managers to think outside the boundaries of their organization.

Level 4 – Workforce Development

Measurement
An important part of developing a scientific workforce is to develop a working knowledge of how and when to measure. The use of measures promotes data-based driven problem-solving.

Statistical Tools
As the workforce skills mature, the use of statistical tools for problem-solving and process management become more important. The organization cannot effectively move to higher levels of defect prevention without the use of statistics.

Process Analysis
As teams, cells, and workgroups move to higher levels of defect prevention, the techniques of process analysis become more important.

Decision-Making
Teams move to higher levels of maturity and begin to make decisions affecting their own work process. Decision-making skills promote more effective decisions.

THE SEA LEAN ENTERPRISE SYSTEM

Level 4 – Operational Excellence

Critical to Quality Characteristics
An effective improvement system links itself to the voice of the customer. The most critical characteristics in the eyes of the customer are often called "critical to quality" characteristics. Measurement of opportunities for defects depends on a differentiation of each of these characteristics.

Performance Metrics
Leadership develops a high level scorecard to define what organizational measures are important. This is often called a "balanced scorecard". Managers are challenged to craft performance metrics by linking the scorecard to measures within their own departments.

Process Capability
As statistical controls are introduced, a determination of process capability enables a clear understanding of what is possible and where to set control limits.

Variation Sources
Sources of variation become more important as statistical controls gain increased usage.

Action Plans
Action plans are generated by teams that analyze failure sources for root causes of failures.

New Performance Objectives
Performance objectives includes new measures and stretch goals to challenge continuing improvement efforts.

LEVEL 5

Level 5 – Leadership and Culture

Implement Change Management Plan
The leadership team continues to monitor and implement the change plan.

Leadership Development
Leadership development is a year year-round activity.

THE SEA LEAN ENTERPRISE SYSTEM

Level 5 – Workforce Development

Specific and Advanced Development
A sophisticated workforce is one that has continuing needs for development. At higher levels of maturity, a training system is evident and ongoing assessment links performance improvement needs to key performance objectives.

Level 5 – Operational Excellence

Sustainable Results
At higher levels of maturity, measures indicate the self-sustaining nature of continuous improvement. Sporadic results come from sporadic continuous improvement efforts.

THE SEA LEAN ENTERPRISE SYSTEM

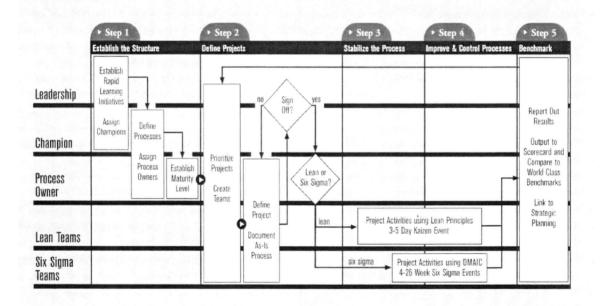

Blueprint for Operational Excellence

How will we manage improvement projects?

Blueprint for Operational Excellence

The cornerstone of Operational Excellence is the improvement system. Organizations can't wait until things "calm down" to turn their attention to improvements. When improvements are needed, there is never enough time to focus on them. Making improvements needs to be like payroll: you do it weekly like clockwork, or the whole system falls apart. What stands in the way? Survival. If you create an organizational context that you're always in survival mode, then everyone is excused to go spend twelve hours a day putting out fires. The time to dig your way out is always now. Later could be too late.

THE SEA LEAN ENTERPRISE SYSTEM

Examinations of some of the best companies find that world world-class companies not only do all of the right things, but they also link their activities and operate them as a coherent system, a step by step process where roles and responsibilities are clear and required actions have been defined.

The SEA Blueprint for Operational Excellence embodies the best practices of Baldrige award-winning companies. The aerospace prime members of SEA contributed to this model and validated parts that have already worked for their best-in-class suppliers.

Step 1 – Establish the Structure

This step is often skipped by organizations and it is common to see project improvement activities that are not well-linked to goals and top-level measures. Setting the structure establishes sponsorship and ownership. It lays the groundwork for accountability for process improvement. It is the structure for establishing a broad range of employee involvement activity linked to key improvement efforts.

Establish Rapid Learning Initiatives
All improvement efforts are also learning efforts. You set a goal to improve time to time-to-market on new products. You assign a champion and a Process Owner. They map the process and believe that they can achieve a 20% reduction by implementing several new ideas. They try it. Sometimes it works right away. More often it doesn't and they learn things. Many Rapid Learning Initiatives rely on Rapid Learning Events or Kaizens. These speed up the learning because they often take the form of a 4-5 day intensive project. The idea is to speed up the experimentation and learning. The leadership team establishes the Kaizen events that will drive overall improvement efforts.

Assign Champions
As important as developing a Kaizen culture is assigning a champion to take on the initiative. Most initiatives are cross-functional and therefore champions are challenged to work outside their normal functional boundaries. Champions are most often members of the leadership team. Their job is to provide resources and clear away barriers to improvement.

Define Processes
The first step in establishing a process improvement effort is the development of a high-level Value Stream Map. This map defines the key elements of the process and helps to ensure that duplication doesn't occur. The champion and Process Owner work together on this step.

THE SEA LEAN ENTERPRISE SYSTEM

Assign Process Owners
The Process Owner is the day-to-day driver of improvement. While the champion's job is to clear the way and provide resources, the Process Owner builds a team and sets the pace of improvement. The champion selects the Process Owner with the agreement of the leadership team.

Establish Maturity Level
The first time a process maturity level is set, it is self-evaluated by the Process Owner and champion. Later, a more rigorous process of auditing and inspection can be established. The main purpose of using a process maturity system is to provide a method by which improvement efforts can be accurately categorized and used in the performance management system. Process Owners should have incentives for achieving higher levels of process maturity and goals in their performance plan related to process maturity.

Step 2 – Define Projects
Project definition is often a haphazard affair and can often be executed by one person in a vacuum. Careful consideration of projects can lead to less wasted effort and more usable output.

Prioritize Projects
Prioritizing projects is an important activity for leadership, champions, and Process Owners to collaborate on. Dedicating people's time to process improvement is an investment decision because it allocates significant resources and therefore deserves leadership attention. And yet decisions about project priorities are often made poorly, without any criteria, or without input from all individuals affected. Project priorities should be set in light of key customer priorities and a good estimate of the return on investment.

Create Teams
Team selection should occur after project prioritization. The team should be made up of at least 50% of the people who work in the process, 25% of those who either supply the process or are customers of the process, and the rest are those from outside the process altogether. The reason for including people who are outside the process and know little about it is that people inside the process often cannot see solutions outside of their prevailing paradigm.

THE SEA LEAN ENTERPRISE SYSTEM

Define Projects
The Process Owner and the team define the project. Two initial project-definition steps that are very important are (1) setting the project scope correctly, and (2) establishing the measurable goals.

The scope of the project should be intentionally "tight" so as to ensure that the project is achievable within the timeframe allowed, usually no more than 5 days. The best improvement projects are those where 80% of the improvements are made during the project time itself. Walking away from a project with a long list of action items is the kiss of death for most improvement efforts. People have work to catch up on when they leave an improvement project. Generating a long list of things to do sets the team up to experience failure. The events should be engineered to experience achieve success.

The measurable objectives of a project are derived from the concept of the improvement project as a scientific experiment. Improvement projects are not searches for the unknown. Rather, they are scientific experiments well thought thought-out and planned before they begin. In an experiment, we have a theory. If I believe that I can achieve A, then I have a theory that by doing B and C, I will achieve A. Thus the best improvement projects proceed as an experiment where we know that we will be doing B and C, and we expect to achieve A within the specified time of the project.

Document As-Is Process
Start with understanding. It is a well-established fact that most teams do not agree initially on how a process actually works. Even worse, they truly do not know. The task of mapping the Current-state process establishes how the process is actually performed and often uncovers an unbelievable amount of variation in how the process is actually performed.

Sign-Off
With the basics completed to define the project, leadership is asked to sign-off on the project or projects. Most improvement efforts consist of a series of short projects and therefore the best approach is to seek sign-off on the plan and schedule for the next year.

THE SEA LEAN ENTERPRISE SYSTEM

Lean or Six Sigma?
The decision about what approach to use is often easy for those who understand the process and its level of maturity. The lean approach involves one or more short improvement projects called Kaizen Events. These events are typically five days or less. The Six Sigma approach involves projects that are often longer in duration. Although they can be shorter, they are most often in the range of 13 to 26 weeks.

In general, the guidelines for selecting the lean approach suggest that if a process is Maturity Level 3 or below, the lean approach is best. The lean approach is also indicated if a process has not been through 5S, or if a major layout change is planned.

Step 3 – Stabilize the Process
A stable process is one that produces fewer errors and has a higher level of predictability. Stable processes have fewer special causes of error. An example of a special cause might be someone performing the process slightly differently than the normal method. This might result from a training deficiency or a lack of training altogether.

Project Activities using Lean Principles
Lean projects often remove steps that don't add value, re-arrange work areas and process flows, and generally work to optimize effectiveness within a particular work area. In this step, lean projects focus on lean methods that help to improve stability such as standard work, job certification and cross-training, visual workspace, and pull signals.

Project Activities using DMAIC
Six Sigma projects generally seek to reduce variation in a process that is stable and highly mature. The distance from three-sigma to six-sigma is one that is often a result of changing the metrics and analytical approach used to manage and improve the process. For instance, a process that formerly used "yield" as a measure might change to using "rolled throughput yield" in order to uncover the hidden operations and the lack of "first pass" quality throughout the process. Lower error rates require new and more advanced approaches to analysis and improvement.

The DMAIC model stands for Define, Measure, Analyze, Improve, and Control. In this step, this model is used to promote better process stability and predictability.

THE SEA LEAN ENTERPRISE SYSTEM

Of course, the overall goal of Six Sigma is equally as important, and a culture change that must be managed by leadership. The goal of uncompromising quality throughout the enterprise can continue the reduction of cost of quality throughout the enterprise long after most visible methods for identification of improvement projects has disappeared from leadership's view.

Step 4 – Improve & Control Processes
In this step, lean and Six Sigma projects begin to focus on process control more than stability because stability, for the most part, has been achieved.

Project Activities using Lean Principles
Lean improvement projects activities focus on self-management and team control of processes. Statistical process controls can be used in appropriate areas. Capability studies lead to control charts as a foundation for the process control system. Regular "stand-up" reviews of work areas and cells gives the team the opportunity to demonstrate their self-management skills.

Project Activities using DMAIC
In this step, the focus of projects begins to turn to process controls as processes gain more and more stability.

Step 5 – Benchmark
Highly mature processes often get classified as "world-class" and improvement stops. But when world-class benchmarks are identified and compared to current levels of performance, improvement starts again.

Report- Out Results
As important as the improvements themselves are the "report-outs". Building enthusiasm and giving recognition for improvement efforts is a key role for leadership. Teams should be assisted in the development of their presentations. Report-outs occur on the final day of the project and focus first on measurable results.

The bigger the audience, the better, but it is absolutely essential that the management team attends report-outs and be highly visible. Report-outs are an opportunity for senior leaders to re-enforce the role of improvements in the bigger picture of the division and company.

THE SEA LEAN ENTERPRISE SYSTEM

SEA Lean Enterprise System

What are the key elements of the lean enterprise system?

Operational Excellence
- Pull Systems
- Standard Work
- Flexible Layout
- Rapid Changeover
- Visual Factory/5S
- Six Sigma
- Value Stream Mapping
- Supply Chain Development
- Total Productive Maintenance
- Mistake Proofing/Corrective Action
- SPC, FMEA, DOE
- AS9100
- Process Maturity Model

Workforce Development
- Lean Measurements
- Job & Process Certification
- Change Management
- Work Area Teams
- Problem-Solving
- Kaizen Events
- Leadership From Within
- Leaders As Coaches

Leadership & Culture
- Performance Improvement Team
- Process Owners
- Team Leaders
- Balanced Scorecard
- Strategy Deployment
- Change Management

THE SEA LEAN ENTERPRISE SYSTEM

Output to Scorecard and Compare to World World-Class Benchmarks
Although overall scorecards are more likely to show change and improvement more slowly, it is important to keep a running picture of progress against world-class benchmarks.

Link to Strategic Planning
Overall improvement efforts should be linked to strategic plans. Strategic planning efforts should define specific improvements that support overall goals, competitiveness, and customer satisfaction.

The SEA Lean Enterprise System

The SEA Lean Enterprise System captures the best practices for manufacturing enterprise improvement with a model with three key focus areas. The reason for these three areas is to emphasize the importance of a total organizational approach to managing the transformation. Large-scale changes that do not address all three areas often fail. Implementations of lean that address all three take less effort and are more often successful.

If lean manufacturing is proactive and preventive in nature, then this model for change is also proactive and preventive. It asks senior management to anticipate the cultural barriers to change and to organize a plan to address these barriers. And it also asks management to build a workforce with the competencies to implement the lean system.

Baldrige Award-winning companies have distinguished themselves for years in financial performance by addressing improvement as an enterprise-wide process. They have continuously improved their leadership system, the competencies of their workforce, and processes throughout the enterprise. The SEA Lean Enterprise System follows these excellent examples by addressing all three areas as critical to successful implementation.

Leadership & Culture
Every company is making improvements. Nobody is standing still. But often we find that certain elements of an improvement system have been missed, and that gap makes it

THE SEA LEAN ENTERPRISE SYSTEM

harder to accelerate improvement to the pace needed to ensure competitiveness. It is therefore the speed of improvement that is the primary issue, not the fact that improvement efforts are being made.

Take for instance the absence of Process Owners. Process Owners are a method for developing and involving employees in the overall improvement process. It is also a method for deploying accountability for improvement. Many senior leaders complain that people have not taken "ownership" for the enterprise. This is another way of saying, "They aren't accountable."

But Process Ownership deploys accountability. If a Process Owner has been trained to improve processes, if they have been given the time and resources to make improvements, and if their performance management plan has objectives for improving their process along with rewards for doing so, then an effective system for accelerating improvement has been deployed and is likely to be very successful.

Most organizations must also address company culture in order to be successful. You could suggest that the reason process improvement hasn't been deployed to Process Owners in the past is because management didn't believe in this approach to employee involvement. Unless the culture can change, the Process Owner system will fail, because senior management will, through lack of direct support, allow it to fail without consciously knowing their role in the failure.

Every major effort to implement improvements eventually runs into the culture barrier, whether it's ISO, MRP, TQM, and so on. Most companies can try a number of times to implement these disciplines only to eventually decide that they do not work. The truth is hidden, although Pogo discovered the truth of the matter many years ago when he said, "We have found the enemy, and he is us."

The ways that our culture resists change are very subtle. I recently reviewed a lean assessment report with a team of senior leaders. The report showed that this $50 million per year company could avoid $500,000/month in costs if they would implement lean. Although they believed the report and could not argue with its findings, they asked that we wait six months until the implementation of their MRP system was complete. The MRP system had no immediate payback projection and used the same out-dated

THE SEA LEAN ENTERPRISE SYSTEM

procedures and processes that were used before the system was purchased. When a management team lacks urgency in changing priorities to achieve better performance immediately, because that lack of urgency is agreed upon by the members of the senior team, we can define it as a cultural barrier. Note that this particular barrier affects the rate of improvement, but not the fact that they are improving.

Workforce Development
Another subtle barrier to change is the skills of the workforce. Many smaller companies do not have a formal method for ensuring that someone is fully certified in the skills they must employ, to follow the process and minimize errors. Few companies of any size have a formal system for assessing training needs and developing a training plan and resources on a regular basis.

Although you can often find pockets of expertise within the workforce, it is rare that you will find a high level of knowledge about statistical process control, lean production methods, setup time reduction, and other such advanced process methods.

Managers have a high level of interest in seeing teams begin to take charge and exhibit higher levels of accountability. They yearn to see teams lead themselves, solve their own problems, and make decisions affecting their day-to-day processes. In order for the workforce to have the confidence necessary to achieve these aims, the training system must anticipate the future needs of the workforce and provide training and practice in these skills. It is pride that drives us to learn new skills and try new things. Why would I want to make decisions and risk making a mistake when I can continue to rely on my supervisor and let him take the risk?

A training system that uses a learn-do approach can build knowledge, skills, and confidence at the same time.

Operational Excellence
All of the methods and techniques of lean production, flow manufacturing, Six Sigma, and more, are contained in this category. Many of the most important techniques will be explained elsewhere in this book.

NOTES

CHAPTER

1 AEROSPACE FLOW

The success of the aerospace industry in the 21st Century is linked closely to its ability to reduce response time and eliminate waste.

AEROSPACE FLOW

The aerospace industry in the United States and in Europe represents a sizable percentage of the GNP. Fifteen percent of the U.S. economy is tied to the aerospace and defense establishment, and this industry is the second largest employer in Southern California.

Given the importance of aerospace in economic value, in jobs and in support of the national defense, it is not surprising that there is considerable interest in adapting the tools and techniques of flow and lean manufacturing. Elimination of waste has been a longstanding concern in military and defense procurement. In the 1980's, as defense spending expanded under President Reagan, stories about $7,600 coffee makers, $435 hammers and $640 toilet seats began to surface in the media. The government's response, however, was to increase the level of oversight over government procurement, and introduce a host of new regulations and regulatory agencies. Very little attention was paid to the root causes of waste, inflated costs and long lead times.

By the early 1990's, however, flow and lean manufacturing methods had made strong inroads into many major U.S. industries, including automotive, computers and electronics, air conditioning, and a host of others. Interest and excitement regarding the application of flow methods to the aerospace industry began to grow, and companies like Boeing, Lockheed and Raytheon began to introduce flow/lean practices in many of their plants. One of the organizations that was created in support of this movement was the Lean Aerospace Initiative (LAI), formed in 1993 to promote the introduction of aerospace lean manufacturing. With the U.S. Air Force and the Massachusetts Institute of Technology as sponsors, the LAI has hosted many conferences and seminars, maintains a large web site, and is a repository of a large amount of information

AEROSPACE VELOCITY

The common snail travels at MACH .0000094 (0.007 miles per hour). This is more than 10 times faster than the average velocity of the fastest part flowing through a fighter aircraft production system.

Lean Enterprise Institute
Aerospace Expo 1998

AEROSPACE FLOW

JOB SHOP?

It is common for aerospace companies to think of themselves as *job shops*. "We never do the same thing twice" is an oft-heard saying. From a process perspective however, this is rarely true.

A connector manufacturer in Southern California, for example, bemoaned the reality of over 2,000 different SKUs, and the large variety of different customer requirements they were forced to meet. Orders were processed in batches, and although the lead time had come down (due mainly to a down-turn in business), it still remained at 3-4 weeks.

An analysis of the process steps required to build the connectors revealed an extremely high level of process commonality. With few exceptions, all of the connectors went through the same manufacturing steps. This environment is very well suited to the flow manufacturing methods described in this book, and the potential lead time for these items could be reduced to several days.

related to aerospace lean. A Google search of the internet for the terms "aerospace" and "lean manufacturing" yielded over 18,000 references.

So, after at least 10 years of effort, how is the U.S. aerospace industry doing? One of the measurements we can use is *inventory turnover*. Inventory turnover is a measure of material velocity, the time it takes for materials to move through the various manufacturing processes. We would expect that an industry embarking on a serious lean initiative would be in the process of reducing queue time, eliminating non-value-added work steps, and introducing material pull methods. We would expect material velocity to increase, along with inventory turnover.

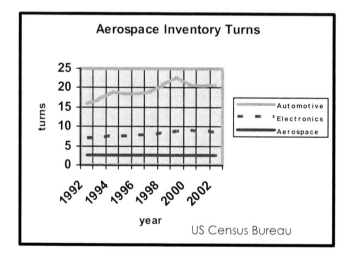

If we use inventory turnover as a key measure of "leanness", it is clear from the graph above that while the electronics and automotive industries have shown steady progress over the last 10 years (with a dip reflecting the 2001 economic slowdown), the aerospace industry has remained essentially unchanged. Over the same period of time there has

AEROSPACE FLOW

been no significant reduction in the cost of doing business, and the debt to equity ratio for aerospace as a whole has doubled. The picture that emerges from the current financial data is of an industry stuck in a status quo, with serious structural issues that need to be addressed. Changes in the global aerospace industry since the end of the cold war mean that aerospace companies must now compete in the global marketplace and sometimes face subsidized foreign competition. Commercial space sales, for example, peaked in 1997 at $6.0 billion dollars, and had fallen by nearly 50% by the end of 2002. Employment in the aerospace manufacturing sector is at its lowest level since World War II, and over 500,000 aerospace jobs have been lost in the U.S. since 1990.

The aerospace industry is made up of a very large number of companies, and an examination of individual firms will also show a range of performance results. Many smaller aerospace suppliers provide innovative or proprietary products, and enjoy a sole-source supplier relationship with their customers. In these conditions, profit margins can remain strong, even if performance fundamentals like velocity are not improved. Larger aerospace/defense contractors experience more direct competition and thinner profit margins, and have been experiencing a continuing deterioration in their performance metrics.

The opportunity for the aerospace industry, and the subject of this book, is that by focusing on *flow* three goals are accomplished:

- Product cycle time is reduced to a minimum. If the product can progress continuously and without delay from start to finish, then it will arrive in the customer's hands in the minimum time possible.

- Quality goes up, and scrap and rework go down. This happens because in order to achieve continuous flow, we are required to analyze in

AEROSPACE/DEFENSE PROGRESS REPORT

"Everybody has been talking a good game, but translating strategy into measurable results across the enterprise has proven to be far more challenging. Based on this year's (2002) study, I would have to conclude that the industry in general has done more posturing than actively pursuing improved competitiveness."

Scott Robertson
Partner, Pricewaterhouse Coopers

AEROSPACE FLOW

GRIM FUTURE FOR AEROSPACE?

The U.S. aerospace industry is in "dire" shape and the federal government needs to come to its rescue - and fast, says the final report from an exhaustive assessment funded with about $3 million from Congress and federal agencies.

The 12 members of the Commission on the Future of the United States Aerospace Industry agreed that there is an economic "crisis" afflicting the U.S. aerospace industry. Its final report represents an "urgent call" to the nation to address "systemic failures" that threaten the industry's survival, says panel chairman Robert Walker.

Manufacturing and Technology News
November 2002

detail each work step along the way, and ensure that each step is error-proofed.

♦ Cost goes down. By progressing in the direction of flow, waste and non-value-added work are squeezed out. The aerospace industry is being pushed hard to reduce costs while maintaining profit margins.

So what are some of the key challenges to the implementation of flow/lean manufacturing in the aerospace industry that have made this necessary transition apparently so difficult?

LEAN AEROSPACE: THE 10 BIGGEST CHALLENGES

I. Management and Aerospace Culture. Aerospace management has been slow to understand and insist upon flow methods. The forces of the status quo are numerous and strong: antiquated customer procurement methods, onerous product validation processes, a comfortable "good ol' boy" network, real and imagined regulations.

One is reminded of the Russian Czar Peter the Great's statement about bringing Russia into the modern age: "I will move these people into the future willingly, if possible. Kicking and screaming, if necessary." A strong process improvement champion is a required element in *every* successful flow manufacturing implementation that we have been involved in, bar none. Need a champion in your company? How about you?

II. Low Volume, High Mix Production. Quantities of any one product tend to be low, which is perceived as a barrier to achieving flow and making large investments in process improvement. After all, there are only so many F-16's in the world. This has led to the common impression that flow/lean manufacturing is primarily applicable to high volume, repetitive manufacturing, and doesn't fit the aerospace industry very well.

AEROSPACE FLOW

A closer look at an aerospace company's products and processes, however, usually reveals a high level of process commonality, albeit across a large number of products. Taking a process view allows us to group products into product families (Chapter 6 of this book) and create lines or cells that greatly improve material velocity, quality and productivity.

III. Project Orientation. Aerospace companies tend to be organized along project or individual contract lines, tied to a particular contract or customer. The effect is to discourage communication and cooperation across projects. In some cases the customer adds fuel to this fire by insisting on dedicated production lines and inventory for their products.

Flow manufacturing takes a process view, based on the development of Process Flow Diagrams (Chapter 4). A Process Map matrix can then be created to analyze the level of common processes, which is typically high. What at first blush is a confusingly large number of products can be reduced to a manageable number of product families.

IV. Prime Customer Procurement Methods. The large aerospace contractors themselves contribute to the long lead-time, batch manufacturing mentality in their suppliers. Contracts are typically specified with a fixed delivery date and quantity, unrelated to the rate of actual consumption or need date on the factory floor. Long lead-times are dealt with by increasing the order quantity. This practice will in turn lead to even longer lead times and what is called the "response time spiral", the tendency for lead times to grow as a result of the effort to deliver on time.

Aerospace companies pursuing a flow manufacturing strategy will need to partner closely with their customers

AEROSPACE LEAN

When cost-plus contracts came to an end in the defense industries, there was a jump in interest in implementing lean manufacturing, even though the production methods didn't resemble the high-volumes of the auto industry. If wasteful aerospace manufacturers can indeed cut out the obvious and the not-so-obvious waste steps in their process, and actually develop a flow to their work, then anyone with the will and a willing workforce can do it. Then working in manufacturing might actually become fun.

Frederick Mason
"Lean manufacturing principles reach aerospace job shop"

AEROSPACE FLOW

PROGRESS PAYMENTS

Some of the challenges that many aerospace companies face include high debt levels and a lack of working capital. Servicing a large debt overhang while struggling to maintain sufficient cash flow can suck management energy away from the seemingly optional task of process improvement. Flow Manufacturing can be a life-saver in freeing up working capital currently tied up in raw materials, WIP, and Finished Goods inventories. And allow companies to wean themselves from progress payments.

and suppliers to understand actual demand patterns and requirements. World-class companies often allow their key suppliers access to actual production schedules, so that the suppliers can better plan their own internal resources. This strategy will require a higher level of trust between suppliers and customers than often currently exists.

V. Progress Payments for Material Procurement.
Aerospace companies are often reimbursed, in the form of progress payments, for the procurement of material. This practice tends to blur the focus on cycle time, inventory turnover, supply chain and velocity goals. After all, the reasoning goes, it's not "our" inventory. These progress payments are even reported as income on the Profit and Loss Statement.

World-class aerospace suppliers would be best served by refusing progress payments and the layers of overhead cost that accompany this so-called benefit. While this would be painful at first, a refusal of progress payments can also be a powerful motivator to improve velocity, inventory turnover and response time, and to accelerate the necessary culture change.

VI. Batch Processing and Shared Resources.
Aerospace products are often designed for (or require) large scale and batch processes. Aircraft antennas that require bonding, for example, are often sent through an autoclave process that is highly effective but also expensive and batch oriented. Long setup times on presses, paint booths and milling machines also encourages the processing of material in batches. Expensive and complex machine resources drive a need to share the equipment among various internal customers, and to attempt to maintain high utilization. Both of these factors contribute to excessive queue time through the factory.

Once a company begins to *think flow*, they also begin to change the way that products are designed and built, including the equipment used. The focus shifts from a concern with piece-part cost and resource utilization to one of improving speed and flexibility, and minimizing the product cycle time. The ideal is to be able to build products one at a time, although this is not always possible.

VII. Material Accountability by Project. For many government controlled projects, materials are procured, stored, tracked and consumed by individual contract. The customers, in the form of periodic audits, want to put their hands on "their" material. The inventory system takes several quantum leaps up in complexity, where the same component may be stored in 10 or 20 different locations, even with different part numbers.

In this environment it is virtually impossible to implement a traditional Kanban system, as discussed in Chapter 9 of this book. The printing of pick lists and the preparations of material kits is the norm, along with the inevitable work order reconciliation, high number of inventory transactions, and less than stellar response time to the consuming workstations. Simplifying the material delivery system will reduce material handling costs, reduce down-time due to parts shortages, and improve inventory accuracy.

VIII. Individual Year Contract Process. Aerospace contracts are often negotiated on a year-by-year basis, with an expectation that the price will come down on following-year contracts. Cost reduction programs and process improvements resulting in improved margins are often simply lost during follow-on contract negotiations where actual cost information is disclosed. There is little benefit for the supplier, therefore, if efforts to reduce cost simply result in a lower selling price.

The win-win scenario is to create a formal agreement to share the benefits of process improvement, allowing the

LEAN MANUFACTURING AND DEFENSE

All the prime contractors that participated in this study reported some experience in the use of lean manufacturing on the factory floor, and many contended that these early efforts had already yielded considerable savings. In a sample of 20 pilot programs, for example, manufacturers reported that the direct labor hours required to produce parts had declined between 5 and 81 percent following the institution of lean practices. Similarly, it was claimed that lean procedures had diminished the cycle time required to produce parts by 13 to 93 percent. Such results offer preliminary evidence that lean principles have the potential to reduce aircraft manufacturing costs. At the same time, however, it is not yet clear whether the savings achieved in these limited efforts can be extrapolated to the implementation of lean principles throughout a manufacturing facility.

Rand Corporation Brief
Lean Manufacturing and the Defense Industry

AEROSPACE FLOW

MRP AND THE RESPONSE TIME SPIRAL

"If only we knew where each job was at each moment, and if the computer could tell us what to do next to help keep jobs on time, we would never be late," thought many manufacturing executives. Sophisticated and expensive shop floor scheduling programs became all the rage...I personally had the misfortune to witness the quoted lead time for a company in the aerospace industry go from 6 months to 9 months, then to 15 months and finally to 24 months as the spiral unfurled at this company.

Rajan Suri
Quick Response Manufacturing

customer to enjoy price reductions and the supplier to keep a portion of the savings and maintain or improve profit margins. Suppliers are allowed to recoup capital investments required to earn the savings, prior to sharing them with the customer.

IX. Lack of Competition. Although there is some competition within the industry, especially for the larger prime contractors and increasingly from abroad, all of the players are operating with basically the same assumptions. There is no "Toyota" on the scene to shake up the existing paradigm.

The potential for huge improvements is there. A simple physical walk-through of the steps required to build many aerospace products can be an eye-opener. The typical part or product is waiting, not being worked on, for up to 98% of the elapsed time! Taking large chunks of this queue time out through the methods of flow manufacturing will enable aerospace companies to radically transform the industry and chalk up large improvements in customer response time, working capital, inventory reduction, productivity, quality and floor space.

X. Use of MRP/ERP Shop Floor Control. It was not unusual in past years to find aerospace companies with *no* formal manufacturing systems, or with home-grown systems that had evolved over time. Today some of these firms are attempting to play catch-up by installing new MRP/ERP systems, with the expectation that this methodology will allow them to reduce lead times, more tightly control the movement of material, and improve productivity. The unfortunate reality is that the ERP/MRP scheduling methodology is itself a prime contributor to the "Response Time Spiral", the tendency for lead times to grow using scheduling techniques.

There are many valid uses for ERP/MRP systems, in the functions of long-range material planning, inventory control, purchasing and engineering data

AEROSPACE FLOW

management. Shop floor and material delivery processes should be controlled not by a computer, but by a visual pull system that responds quickly and flexibly to changes in mix and volume. Much of this book addresses the details of implementing a pull system for work and materials.

The good news is that all of these challenges can be overcome. Given the less-than-stellar improvement results for the aerospace industry over the last decade (with some exceptions), it is also clear that piecemeal and half-hearted efforts will not suffice. *Pockets of excellence* will not achieve the radical response time and cost reductions that will be necessary to sustain and grow the industry. Aerospace management must embrace the philosophy of rapid response as a total business strategy, involving all areas of the business: manufacturing, product development, customer service, information systems, administration, quality, sales and marketing.

Aerospace Flow Manufacturing and the Supplier Excellence Alliance (SEA) roadmap present a logical, data-driven and proven method to achieve these objectives. It will be necessary, however, to adapt flow methods to the realities of your products and processes, rather than regarding flow/lean manufacturing as a religion that cannot evolve, or as a cookie-cutter approach. The fundamental goal remains unchanged: the acceleration of customer response time as a key metric, and the elimination of waste. The specific tools used will vary. The techniques of material Kanban, for example, work very well in a repetitive manufacturing environment but may not be the material delivery method of choice in a high mix, low volume environment. The ideal of a single-piece flow, mixed-model line may need to yield to the concept of overlapping cells and small batches. The fruit is still hanging low to the ground. Best wishes for a fruitful harvest!

LESSONS LEARNED

1. **In order to survive and prosper, the aerospace industry must radically improve. Flow/lean manufacturing provides a powerful and proven path.**
2. **Although the aerospace industry is unique in many ways, there are no insurmountable obstacles to implementing flow manufacturing if the leadership is present.**
3. **The tools and techniques of flow manufacturing will need to be customized and adapted to fit specific environments. There is no 100% canned solution.**

NOTES

CHAPTER

2

INTRODUCTION

Every day, another visionary manager realizes that the tools and techniques of flow manufacturing are as powerful as they are simple.

INTRODUCTION

The way that work is done is being transformed for both manufacturing and service-based industries. The method being adapted across the world is called *flow manufacturing*.

The first exposure to the concepts of flow manufacturing is often a shock. The initial reaction is frequently a combination of "Wow!" with "Why didn't we do this sooner?" The overriding feeling is that adopting flow methods is something that makes sense, and something that makes a positive difference in the way we organize our work and run our businesses.

As the message spread through word of mouth, books and publications, flow manufacturing and flow processing methods gained a great deal of popularity during the 1990's. Today, flow practitioners are reporting significant, sometimes amazing, financial and performance benefits. Every day, a new visionary manager realizes that the tools and techniques of flow manufacturing are as powerful as they are simple. The benefits realized by companies who have adopted flow techniques usually include:

- Inventory reduction. It is common to see a 90% reduction in Work-In-Process inventory when moving from a traditional manufacturing to a flow environment.

- Quality improvements. A requirement to document and standardize work, error-proof processes and focus quality to the point where the work is performed, results in a dramatic decline in scrap and rework.

- Improved productivity. Training employees to perform standard work, with a special focus on quality, results in impressive productivity gains, even in so-called *mature* industries.

NEW ASSUMPTIONS

The assumptions of previous manufacturing methods no longer apply:

- **Material cost is the primary cost component**
- **Customized products are expected**
- **Product lifecycles are short and shrinking**
- **Competitors are improving customer service, productivity, and quality while reducing inventory**

Flow manufacturing is based on new assumptions.

-Dan Natchek
Oracle Corporation

INTRODUCTION

- ◆ Improved response time to customer orders. In today's world, the ability to respond quickly to customer requirements is no longer a competitive *advantage*, but a competitive *necessity*. Driving out waste in the form of queue time allows a flow manufacturing line to make a product in a fraction of the time required by traditional manufacturing methods.

- ◆ Reduction in the working capital needed to run a business. The availability of working capital can be a key constraining factor, or even a cause for business failure. Flow manufacturing companies dramatically drive down (or even eliminate!) the need for working capital.

COMPETITIVE NECESSITY

In the early stages of the reintroduction of flow techniques in North America in the late 1970's, flow manufacturing was considered a competitive advantage. Today, after two decades of wide-spread application, flow manufacturing has become a competitive necessity.

- ◆ Floor space and capital asset utilization improvement. The linking and balancing of manufacturing processes together into flow lines or cells, the related reduction in WIP inventory, and a thorough housekeeping effort, will typically result in a 20%+ reduction in the amount of factory floor space required.

All companies have several goals in common: the desire to achieve a competitive advantage, make a profit, and increase market share. They all know that customers expect high quality products, delivered on time, configured to their specification. Companies know that more and more of their customers are no longer brand loyal, and will seek out the supplier who can best meet their requirements for quality, delivery and price. Companies also know that in today's global economy, competition can come from anywhere on the planet, often from low labor cost countries.

Visionary managers are not discouraged by these challenges. Rather, they see the ability to meet or exceed their customers' expectations as a significant

INTRODUCTION

competitive difference. A growing number of companies are looking to flow manufacturing as *the* method to help them achieve this competitive advantage. Throughout the 1990's entire industries converted en-masse to flow manufacturing. In fact, many companies would not be in business today, had they not embraced flow manufacturing methods.

Flow manufacturing is not a new concept. Although the flow solution is surprisingly simple, many interpretations exist as to what flow manufacturing is. The *flow* type of manufacturing has been described and packaged in many ways. These are just a few:

- Lean manufacturing
- Continuous flow manufacturing (CFM)
- Repetitive manufacturing
- Just-in-Time (JIT)
- Assembly line manufacturing
- Agile manufacturing
- Toyota Production System (TPS)
- Kanban manufacturing
- Cellular (or cell) manufacturing
- Flow Processing

Many readers at this point may be confused about the use of the word "flow". *Lean manufacturing*, for example, is a commonly used term these days, and many companies today say they are implementing "lean". Is lean the same as flow? The answer is that what we are calling *flow* may contain elements from all the above listed buzz-words and programs. And, of course, the label *flow manufacturing* can be as misleading and inconsistent as any of the labels listed above.

The key point for the business professional is this: any manufacturing method must be consistent, repeatable, and achieve the desired results. The flow manufacturing techniques presented in this book are consistent,

VELOCITY

"As Dell Computer exchanged inventory for information, they increased velocity, or the rate at which their business processes happen. Velocity is a critical focus for Dell management. In order to manage the changing requirements of their customers and the changing technology critical to their products, it was necessary to be able to quickly and effectively respond. This was termed *velocity* at Dell. Michael Dell expressed this as a 'time driven' culture, where the focus was on how fast inventory is moving rather than on how much inventory there was."

- Pearlson and Yeh
The Zero Time Organization

INTRODUCTION

repeatable, and are being used every day, for the manufacture of many different kinds of products, always with superior results. This book presents the concepts of flow manufacturing, their application to manufacturing and administrative processes, and a glossary of standard terminology. This book is not intended to be an implementation manual or cookbook for prospective flow manufacturing practitioners, but it can be a first step in the journey. As the experienced travelers we are, we now invite you embrace the power and simplicity of flow manufacturing. Enjoy the trip.

EVERYTHING I KNOW ABOUT FLOW, I LEARNED IN MY MOM'S KITCHEN

As the son of an Industrial Engineer and a stubborn but excellent cook, my mother, I was exposed to the tools of flow manufacturing at a very young age. When I was only 14 years old, my sister got married, the first of eight children. The wedding reception had to be extra special. I do not know if it was special, but it was *big*. Mom decided that she was going to bake *all* the pies to be served at the reception. Needless to say, she was not planning on doing this alone.

A few weeks before the wedding, Mom gathered all her sons together in the kitchen and shared with us her plan. Since we had invited approximately 250 people, she figured we would need 42 pies (1/6 of a pie per person). Since pies can spoil, we could only start baking 4 days before the wedding, resulting in a daily production volume of 11 pies per day (42/4, rounded up). We wanted to spend only 4 hours (240 minutes) a day cooking, so we needed to achieve a production rate of 22 minutes per pie (240/11, rounded up). Since every pie has a work content of 60 minutes, Mom calculated that she needed 3 helpers (60/22, rounded up). The work content for a pie was then divided into 3 sequential increments of approximately 20 minutes each, and each workstation was staffed by one of us brothers. To ensure that we would not get ahead of each other, we were instructed to finish one pie, do one more, and then help the slower brother. When baking day arrived, success! Pies were flowing one at a time to my Mom's workstation for the final touches, before going into the oven.

Sequential work, linked and balanced to a pre-established rate. Sounds like flow to me.

CHAPTER

3

WHAT IS FLOW MANUFACTURING?

Flow in manufacturing is a technique by which products are manufactured one unit at a time, at a formulated rate, without wait time, queue time, or other delays.

WHAT IS FLOW MANUFACTURING?

In flow manufacturing a product progresses through its manufacturing processes without stopping, like water in a river, hence the term "flow".

The Mississippi River begins its journey to the Gulf of Mexico as a modest stream in northern Minnesota. Moving steadily southward, joining with small and later larger streams and rivers, the Mississippi quickly grows to between 1,000 and 2,000 feet across. Over 250 tributaries join the main river: the Ohio, the Missouri, the Arkansas. The water is in constant motion, always moving forward. The tributaries are all physically connected. Unless man intervenes with dams and water projects, the water follows a never stopping path. The river, therefore, is our metaphor for flow manufacturing.

If products can be built one at a time, without waiting between processes, then the elapsed time required to progress through the manufacturing processes will always be significantly less than the time required to route products through a factory in batches. Reductions in manufacturing lead-time drive many of the benefits associated with flow manufacturing: inventory reductions, quality improvements, productivity improvements, and floor space optimization, to name a few. It is from this ability to build a product in a time closer its actual work content time that the benefits of flow manufacturing are realized.

The goal of the flow manufacturer is to design and create a manufacturing line capable of building different products, one at a time, using only the amount of time required to actually complete the work. Wait time, queue time, and other delays are largely eliminated in flow manufacturing. The gains in manufacturing response time are not achieved by working harder or faster, but rather by implementing the tools and techniques that connect processes together, eliminating the traditional "batch and queue"

THE "HOT ORDER" TEST

Have you ever been in a situation where there is a "hot order", which MUST be completed in a time far shorter than your normal delivery lead-time? Did that order get done on time for delivery as requested? The answer is usually yes. So how did you manage to finish an order in 50%, 25%, or even 10% of the time it takes to complete a normal order?

The technique used is called *expediting*. By walking the hot order from workstation to workstation, and from machine to machine, skipping queues and breaking priorities from the first to the last manufacturing process, the hot order is completed much more quickly.

If that could be done with one order, why not *all* orders? In a batch environment, constant expediting would be a source of spiraling chaos. In a flow environment, a delivery time close to or less than the product's work content time *is the norm*.

WHAT IS FLOW MANUFACTURING?

TAKT TIME

The line's maximum production rate. Takt time is used to calculate resources at capacity, and to balance the line. Takt is a German word meaning *a precise interval of time*, or *beat*.

WORKSTATION DEFINITION

Work tasks grouped together with a total work content of a takt time or less define a *workstation*.

production. The benefits of eliminating delays in the manufacturing process are far greater than simply trying to speed up the actual work process itself.

The rate at which work progresses through the factory is called the *flow rate* or *takt* . The flow of a product is achieved by grouping and balancing all of its work tasks to a calculated takt time. Working with this method, a person or a machine will perform a group of tasks equal to one takt time worth of work. The partially completed unit is then passed to the next workstation down the line, where the next takt time worth of work tasks are performed. The materials progress in a flow through all the manufacturing processes until all of the required work has been done and the product is complete.

Flow manufacturers may choose to regulate the output of the line to closely match the current mix and volume of customer demand. With a flow line designed to build products at a formulated takt time, the flow manufacturer also has the ability to regulate the rate of the line. The desired rate is identified every day based on that day's customer orders. The rate of production is adjusted by changing the number of labor resources on the line, i.e. by adding or removing people, not by changing the physical design of the line itself. Takt time cycles will therefore be missed or completed during the day. The number of takt times completed is matched to the number of units required that day. The ability to change output rate every day, driven by changes in customer order requirements, is a powerful tool for managing productivity, work in process and finished goods inventories.

WHY DO COMPANIES USE FLOW?

Global manufacturers have had to achieve productivity increases, operating cost reductions, quality improvements, and shortened customer lead-times in order to stay competitive. Many companies have

WHAT IS FLOW MANUFACTURING?

chosen the tools of flow manufacturing as a solution to these challenges. Products coming from flow manufacturers are delivered on time, with the highest quality, and the lowest cost. Following are some examples of the potential benefits resulting from the implementation of flow manufacturing.

INCREASED PRODUCTIVITY

The number of units produced by a group of people in a given period of time is generally accepted as the measurement of a factory's labor productivity. By linking and balancing the work to be performed, and by error-proofing the work processes, operators can spend more time building good products and less time on rework and delays. Also inherent to flow manufacturing are the continuous process improvement strategies known as Kaizen or Rapid Improvement events. These tools systematically focus on the reduction and elimination of move time, queue time, changeover time and other non-value-adding activities. By eliminating waste, production employees can spend more time building products, and productivity will improve.

Many traditional manufacturers focus on direct labor productivity as a primary performance metric. While direct labor is undoubtedly one element of product cost, for many products it is the smallest component, often less than 5%. The much larger elements of product cost are direct materials and overhead. Labor productivity improvements should be considered a by-product of flow manufacturing methods, resulting from a correct focus on balanced work, process velocity and elimination of waste.

During the 1990's many mature industries began to report impressive productivity gains. While there are multiple reasons for this, including the introduction of

CASE HISTORY

Improvements in productivity can sometimes create unexpected challenges. A large medical products company in the US, upon implementing flow manufacturing in one of its plants, found that the plant was overstaffed by 100%! Several years of rapid growth and a practice of throwing people at the challenge resulted in the dilemma: what to do with the excess people? The company was smart enough to know that a large layoff would be the kiss of death for any future continuous process improvement activities. Fortunately they were able to make a short-term adjustment by reducing the number of temporary workers being used, and allow normal growth and attrition to complete the remaining adjustments over a relatively short period of time.

WHAT IS FLOW MANUFACTURING?

new technologies like the internet, the introduction of flow manufacturing in these industries is a primary explanation for the improvement.

IMPROVED PRODUCTIVITY

"On the whole, increased attention to world-class performance has delivered broad-based productivity gains. In the U.S. manufacturing sector, productivity climbed nearly 3% a year from 1990 to 1996 -- about three times the productivity growth rate of the economy as a whole. Some people say that the reason for the productivity improvement is all the downsizing and outsourcing that has been taking place. But if you look at the productivity data for the last 12 years -- from 1985 to 1997 -- you'll see that, although employment in manufacturing did decline about 4%, the productivity level improved by 44%. That means that the bulk of the gain didn't come from getting rid of people. Instead, innovation has been a big part of the productivity improvement in manufacturing."

- Richard K. Lester
The Productive Edge: How U.S. Industries Are Pointing the Way to a New Era of Economic Growth

REDUCED OPERATING COSTS

The largest opportunities for most manufacturing companies to lower costs and improve profitability lie in the category of overhead cost reduction. Direct material costs, after all, will only be reduced if products are redesigned or the company pays less for the material. While both these options are possible, it is unlikely that significant gains can be achieved in the short term. Direct labor costs already represent the smallest portion of product cost. For many products even if magical elves would build the product for free, the overall reduction in product cost would be small. What is left as a focus of attention is the 15-25% of product cost called overhead.

A flow factory's operating costs are reduced as a result of the following efforts:

- Total Quality Management (TQM) activities that improve process quality, reduce scrap, rework, and warranty costs.
- Inventory reduction resulting from shortened manufacturing lead-time. Reduced inventory will have a positive impact on material handling overhead, as well as reduced obsolescence, damage, storage space, interest and taxes.
- Total Productive Maintenance (TPM) programs can result in dramatic improvements in equipment up-time, quality, change-over time and capital expenditures.
- Improved resource and floor space utilization through the elimination of waste and unnecessary inventory.

WHAT IS FLOW MANUFACTURING?

- ◆ Reduced transaction costs as a result of pulling materials via Kanban techniques.
- ◆ A simplified manufacturing environment that reduces the need for a high level of computer transactions, complex systems and layers of supervisory and planning support.

SHORTENED CUSTOMER LEAD-TIME

The business world today is moving at a fast pace. Customer delivery times that were once perfectly acceptable are now regarded as painfully slow. Regular mail is now referred to as *snail mail*. Even two-day courier delivery is too slow for some uses: "its gotta go overnight!". The marketplace is expecting a significantly shorter order fulfillment lead-time than it did a decade ago. A factory that arranges its resources in a flow relationship creates, by design, a much shorter manufacturing lead-time. The shorter the manufacturing lead-time, the quicker the response to a customer order, without having to carry finished goods or work-in-process inventory.

Traditionally, finished goods inventory has been used as the method to shorten customer response time. By having the products ready to go on the shelf, shipment to customers can be quick. The downside of finished goods inventory, of course, is the large amount of working capital required to establish it, the risk of obsolescence or non-moving products, storage and logistics costs. And often finding out, even with a large inventory of finished goods, that you don't have what the customer wants. The flow manufacturer would much prefer to shorten manufacturing lead-times to a minimum, and build to customer orders directly, eliminating the need for finished goods.

CASE HISTORY

When trying to understand your delivery performance, do not look just in the factory. A manufacturer of custom-made medical devices had an average response time of 11 days, trailing the market leader who consistently responded in 3 days. After reviewing all the processes within the entire order fulfillment chain of events they found out that it took an average of 5 days *just to process the order paperwork*. Even if they could manufacture in zero time, they would still be 2 days behind the competition. By implementing the tools of flow, not only in the factory, but also in all the office processes preceding manufacturing, they are today consistently achieving a 1.7-day total response time.

WHAT IS FLOW MANUFACTURING?

NO TIME

"Zero value-gaps, Zero learning-gaps, Zero management-gaps, Zero process-gaps, and Zero inclusion-gaps. A Zero-Time organization has a mindset different from other organizations. Zero-Time organizations design and operate with the assumption that processes can be done instantaneously if information technology and people are creatively combined."

- Pearlson and Yeh
A Zero Time Organization

OPERATIONAL BENEFITS

Production planning in a flow line is simplified, because planning occurs only at the end-item level. Subassembly production planning is virtually eliminated by linking processes together and creating direct *feeder* lines. Multi-level Bills of Material can also be dramatically simplified or flattened, since many subassembly part numbers are no longer used or transacted against. Variable staffing levels, driven by actual customer orders, control the flow rate of the line. The daily production schedule is matched as closely as possible to the actual customer orders.

Cost accounting methods can be simplified with flow manufacturing. Because the lead-time through a flow facility is consistent, repeatable, and not volume sensitive, Activity Based Costing (ABC) can be more easily introduced. Labor costs for the flow manufacturer can become elements of the overhead that is applied proportionally to each product. A variable overhead cost may also be created to account for extraordinary conversion costs driven by the use of special machines or resources.

Production reporting in flow manufacturing is simple and direct. Some of the typical reports in a flow environment are:

- ◆ Actual backflush units versus planned completions. Backflush eliminates the need for excessive shop floor transactions, work order reconciliation and pick lists.

- ◆ Kanban material usage variance. Work order reconciliation is eliminated.

- ◆ Resource utilization reporting. Labor tracking at the work order level is not done, although overall productivity is still reported.

WHAT IS FLOW MANUFACTURING?

Given the long list of benefits, it is not surprising that flow manufacturing has become a competitive necessity for most industries. The extension of flow methods to non-manufacturing processes and industries, like banking, software development, health care and construction is the next frontier, just getting started.

DISCRETE MANUFACTURING

Discrete manufacturing is the most common production method for the application of flow manufacturing. Shippable end items are usually measured in individual units or "each". The production quantities produced in manufacturing can vary from one to large order quantities. In contrast to process intensive factories, discrete manufacturing usually requires more people than machines.

Traditional factories usually organize resources functionally, into departments or work centers. These areas include resources, people and machines, grouped together based upon the type of work that they perform or the machines that are used. Factory layout and product flow is often sub-optimal. The movement of materials between resources may be indirect, and the distances traveled by the material may be long. Because semi-finished products have to travel across departmental boundaries, large quantities of inventory tend to build up throughout the factory.

The traditional plant layout, based on a functional orientation, satisfies a requirement to collect *earned hours* for people and machines in departments. Little or no attention is paid to the need to balance the work across resources or work centers. Each resource works independently to its own pace or beat. Individual resources do not inherently consider the supplying process's ability to feed them, or the consuming process's ability to consume what is being produced. The result: excess inventory in the system.

EARNED HOURS

Earned hours, the calculated number of machine or labor hours that would have been consumed if the factory had been working to standard, is used to track labor and machine efficiencies, and to allocate overhead costs.

WHAT IS FLOW MANUFACTURING?

Industry	Industry
Aerospace and Defense products	Injection molding and die casting
Automotive Assembly	Insulation materials
Automotive parts and accessories	Machine tools
Castings and forgings	Machining job shops
Ceramics	Material handling equipment
Clothing and shoes	Metal fabrications
Computers and peripherals	Medical equipment
Digital Imaging equipment	Photocopiers
Electric motors and controls	Paper products
Electronic / Circuit Card assembly	Pharmaceuticals
Fabrication job shops	Plastic resin
Glass products	Plumbing Products
HVAC products and accessories	Printing
Household appliances	Semiconductor Equipment
Mobile Refrigeration Equipment	Subcontracted assembly
Snow Plows	Shampoo
Hearing Aids	Windows

WHAT INDUSTRIES USE FLOW?

It is interesting to note the domination of flow manufacturing techniques in many industries. As the word regarding the many benefits of these proven tools spread in the 1990's, many industries converted across the board to flow manufacturing. The heating and air conditioning industry, electronic assembly, automotive, plumbing products are some examples. A visit to virtually any company in these industries will show the implementation of flow methods. The reason, of course, is that they *had* to in order to remain competitive.

WHAT IS FLOW MANUFACTURING?

In order to replenish the material consumed, discrete batch manufacturers generally use computer generated *pick-lists*, lists of components and assemblies required based on the current production plan and released work orders. Customer orders or demand forecasts are entered into the manufacturing system, and the system will then determine material requirements based on each product's Bill of Material. Computer generated reports will then call for the allocation of materials to the associated work order, shop order, or schedule. The timing of the data entry of a customer order into the system will determine when the materials will be allocated to the order. This can sometimes turn into a "battle of wits" among production schedulers trying to get their orders first in line. This material allocation methodology by its very nature is almost guaranteed to cause material imbalances resulting in shortages.

PROCESS MANUFACTURING

Process manufacturing tends to be highly automated. Upon arrival to a process factory, one of the first things noticed is the size and apparent complexity of the machinery in use. The second distinct feature is that relatively few people operate the factory. The factory layout is usually determined by the order of the processing steps required to make the products. Commonly only one type of product is being manufactured at a time, in batches or lots. The manufacturing process may be a *black box*, with interconnected pieces of machinery linked by conveyors.

In process oriented factories, products are nearly always produced in units of measure that are not "each". Typical units of measure in a process factory relate to:

- ◆ Weight (Oz, Kg, Tons)
- ◆ Linear measurements (Feet, Yards, Meters)

FLOW IN PROCESS INDUSTRIES

Mini-mills are engaging in innovative worker training programs including "Pay for Skills," "Commitment to Excellence," and participation in regional manufacturing training centers. All these efforts are designed to foster worker well being, improve productivity, and enhance worker safety. Training workers in a multiplicity of tasks rather than narrow specializations gives the work crews versatility to maintain and increase productivity, the hall-mark of mini-mill efficiency.

WHAT IS FLOW MANUFACTURING?

MINING INDUSTRY

"[Flow processing] appears to be highly applicable to mining, as it is to many other production systems. Value definition and value stream analysis, standardized work, quality at the source, total productive maintenance, flexible workforce, setup reduction techniques, and continuous improvement approaches could be implemented directly in the mining industry. Techniques designed for flow do not transfer [directly] from manufacturing to mining, but the benefits from flow, nonetheless, should be highly valuable."

- Yingling, Detty and Sottile
Lean Manufacturing Principles and Their Applicability to the Mining Industry

- Surface measurements (Square Feet, Square Yard, Square Meter)
- Volume measurements (Gallons, Quarts, Cubic Meters)

In process factories it is possible that the shipping unit of measure may be expressed in quantities of "each". High volume environments that produce discrete products but are highly automated have many of the same characteristics: a series of machines linked with automatic conveyors. High volume consumer products like shampoo or soap are manufactured in this way. Products are not mixed in this environment, but rather are produced in batches or runs.

Due to the nature of the conversion methods, process manufacturers already "flow" their products with interconnected processes. What differentiates a process manufacturer from a flow manufacturer is that for the process manufacturer, production quantities are processed in large batches or lots. These production lot quantities are usually calculated based on economic order quantity logic that focuses on resource utilization. Lot sizes are sometimes simply the result of a planner's educated guess, rather than the result of intense data analysis.

Two of the biggest challenges that process manufacturers face are equipment reliability and changeover times. Because the manufacturing environment is heavily automated and interconnected, equipment failures will shut down the entire production process very quickly. Intermittent or poorly running machines can have a dramatic negative impact on overall productive capacity. Lengthy setup times between products also drive the need to produce in large batches. After an 8 hour setup, for example, the natural tendency will be to produce a large quantity of that product, so that you don't have to set up for it again anytime soon.

WHAT IS FLOW MANUFACTURING?

Process manufacturers can obtain significant benefits from the tools of flow processing. Inventory management both at the in-process level and finished goods level are a point of focus. Two key flow benefits for a process manufacturer are resource balancing and material management.

The goal of a flow manufacturing line in a process intensive environment is to achieve the following:

- Small batch sizes, ideally linked to customer demand
- Less than 10 minute changeover from one product to another
- Lower capital investment
- Easier maintenance and adjustment

The direct labor requirements may actually be higher, and output per line lower, in a flow manufacturing line than a more traditional automated line. From a flexibility, up-time, reliability and overall operating cost viewpoint, however, these flow manufacturing cell configurations become a necessity if the company wants to produce a high mix of products and reduce WIP inventory.

Material kanban techniques can be used within a process intensive environment to manage and control the transfer of semi-finished product from a supplying process to a consuming process in the factory. Kanban replenishment techniques can also be used for controlling supplied materials consumed at the required processes. Another common application for kanban is as a tool to signal the replenishment of finished goods inventory shipped to customers. Finished Goods Kanban is a simple and easy-to-implement first step that can achieve dramatic finished goods inventory reductions in a short period of time.

FLOWING BATCHES

In a process intensive industry, we cannot entirely get away from building products in batches. The challenge is the optimization of the batch size, with the desire to reduce batch quantities to a minimum. So is it possible to flow a batch? Sure.

WHAT IS FLOW MANUFACTURING?

LESSONS LEARNED

1. *Flowing* work is to connect all of the work steps as closely as possible, and eliminate queue time and delays.
2. A host of benefits are achieved by flowing work: fast response time, inventory reductions, productivity gains, quality improvements, reduction in floor space.
3. Any industry can benefit from flow manufacturing methods, and many industries have already converted en-masse.
4. Both process and discrete manufacturing are candidates for improvement with flow manufacturing methods.

The conversion of a discrete or process-oriented factory from traditional, batch-manufacturing methods to flow manufacturing is a production manager's (and consultant's) dream, because the benefits can be so large. A reduction in WIP inventory of 90% is not unusual, and large improvements in all of the key business metrics are expected.

The toolkit of flow manufacturing methods and techniques is extensive and thorough, and the right tools need to be selected for the right applications. Process industries, for example, will often focus on the reduction of variability and changeover times as a large opportunity. Discrete manufacturing may take on the physical linking and balancing of work, and the organization of the material delivery system, as their initial focus. Administrative and office processes, discussed in a later chapter, look to the reduction of departmental barriers and employee cross-training to get the maximum benefits. Whatever the application, the fundamentals of flow manufacturing will apply.

WHAT IS FLOW MANUFACTURING?

AEROSPACE FLOW: BUILDING A FOUNDATION

The series of steps presented in this book, starting with Chapter 4, offer a roadmap, or series of implementation steps that can be followed in order to achieve process excellence. Before jumping onto the flow manufacturing train, however, we need to make sure we are ready to take the trip. This beginning stage is sometimes referred to as "stabilization", i.e. making sure that we have a stable foundation of basic disciplines that are a prerequisite for future improvements. Some of the stabilization issues that may need to be immediately addressed include:

PROCESS STABILITY

The reduction in variability and achievement of process stability has to be a very high priority if we expect to achieve good process flow. At this stage we are not necessarily referring to a *Six Sigma* level of quality, 3.4 defects per million, as a necessary accomplishment, but process instability will be a major obstacle to process flow. The methods that we can apply to analyze and reduce variability are many, including root-cause analysis tools like Ishikawa or fishbone diagramming, Failure Mode and Effects Analysis (FMEA) or the 5 Whys technique.

5S

The 5S methodology has become well-know in recent years as a formal process for achieving a high level of organization and housekeeping. It is also a necessary part of what are called "Visual Workplace" techniques, and can be considered a prerequisite for a sustainable Kanban system. We normally do *not* recommend 5S as the *first* step in the Flow Manufacturing journey, as an activity divorced from the line/cell design. After all, why implement 5S in an area that will soon be reorganized anyway? In some environments, however, the level of housekeeping and organization has deteriorated to the level that a first-pass 5S activity is needed and recommended at the outset.

WHAT IS FLOW MANUFACTURING?

INVENTORY AND BOM ACCURACY

A high level of inventory and Bill of Material accuracy can be considered a basic manufacturing requirement, whether you are implementing flow or lean manufacturing, or using more traditional ERP/MRP methods. In the past a 95% level of inventory accuracy was considered the bare minimum for Material Requirements Planning (MRP) to work. In a flow manufacturing world, with less inventory available or desired, our minimum acceptable level needs to be 98% or better. A failure to achieve this will result in line stoppages, a high level of replanning, and rising levels of WIP inventory that can't be completed due to material shortages.

Bills of Material establish our product configuration, are used to drive the material procurement process, are used to cost our products and for inventory backflush. The target level of Bill of Material accuracy has to be 100%.

CHAPTER

4

A BRIEF HISTORY OF FLOW MANUFACTURING

Readers who think of flow manufacturing as a Japanese import will be surprised to learn that it actually began in the United States in the 1800's, with the *Scientific Management* movement.

A BRIEF HISTORY

Flow manufacturing is not a new or radical concept for the 21st century, but it certainly has evolved since its humble beginnings in the early part of the 1800's.

At the beginning of the industrial revolution, manufacturing companies were first challenged with the management of new machines and their enormous production output, machine output that could far outpace human beings doing the same work. The textile industry was one of the first to introduce large-scale machinery, large cloth-weaving machines. At that time products requiring the shaping or cutting of metals were still extremely labor intensive, and labor productivity was a serious management concern in those heavy industries.

Around 1885 these technology and management issues started to be addressed formally when Frederick Winslow Taylor began publishing his work. What Taylor proposed was that all manufacturing work should be analyzed and broken down into individual tasks, with a view that the tasks could be shortened or eliminated. The application of this *scientific method* coupled with the time study techniques introduced by Frank Gilbreth, led to great increases in the efficiency of industrial work. Taylor set about proving his methods in different industrial applications, focused on finding the *one best way*, or what we now call *standard work*.

Taylor's methods were put to the test by Henry Ford's large motor car plants. Ford's first successful production model was produced in 1903, but his fame truly grew with the first full production year of the Model T in 1908. By 1913, ten years after launching the company, Ford was producing half of the cars made in America. Ford proposed to build an automobile that would be "a car affordable for every American". The main challenges were productivity, cost, and finished product

FREDERICK WINSLOW TAYLOR

"In 1977, a pair of management scholars, Daniel A. Wren and Robert D. Hay, asked historians of business and economics to rank seventy one contributors to management thought and practice. Taylor won handily, ahead of John D. Rockefeller, Andrew Carnegie, Alfred P. Sloan, Thomas Edison, and Henry Ford. When the same task was put to members of the management history division of the Academy of Management, Taylor again topped the list, scoring thirty-one first-place votes; the next person down had three."

- Robert Kanigel
The One Best Way

A BRIEF HISTORY

NOT INVENTED "THERE"

"The phenomenon that modern authors call 'Japanese-Style Management' is not a recent creation, but a product of the introduction of scientific management into Japan early in the 20th century"

- Daniel Wren
The Evolution of Management Thought

TAYLOR COMES BACK

"By the late 1920's, it could seem that all of modern society had come under the sway of a single commanding idea: that waste was wrong and efficiency the highest good, and that eliminating one and achieving the other was best left to the experts. The 1928 election of mining engineer Herbert Hoover, secretary of commerce in the Harding and Coolidge administrations and author of the influential 1921 report "Waste in Industry" brought scientific management into the White House itself."

- Robert Kanigel
The One Best Way

availability. Productivity was improved by having the car pulled through the plant at a constant speed, while groups of parts were accumulated for the workers to assemble. In this production line, workers would normally repeat one or two tasks. Ford had proposed that 'A man must not be hurried in his work', so the timing and balance of the individual tasks was critical.

Productivity was further increased when Ford introduced the moving assembly line for chassis assembly. Total assembly time was reduced from 12.1 hours to 1.5 hours. Productivity improved and the goals of cost reduction and increased availability were also reached using this method. A remarkable achievement during the production of the Model T was the fact that as the production volume increased, the selling price was continually reduced, beginning at $850 in 1909 and reduced to $260 in the final full production year of 1926.

One of the early visitors to Ford's River Rouge plant was Mr. Kiichiro Toyoda of Japan, who had been asked by the Japanese government to begin to produce vehicles as an extension of his successful textile business. His founding of the Toyota Motor Company in 1937 was said to have been inspired by his visit to the River Rouge site. The huge capital investment that would have been required to fully emulate the Ford plant was impossible for Toyota, and the need to compete with fewer resources provided the motivation for the improvements and changes that were to later come.

Driven by customer demand, product variety became the next goal in manufacturing during the 1920's. Most manufacturing facilities struggled to gear up for production of new product models. Delays of six months for the retooling of assembly lines were common and expected. Ford spent $100,000,000 and took 18 months to introduce the new Model A in 1927. Up until this time, manufacturers had focused primarily on labor productivity to achieve a competitive cost advantage.

A BRIEF HISTORY

Innovations in technology now became the new productivity tool that allowed many manufacturers to remain competitive. This period marked the advent of technological changes in machine tool cutting points, synthetic abrasives, and multiple rotary cutting points, particularly in lathes and milling machines.

Manufacturing through the 1930's and 1940's was still driven by large quantity production runs, although runs like the 17 years for the Model T Ford were no longer possible. Consumers were more and more the drivers of change in a product's life cycle. The demand for specialized products began to grow in earnest following World War II. Not only were products more specialized, but they also had much shorter life cycles. This evolution in production methods, led by improvements in machine and labor productivity, marked the beginning of the mass production era in the U.S., with its flagship production method *batch production*.

In batch manufacturing, production quantities were often based upon what would make the machines most productive, and not necessarily what the market wanted to buy. This subtle change in focus pitted manufacturing departments against marketing departments throughout industry. Batch manufacturing allowed machines to be productive when building large quantities of the same product, but batch processes also created problems for manufacturing when building a mix of different products. Solutions to this dilemma were found in the 1950's in a discipline called Group Technology. Group Technology proposed that manufacturing processes should focus on the similarity of material shape, size, or method of manufacture. The focus on materials gave limited advantages, so the discipline was expanded to include machines and operations. This evolved into what we know today as Cellular Manufacturing, where a group of machines and people have autonomous authority over administration, planning, and operations to build a specific family of products.

BATCH MANUFACTURING

The functional layout is used for batch production where batches of identical components undergo an operation and, when all parts in the batch are complete, they are then transported on to the next location. This has two implications:

1) it takes a long time to complete each batch as every component has to wait until the whole batch is complete before moving on to the next operation.

2) there is a fairly high level of work-in-progress (WIP) in the workshop and, unless strict controls are in operation, WIP can very quickly fill all the available physical space.

- Ford Suppliers Program

A BRIEF HISTORY

MANUFACTURING SECRETS

The Mitsubishi Electric Company sent dozens of people to Westinghouse in the United States, as part of a technical cooperation agreement, to learn time-study methods and standard work documentation. The techniques were then quickly spread throughout Japan, starting in 1923. A fictional pamphlet in Japan, "The Secrets of Saving Lost Motion", sold more than a million copies. During the 1920's American experts Lillian Gilbreth, Barth Hathaway, Wilfred Lewis and Harrington Emerson all traveled to Japan to give lectures, inspect factories and help guide the new movement. By the time W. Edwards Deming arrived after World War II, the path had been cleared by the previous American management leaders.

While many companies in the United States pursued these disciplines, a different set of techniques was maturing in Japan, lead by the Toyota Motor Company. At Toyota it was contended that the standard thinking of *Cost + Profit = Sales Price* was incorrect. Toyota believed that *Profit = Sales Price – Costs*, highlighting the manufacturer's market role as a "price taker", rather than an influential force in price setting. From this premise Toyota began to create a manufacturing system that would focus on the management of costs. Cost became translated as "waste" and wastes of all varieties were targeted for elimination. Target areas included work in process inventory and safety stock. While many companies in the United States and Europe were attempting to calculate the optimum batch sizes for production, Toyota was working diligently toward the goal of being able to build a mix of products in a one-piece-flow, i.e. a batch size of one. Building a mix of products in a one-piece-flow satisfied many key objectives for Toyota: raising productivity, reducing costs, reducing the need for working capital, and fast customer response.

From an almost bankrupt position in 1949, and a modest total production of only 3,000 vehicles in 1950, Toyota began to gather and document all of the information in the field of manufacturing that was available. In that year Taiichi Ohno became the manager of Toyota's Honsha machining plant, and Shigeo Shingo began his work as an engineering consultant within that organization. One of the key documents uncovered by Mr. Ohno was a 1912 Japanese translation of Frederick Taylor's *Shop Management and the Principals of Scientific Management*, published in English in 1911. Drawing on this and other sources, American and Japanese, Ohno began to mature and apply these concepts to what would later be known as the *Toyota Production System*.

A BRIEF HISTORY

During the reconstruction period following the war Japan also received help from several quality experts from the U. S.: W. Edwards Deming, W. A. Shewhart and Joseph Juran. While Shewhart declined the invitation to work in Japan directly, both Juran and Deming spent considerable time there, teaching Japanese managers about statistics and quality. Deming has been credited with the creation of the "Japanese Industrial Miracle" and the highest prize for quality in Japan today is called the *Deming Quality Award*.

In Japan in the 1960's, Toyota, Honda and other Japanese manufacturers were preparing for their assault on the American automobile market. In 1955, 95% of the automobiles sold in America were American made; that would soon change. Extending its production philosophy further, Toyota introduced the concept of *Quality Circles* in 1962. Active participation by production workers to analyze and discover the root cause of problems, and then implement a solution, introduced the practice of *Kaizen* or rapid improvement. The company began to receive an average of one improvement suggestion per worker, per week, or thousands per year. Toyota won the Deming Prize in 1965.

Through the 1960's and into the 1970's, the Japanese and American schools of manufacturing developed down separate paths. In the U. S. manufacturing companies were looking for better ways to manage batch production, while in Japan companies were finding ways to allow one-piece-flow of a mix of products. The results of these different techniques came into clear focus during the 1980's, when many product markets within the United States and Europe came under pressure from Pacific Rim manufacturers. Foreign products were introduced into the American market that were unquestionably cheaper and of higher quality. In order to survive, American manufacturers began to search for better ways to compete, and for the manufacturing "secrets" of these foreign competitors. Theories abounded, including cultural

FLOW AT BOEING

One-Piece Flow is the opposite of batch production. Instead of building many products and then holding them in queue for the next step in the process, products go through each step in the process one at a time, without interruption. Producing products one at a time continuously improves quality and lowers costs.

-The Boeing Company web site

A BRIEF HISTORY

GOOGLE PAGES, SEPTEMBER 2003

ERP	4,390,000
Just In Time	1,670,000
MRP	870,000
Reengineering	498,000
Six Sigma	484,000
Enterprise Resource Planning	456,000
Kaizen	180,000
Lean Manufacturing	158,000
Theory of Constraints	31,000
Agile Manufacturing	18,600
Batch Manufacturing	18,000
Cellular Manufacturing	16,800
Manufacturing Resource Planning	15,900
Toyota Production System	13,100
Flow Manufacturing	9,640

LESSONS LEARNED

1. Although there are many buzz-words and varieties of flow methods , they are all very similar. *Flow Manufacturing* is the term used in this book.
2. Flow Manufacturing has its roots in the 1800's with the Scientific Management movement. It later matured in Japan, and was introduced to the U.S. in the 1970's and 1980's.
3. By the 1990's many companies had to convert to flow methods in order to survive. Batch and MRP methods are no longer competitive.

explanations for the differences between Japanese and American products. As time went on, the specific tools and techniques being used by these foreign competitors became more widely known, and in the late 1980's and 1990's many American companies abandoned batch manufacturing in favor of the more responsive method of flow manufacturing, to also pursue the goal of being able to flow a mix of products one unit at a time.

Taiichi Ohno proclaimed in 1971 that his ambition to complete the *Toyota Production System* had been accomplished. As the "secret" information from abroad began to be documented and taught, various schools of thought also began to develop in the United States. One school of thought adheres strictly to the methods presented by Toyota and the Toyota Production System. The school of *lean manufacturing*, similar to the Toyota approach, has been adapted in the U.S. by many companies, especially the automotive industry. A business novel "The Goal" by Eli Goldratt in 1985 launched the concept of *Theory of Constraints*, with a focus on throughput maximization. The list of books and buzzwords continues to grow.

Flow manufacturing today is a widely proven, non-culturally based technique that links elements of work so they are carried out without bottlenecks or delays. Although the products themselves vary in volume, in type, and in mix, the techniques remain the same: definition of the processing flow of a product, standard work definition at a detailed level, and designing the production flow line. When the line has been designed for product flow, a set of tools that balance the work to a calculated flow rate or *takt* are employed. As the design and balance of the line is completed, the flow of material and calculation of material quantities, using kanban techniques, are executed. Using these basic tools, a flow processing line can be created and implemented successfully. This book is an introduction to the basics of this flow manufacturing method.

CHAPTER

5

**UNDERSTANDING
THE
FLOW**

Our objective is to design a multi-product line, capable of building *all* of our products. We need to gather some basic information before making decisions as to what shape the line will have.

UNDERSTANDING THE FLOW

From the manufacturing standpoint, a product is the result of transforming materials through the application of work. Work is organized into processes, and it is *by process* that we will design our line.

The first tool in our design methodology refers to the understanding of the relationships of manufacturing processes required to build every product.

We have, so far, discussed some of the characteristics and benefits of flow manufacturing. We now need to begin looking at a set of tools and a methodology to help us design a flow line. The tools that we will describe in this and subsequent chapters, have been around for a while, and have always been widely used by Industrial Engineers.

When a company sets out to improve its performance through the application of flow manufacturing techniques to its manufacturing or administrative processes, it must do so with a plan to adopt flow as a new way of life. At the highest management levels of the company, there has to be a process-oriented vision of high financial performance through the creation and delivery of value to its customers. In this high-level vision, all processes in the value stream are linked and balanced to allow work to take place without bottlenecks, delays, queues and other forms of waste. However, we need to follow a step by step method, and eat this elephant one bite at a time. A commonly suggested method recommended by experienced practitioners is to break the implementation of flow manufacturing in manageable pieces or areas that need definition, and address them one by one.

FIRST THINGS FIRST

"We've found that there's a logical sequence for the implementation of lean…"

-Jorge L. Larco and Bruce A. Henderson
Lean Transformation

UNDERSTANDING THE FLOW

THE IMPLEMENTATION AREA

So you have decided to take it one step at a time. That is a very good idea. Implementing in smaller, strategically selected areas will ensure success for a number of reasons:

♦ You see results quickly.
♦ You get an opportunity to learn from experience and improve upon the implementation methodology for the next implementation area.
♦ If you use consulting support, you have a chance to see the experts in action without waiting for an extended period of time. You also have an opportunity to learn from their experience, which will enable you to become self-sufficient sooner.
♦ You can adapt the implementation methodology to your company's culture and test it again.

The implementation area can be defined in terms of its physical location within the company, by the products built in the area, or by the manufacturing or business processes within its boundaries. Financial performance is the usual guide for picking the physical location of the first implementation. It is very common to see that a plant within a corporation is chosen because of the potential financial gains derived from the application of the tools of flow manufacturing. It is also recommended to start at the processes closest to the customer, since that will provide us with a clearer picture of our customer's demands as well as an almost immediate impact on customer satisfaction. The two next sections of this chapter analyze the products in the implementation area, and demonstrate how to document these products from a process perspective.

As a practical example, we will create a fictional factory that manufactures hand-held power tools, where we will build a variety of different products like drills, sanders, jigsaws, chain saws and electric

WHICH PRODUCTS?

The highest volume products (80/20 rule) plus all products with unique processes make up the product list.

WHAT IS A PROCESS?

The term "process" is another way of saying "work". A process is a collection of sequential steps of like work performed by people or machines, usually at constant volume.

UNDERSTANDING THE FLOW

screwdrivers. As in any process design effort, flow or otherwise, we need to know:

1. What do we make? This is our *Product List*.
2. How do we make it? This is what we call *Process Flow Diagrams*.

THE PRODUCTS

The first step in gathering the information to create a line design is to identify the products we expect to build on our line. Table 4.1 displays the list of products we will use for our power tools line design.

Our objective is to design a multi-product line, capable of building all of our products. We need to gather some basic information before making decisions as to what shape the line will have, and which products can be combined.

Our list of products does not need to be exhaustive, that is, not every single product we plan to build in our line needs to be included in our analysis. We will always approach the design by looking at the group of products that drives the highest production volume. Companies often have a very long list of products that they *could* build, but the active list is typically much smaller.

Designing for the high volume products does not mean we ignore the rest of the product offerings. Our line will be designed to manufacture *all* the products within our target area. It is also very important to ensure that all the products that have unique processes or manufacturing resources associated with them are included in the product list, regardless of their volume. It is a common practice to begin the transition to flow manufacturing by conducting a pilot project for a section of the factory. If we want to start by creating a pilot implementation, the product list could be one of the

HOW MANY?

How many products should we try to combine? In general terms, the more products we have on our line, the less vulnerable we are to swings in customer demand.

TABLE 4.1 PRODUCT LIST

Part Number	Description
16445DR	Drill
16456DR	Drill
16467DR	Drill
16878SD	Sander
16865CS	Circular Saw
16227OS	Orbital Sander
16238OV	Orbital Sander
16144CS	Chain Saw
16155CS	Chain Saw

UNDERSTANDING THE FLOW

factors in determining the boundaries of the design scope.

In office process designs, the determination of the product list is one of the more challenging aspects of the project. What is the product of office work? Look for discrete units of output. These units of output could be a customer order ready to be transferred to manufacturing, a request for a product return, or a processed credit application. We will address some of these topics in the chapter on Administrative Flow.

THE PROCESS FLOW DIAGRAM

START AT THE END

When documenting the relationship of processes in a PFD, start at the end, in the shipping department or at the end of the line. The reason for this is simple: a product will have only one completion point, but could have many starting points.

Use a river as an analogy. The Mississippi ends in the Gulf of Mexico, but it has many tributaries and potential starting points. So start at New Orleans and work your way upstream.

Once we know our products, the next step is to understand how those products are built. A product is the result of transforming materials through the application of work. The work applied to a product comes from a number of different resources; sometimes the resource can be a person, sometimes a machine, sometimes both. Production resources are grouped into processes, and it is by process that we will design our line. The relationship of manufacturing processes to make a product is depicted in its product's Process Flow Diagram (PFD). Each PFD shows how the materials flow from process to process to build one unit of product.

The manufacturing processes in our sample factory include final assembly, test, pack, and injection molding. We must go to the factory floor, and draw a PFD for every product in our list. With a PFD, we are documenting the relationship of manufacturing processes, with an emphasis on the volume of product going through each process. The PDF format is similar to a simple relationship diagram, with the sequence of processes going from left to right on the page.

Let's take a look at two sample PFDs for four products in our power tools factory in Figure 4.1.

UNDERSTANDING THE FLOW

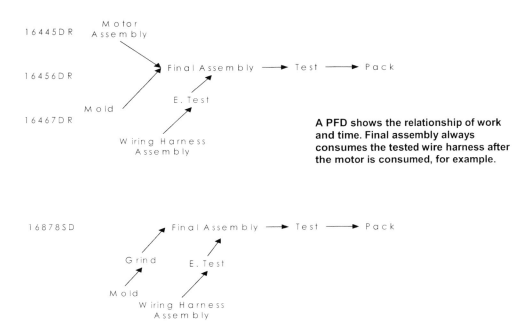

A PFD shows the relationship of work and time. Final assembly always consumes the tested wire harness after the motor is consumed, for example.

FIGURE 4.1, PROCESS FLOW DIAGRAMS

Notice the product part numbers, from the original product list, on the left side of each PFD. It is very common to find that a PFD applies to multiple products. A PFD must document all the paths the product follows as it is manufactured. Sometimes a product does not advance forward as we would hope, so we need to document any loop-backs of rework that may exist. The process flow diagram for a product also shows the relationship of work and time, as the processes are physically placed in the order in which they occur. One PFD at a time, we are gathering one of the most critical pieces of information for our flow implementation. The PFD will allow us to understand the number of units flowing through any individual process.

HOW MANY PFDs?

A Process Flow Diagram can apply to one or many different products. Two products that share the same process relationships, including yield and rework, would share the same PFD.

UNDERSTANDING THE FLOW

LINEAR EQUATION

Each PFD can be seen as a graphical linear equation in a mathematical model. The solution to that mathematical model is the number of resources required to support the Daily Forecasted Volume.

THE REALITY CHECK

Do not attempt to draw the Process Flow Diagrams from a desk in an office. Chances are, you will miss something. That is what happened to a manufacturer of power generators. While an audit of the PFDs was being conducted in the shop floor, an operator walked by the auditing group, looked at a PFD and casually commented: "That's not the way we do that job. That's the way we were told to do it, but if we were to do it that way, the product would never move."

Make sure that the PFDs are an accurate reflection of the factory. Routings, Bills of Materials, and subassembly definitions may serve as supporting documentation, but relying only on legacy data will lead you to an inadequate, if not flat-out wrong, line design. So when working on your next multi-product flow line design, wear comfortable shoes, and be prepared to walk the factory floor.

Having completed the documentation of all the process relationships in the form of process flow diagrams, we now have a stack of paper that, at this stage, is not terribly helpful. To make sense out of the PFDs, we must organize them in a form that allows us to see patterns of flow paths followed by all the products. The tool we use for organizing the process relationship data is the *Process Flow Map*, discussed in the next chapter.

VALUE STREAM MAPPING

A term much in vogue today is Value Stream Mapping (VSM). The concept of a VSM (love those acronyms!) is to develop an overall picture of the enterprise that includes all of the essential processes required to build a product. This scope includes not only the manufacturing processes, but typically includes raw material procurement, warehousing, product design, administration and customer service, computer processes, etc. It covers the flow of information as well as material. It documents the big picture, with a view towards optimizing the entire flow, not just a piece of it. As such, the Value Stream Mapping effort is often a starting point for a company implementing flow manufacturing.

Is a PFD the same thing as a VSM? From the standpoint that they both pursue the same objectives we can say the answer is yes. However, while VSM is a high level depiction of the relationship of business processes, a PFD is a tool within a practical methodology that will lead us toward the physical design of a set of business

UNDERSTANDING THE FLOW

processes with precise locations for all the resources within each process. Often, the scope of a PFD is limited to the direct manufacturing processes only, and does not include other support processes. This is done not because other processes are unimportant, or do not have a significant impact on customer response. The factory floor is where we typically start, however, because if our manufacturing processes are not in a flow, this will have negative repercussions on all of the supporting activities. Most of the added value usually takes place in manufacturing, although significant components of lead-time can also occur elsewhere. Is Value Stream Mapping important? Absolutely, and it should be done. Where do we start implementing? In manufacturing.

VALUE STREAM MAPS

"Taking a value stream perspective means working on the whole, not just optimizing the parts. Value Stream Mapping covers 'door-to-door' production flow inside a plant, including shipment to the plant's customer and delivery of supplied parts and material. This is a good level at which to begin…"

- Rother and Shook
Learning To See

LESSONS LEARNED

1. We begin our process design with a preliminary product list, and by creating a process flow diagram for each product.
2. The process flow diagram documents the processes required to build each product, and how those processes are related.
3. Our goal is to design a flow line that can build multiple products in the minimum elapsed time and with maximum quality. We will use the process flow diagram to help calculate the number of resources required by each process, and to give us an idea of the optimal line layout.
4. Value stream mapping is another common term, and process flow diagrams is a similar concept. The scope of the diagram will vary, depending on our goals. Value stream mapping is recommended to develop a big picture view of the enterprise.

UNDERSTANDING THE FLOW

VALUE STREAM MAPPING VS PROCESS FLOW DIAGRAMS

One of the most difficult things to grasp is the right level of detail for Value Stream Maps and Process Flow Diagrams. Both are high-level depictions of the process flow, at the 30,000 foot level, and a failure to understand and document the right level of detail can yield a result that is essentially useless. If the document is not detailed enough it will be hard to use from a practical perspective, i.e. it won't contain enough information to be able to truly understand the environment. A Process Flow Diagram that is too detailed, on the other hand, will be much more difficult to create and understand.

The key is to understand the definition of a "process" as the word is being used in this book. A process consists of a grouping of work steps that are 1) logically related and 2) can *flow* within the process. Logically related work steps are often performed sequentially, are physically co-located and represent the same type of work. A process that can *flow* can go from the first step to the last within the process without delay, and without a change in the number of units being processed.

An example of a correctly defined process might be *Final Assembly*, a grouping of work that is logically similar, sequential, physically co-located, and can flow (proceed uninterrupted) from start to finish. There may be hundreds or even thousands of detailed work steps included in Final Assembly, but it is still only one process. Another example, from the automotive industry, might be *Wheel Assembly*. Note that Wheel Assembly and Final Assembly would not be good candidates to combine into a single process since the volume of wheels exceeds the volume of cars by a factor of 4 or 5 to 1. Individual unique machines are usually identified on a Process Flow Diagram as separate processes.

When should we use a Value Stream Map vs. a Process Flow Diagram? We recommend the Value Stream Map as a initial analysis step that will give you a roadmap of the entire enterprise, or at least larger sections of it. The Value Stream Map can be used to identify areas of opportunity for process improvement teams and for line/cell design projects. The Process Flow Diagram, adhering strictly to the definition of a process described above, is needed at the line or cell design stage and is usually includes a more limited number of processes. A Process Flow Diagram is needed for *every product* that you want to include in your design! Remember that Flow Manufacturing is a specific and powerful *method,* and that the Process Flow Diagram document is a key ingredient.

CHAPTER

6

DEFINING
PRODUCT
FAMILIES

The family designation dictates the dedication of manufacturing resources to specific products and production lines.

PRODUCT FAMILIES

A product family is a group of products that require similar processing steps and share common equipment. Many manufacturers organize their products into families. These families define which products will be run on which production lines.

THE PROCESS FLOW MAP

A process flow diagram displays the relationships of manufacturing processes to make a product. Having gathered the PFDs for all the products involved in our line design, we have acquired the necessary information to understand the links between all the process and the products in our target area. The product/process relationships will aid us in establishing groups of products that are likely candidates to be built on the same line, as well as other critical information necessary to create the multi-product flow line design. The tool we are going to use to help us display the relationships between the products we build and the processes we use to build them is the *process flow map*.

A process flow map is a matrix that lists the products in rows and the processes in columns. Each cell at the intersection of a row and a column indicates a process/product relationship. Once we have drawn the basic grid we will begin filling in each cell. One PFD at a time, we will place an "X" in the appropriate cell every time the PFD for a product shows the use of that process. In the example in Figure 5.1, we have three products, A, B, and C. Each product has a different PFD indicating the sequence of processes the product goes through. It is *not* usual for every product to have its own unique PFD, as in this example. In most cases, products share manufacturing resources and manufacturing paths, and so they also share process flow diagrams. Every X you see on a process flow map indicates that a product requires the process indicated in the column heading.

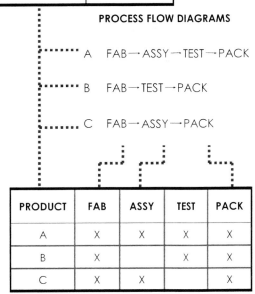

PRODUCT	DESCRIPTION
A	PRODUCT A
B	PRODUCT B
C	PRODUCT C

PROCESS FLOW DIAGRAMS

A FAB → ASSY → TEST → PACK

B FAB → TEST → PACK

C FAB → ASSY → PACK

PRODUCT	FAB	ASSY	TEST	PACK
A	X	X	X	X
B	X		X	X
C	X	X		X

FIGURE 5.1 PROCESS FLOW MAP

PRODUCT FAMILIES

FIRST PRODUCT FAMILY CRITERIA

First criteria for family definition is *process commonality*.

HOW MANY LINES?

Product families may indicate whether we have one or multiple lines. Other drivers of family definitions can be common materials, setup times, and common tooling.

Each X in the process flow map also identifies the existence of work content for that model. The work content could be labor, machine work, or a combination of both. We will later document the work content for every product using *standard work definitions*. Another look at Figure 5.1 shows that there are some processes that are used by *all* products. These processes with a rich mix are very important to identify, since they are the highest volume processes and the ones we design the line around. Conversely, make sure that you identify the processes with a very poor mix, for those can pose a challenge in our ability to make the line flow properly.

In Figure 5.2 below we have created a matrix with 9 rows and 9 columns, based on the number of products from Table 4.1 and the processes documented in the PFDs from Figure 4.2 for our power tools factory, discussed Chapter 4. We have a potential maximum of 81 instances of work content that will have to be

FIGURE 5.2   PROCESS FLOW MAP

Part Number	Description	Mold	Grind	Motor Assy	Wiring Harness Assy	E Test	Mandrel Assy	Final Assy	Test	Pack
16445DR	Drill	X		X	X	X		X	X	X
16456DR	Drill	X		X	X	X		X	X	X
16467DR	Drill	X		X	X	X		X	X	X
16878SD	Sander	X	X	X	X	X		X	X	X
16865CS	Circular Saw						X	X	X	X
16227OS	Orbital Sander	X		X	X	X		X	X	X
16238OV	Orbital Sander	X		X	X	X		X	X	X
16144CS	Chain Saw						X	X	X	X
16155CS	Chain Saw						X	X	X	X

PRODUCT FAMILIES

documented in much finer detail at a later step. Notice that we have shaded two groups of products that share the same or similar process patterns, and possibly have the same manufacturing paths. We will refer to each group as a *Product Family*. A family of products is our first indication, although not the only one, of products that can be built on the same line.

A *process flow map* tends to be more helpful when the manufacturing processes (columns) are organized in downstream sequence left to right, as shown in Figure 5.3. The last processes of the line would be placed on the right-hand side of the matrix. Organizing the processes in that fashion can provide you with some early indications of the potential number of flow paths the products will follow, while answering questions such as: Is it one line or multiple lines? Are there any optional paths that separate from the main line at any point? Are the options mutually exclusive, or do they share resources? Are there common resources between feeder processes? Being aware of these issues is critical in the allocation of manufacturing resources for the line.

FIGURE 5.3 ORGANIZING PROCESSES

First ⟷ Last

PRODUCT	FAB	ASSY	TEST	PACK
A	X	X	X	X
B	X		X	X
C	X	X		X

PRODUCT FAMILIES

A product family is a group of products that require similar processing steps and share common equipment. Many manufacturers organize their products into families. The family designation often dictates the dedication of manufacturing resources to specific products and production lines. However, in many cases these families have not been defined by the manufacturing function. The sales, marketing, or financial departments often define families, with little or no regard to the flow of the product through the manufacturing processes. Traditional family definitions are usually based on the uses or sales channels for the finished product, rather than the manufacturing processing paths and resource usage of the products. When we are in the process of analyzing the

PRODUCT FAMILIES

SECOND PRODUCT FAMILY CRITERIA

Work content times may help us to further refine family definitions to achieve better balance.

manufacturing paths our products follow, we must not assume that the existing family definitions are to be taken as they are today.

Flow manufacturers design lines and build products using family definitions. Family member selections for multi-product flow lines are based first on the commonality of their processing paths from the product's individual process flow diagrams. Multi-product flow lines are designed to build a family of similar products sharing common manufacturing processes. By grouping products in this manner, the flow manufacturer optimizes resource utilization, while facilitating the advance of products through their required resources one unit at a time.

Commonality of processes is not the only basis for product family definitions. A second characteristic that needs to be examined is the work content per product in a process. Large differences in labor and/or machine times among products in the same process will make it difficult to achieve a smooth work flow. Although time differences are normal and expected in a line building a mix of products, large swings in work content will cause imbalances and constraints that may be very difficult to overcome. Large work content differences from product to product within a process may require us to create sub-families of a process or group of processes. As a general rule of thumb, work content times should be within a 30% range, with no individual model being greater or less than 30% of the average time. If the work content within a family can be kept within this range, line balancing is much easier. In Chapter 7, we will take a look at refining family definitions for our power tools factory based on *standard work content times*.

A third potential factor to be considered in the definition of product families is the degree of common materials consumed. Each product will have *some*

PRODUCT FAMILIES

material that is unique, but a lack of material commonality between products will increase greatly the amount of physical space required for material presentation. Material handling challenges alone could put a limit on the number of different models that can be produced on the same line. Some family definitions are driven almost entirely by material considerations. High volume environments must also give serious consideration to the issue of material presentation, and the frequency of delivery. The physical space required for material delivery in a high-volume line is often a constraint on the number of models that can be produced on one line.

Building multiple products on the same line has many benefits for the flow manufacturer. A multi-product flow line can build a wider variety of products in a smaller factory floor footprint. Floor space utilization is important to any manufacturer, for it alleviates the costs of brick and mortar expansion. Different products also usually have different sales cycles. If product lines are dedicated to a small number of products, the alternating peaks and valleys of the products' sales cycles can lead to severe underutilization of assets, or to the "hire/fire" cycle of operators in an attempt to match production capacity to market conditions. The larger the number of products we can build on a single line, the less vulnerable we are to swings in the sales cycles.

Producing in a multi-product mode also helps reduce daily demand variability that naturally occurs for individual products. Forecasters know this phenomenon well: the forecast for families of products is typically more accurate than forecasts for individual products. On any given day, for example, it would be unlikely that demand for *all* products is up. Some may be up, others down, and when we add them together the volatility tends to be smoothed out. The more products that we can combine on the same line, therefore, the smoother the overall demand we expect to see on a day-to-day basis.

PRODUCT FAMILIES

FIGURE 5.4 PROCESS FLOW MAP

PRODUCT/ PROCESS	FEEDER	ASSEMBLY	OPTION 1	OPTION 2	TEST	PACK
1223-0957	X	X	X			X
1872-3099	X	X	X			X
6283-2938	X	X	X			X
4121-0289		X		X	X	X
6372-3092		X		X	X	X
1209-2020		X		X	X	X
1827-3911		X		X	X	X
1029-2029		X		X	X	X
8347-2029		X		X	X	X
0398-2039		X		X	X	X
4928-2093		X		X	X	X
2992-1928	X	X	X			X
3928-2093	X	X	X			X
2938-2993	X	X	X			X

If the mix of products and processes is complicated, you can rely on a process flow map to help analyze these relationships. Products sharing the same processes are good candidates for combining into a product family. In Figure 5.4 we can easily see two logical groupings of products. Although both assembly and pack are shared processes, the differences in other processes may cause us to separate and build the products on two different lines. These products could also be combined into a single line with option feeder lines connected.

THE ROUNDING FACTOR

Too many families can lead to underutilized productive capacity and space. Compare these two possibilities:

LINE	RESOURCES	STATIONS	VERSUS	LINE	RESOURCES	STATIONS
A	2.5	3		A+B	6.9	7
B	4.4	5				
TOTAL		8				

By combining lines A and B, we reduce the number of workstations required from 8 to 7.

PRODUCT FAMILIES

It is important not to go overboard in defining too many families, or to think that small differences between products justifies a new family definition. Too many lines, with insufficient volume in any one line, will consume floor space and require workers to shut down one line and move to another on a daily or hourly basis. A failure to combine products well can also result in inefficient use of resources, since we normally round up the number of resources required per line.

The creation of product families is an important implementation step that will help ensure a successful line design. Simply sharing common processes is not the only family definition criteria, and we will be looking in upcoming chapters at other considerations. The family definition needs to be thought of as an iterative process, one that we will come back to as we continue on our line design journey.

LESSONS LEARNED

1. Intelligent organization of our products into logical families is an important success factor in our line design. Not all products can be combined.
2. Combining products into multi-product lines, as opposed to dedicated lines, will yield many benefits, including demand smoothing and floor space savings.
3. Several factors are included in our criteria for family definition: common processes, common work times, and common material.
4. The *process flow map* is our tool of choice to analyze common processes across all of our products.
5. Family definition is an iterative process that we will return once we have gathered additional data.

FAMILY DEFINITION CASE HISTORY

A manufacturer of building system controls had been in business since the early 1950's, and was still producing some of the early products. The company had pursued a strategy of "outsourcing" for quite a few years, and the only work remaining in the plant was final assembly and pack. Family definition in this plant was often limited to a single product, or a small grouping of very similar products. Specialized test equipment put a constraint on the physical space required in their assembly and packaging cells, and limited the number of products that could be produced in any one cell.

Demand for any individual product, however, was quite low. Orders for the week might be produced in a few hours. Over 60 assembly cells had been set up, but at any given time most of these cells were not running. Workers were required to move from cell to cell on a daily basis, and the factory floor space was highly underutilized.

The solution: combine products that may look different and have different end-use, but share the same processes (assembly and pack) and have similar work content times. Investigate ways to deliver test equipment and tooling as needed, rather than setting up a permanent work space for this equipment.

PRODUCT FAMILIES

CREATING THE PROCESS FLOW MAP

In the high-mix, low-volume environment found in many aerospace companies, the Process Flow Map is an essential tool to begin to define future families, lines and cells. The key data input is the availability of a Process Flow Diagram for every product, discussed in the previous chapter. Simply list all of the product part numbers on the left-hand column of a matrix, and create a column for each of the processes found on the Process Flow Diagrams. We normally organize the process names not alphabetically but in order of flow, moving from left to right. Place an "X" in the product/process cell if that product requires that process.

In an aerospace environment that often involves many different products, the Process Flow Map is an invaluable tool. One aerospace company that we visited had an active product list of over 9,000 items. The grouping of products into families is an essential step in this type of environment. The end-result or output of the Process Flow Map step is a definition of products that can be intelligently combined into multi-product lines and cells. Multi-product processing is one of the most important methods for the industry to implement, in the pursuit of reduced costs and cycle time.

CHAPTER

7

TAKT TIME

I n a flow manufacturing line, products progress through the required processes at a formulated rate. This rate is called takt time.

TAKT TIME

Designing a multi-product flow line is a proactive process. We do not simply react, but rather we attempt to put in place a set of resources that can respond flexibly to changes in customer demand in the future. One of the key inputs to our line design is a clear understanding of customer demand.

When we set out to design a multi-product flow line for our target area, we do not know ahead of time exactly how many units of each product we will build every day once we go "live". The production volume will vary from day to day, as customers place their orders for the products they want. However, we need to make a determination as to what production capacity will be required to support our expected customer demand. We need to make an assumption of future mix and volume, that we will then use to calculate a number of resources (people, workstations, and machines) required to support that mix and volume. It is at this point in the design project that we need to contact our friends in the sales and marketing department, to see what level of output they need from our manufacturing line to support their sales plans. As we review production volume estimates by product, and the capacity needs for the line, the strategy of building as many products as possible on the same line will become even clearer. Our goal is to set up a series of sequential workstations that build products progressively and are balanced to a target rate; it is only logical to see that the smoother the demand pattern, the simpler the balancing of those resources will be. At the individual product level, the demand patterns could be highly variable. That product-level variability would not pose a problem for a flow manufacturer building in multi-product mode. As shown in Figure 6.1, individual products display volatility in their individual demand patterns, but are smoothed when combined as a group.

FORECASTS

You've probably heard the joke: There are only two kinds of forecasts, lucky and lousy. So, are we really talking about using a forecast here as a basis for our line design?

Simply put, yes. We do not, however, expect to *build* to forecast once we have the line in place. We would like to build to actual customer orders. By using a future-related volume, we are attempting to be proactive, and not design a line that will quickly be obsolete. We don't want to be redesigning the line every few months because we ran out of capacity.

MULTI-PRODUCT LINES

The more products we can combine, the smoother the overall demand pattern.

TAKT TIME

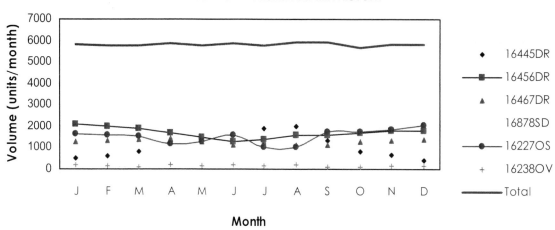

Volume/Mix
FIGURE 6.1 VOLUME AND MIX HISTORY

P/N			
◆	16445DR		
■	16456DR		
▲	16467DR		
	16878SD		
●	16227OS		
+	16238OV		
—	Total		

FIGURE 6.2 PRODUCTION VOLUMES

P/N	Description	Annual	Daily
16445DR	Drill	13,440	56
16456DR	Drill	20,160	84
16467DR	Drill	15,600	65
16878SD	Sander	768	3.2
16865CS	Circular Saw	15,360	64
16227OS	Orbital Sander	18,240	76
16238OV	Orbital Sander	1,920	8
16144CS	Chain Saw	12,960	54
16155CS	Chain Saw	11,040	46

Since we want to design a line for future needs, and not simply base our line design on the volumes we are producing today or we produced in the past, the production volume per product must be a future volume. The analysis has to extend to growth trends, product obsolescence strategies, new product introductions, as well as sales cycles and seasons, by product. Once the determination of volume has been completed, we must then express that production volume in daily quantities. It is necessary to express our process and demand data in common units of measure, and we have chosen a *daily* time-frame to reflect our goal of ultimate flexibility and responsiveness.

Figure 6.2 shows a scenario in which we have been provided with forecasted annual volumes for our power tools factory. Those numbers must then be expressed in daily rates by simply dividing the annual volume by the number of working days per year. Let's assume that our

FIGURE 6.3 PROCESS FLOW MAP

Part Number	Description	Forecast Daily Volume	Mold	Grind	Motor Assy	Wiring Harness Assy	E Test	Mandrel Assy	Final Assy	Test	Pack
16445DR	Drill	56.0	X		X	X	X		X	X	X
16456DR	Drill	84.0	X		X	X	X		X	X	X
16467DR	Drill	65.0	X		X	X	X		X	X	X
16878SD	Sander	3.2	X	X	X	X	X		X	X	X
16865CS	Circular Saw	64.0						X	X	X	X
16227OS	Orbital Sander	76.0	X		X	X	X		X	X	X
16238OV	Orbital Sander	8.0	X		X	X	X		X	X	X
16144CS	Chain Saw	54.0						X	X	X	X
16155CS	Chain Saw	46.0						X	X	X	X
Process Throughput (Units/Day)			292.2	3.2	292.2	292.2	292.2	164.0	456.2	456.2	456.2

future factory works 240 days per year, one shift per day. Once the forecasted daily volumes per product have been determined, we know what the *total* volume at the end of the line will be: the summation of all the individual forecasted volumes.

The line design occurs process by process, and we must calculate a maximum production rate by process as well. To do so, the next step is to calculate the individual volume contributions of every product to the total production volume in a manufacturing process. We will refer to this concept as the *process throughput volume*. The tool we will use to calculate throughput volume is the *process flow map*.

VOLUME BY PROCESS

Throughput volume per process (vertical summation) is derived from the *forecasted daily volume* per product.

TAKT TIME

In the process flow map, Figure 6.3, we added a column called Forecasted Daily Volume where we placed the product volume figures from the table in Figure 6.2. Every X you see in the Process Flow Map, indicates that the volume for that product (row) contributes to the volume for that process (column). We can now calculate the throughput volume by process, by adding a row at the bottom of our process flow map for the *process throughput volume*. This additional row displays the vertical summation of all the individual product volume contributions to the process. Every time a process is affected by scrap, rework, or an option percentage, we will also have to account for these volume modifiers. The end result is the target number of units that we would need to build, at designed capacity per day, *by process*.

AVAILABLE WORK TIME

The next step in our line design effort is to understand the maximum production rate or takt time for our line. We will calculate the maximum rate of production as a ratio of work time and volume, using the calculated throughput volume per process. We just reviewed how to calculate the throughput volume per process. The missing element is the actual work time available in our plant. The time element refers to the time a resource (a person or a machine) spends building products within a shift. A person who reports to work at the beginning of a shift and leaves at the end of the shift did not spend every minute building products. For our power tools factory, let's assume that the shift begins at 6:00 am and ends at 2:30 pm, giving us a typical 8.5-hour or 510-minute shift. Does an individual employee work for all those 510 minutes? The answer is clearly no. How many minutes of work does a person or machine actually do per shift? That varies from company to company, but the typical production employee normally takes two rest breaks, one lunch break, and also performs other

HOW MANY SHIFTS?

We design flow manufacturing line for the least possible number of shifts, for the following reasons:

♦ To allow time for preventive maintenance.
♦ To allow flexibility to respond to seasonal demand.
♦ To permit overtime if necessary to meet the daily production goal.
♦ To allow for growth without additional construction.
♦ To reduce overhead costs of staffing night shifts.

WHAT ABOUT OVERTIME?

While overtime work may sometimes be necessary, we design our lines with the intention of meeting our daily production demand within normal working hours.

miscellaneous activities like continuous improvement meetings, morning startup and end-of-the-shift cleanup.

Let's calculate how many minutes are available to do work, shown in Figure 6.4. We are assuming that there is one 30 minute lunch break, two 15 minute rest breaks, an 18 minute continuous process improvement meeting, and approximately 6 minutes in the morning and 6 minutes in the afternoon for startup and cleanup. That leaves us with 420 minutes of hands-on work time available to us to manufacture product in our multi-product flow line.

PROCESS IMPROVEMENT MEETINGS

Of all the deductions to the number of work minutes per shift, the planning for process improvement meetings is usually the least understood by aspiring flow practitioners. A multi-product flow line takes away many of the forms of waste that mask inefficiencies, but it also adds an element of risk. By removing inventory from the process, we could also expose the line to a higher level of "fragility" or potential stoppages if we do not take the appropriate corrective actions. Excess inventory allows processes to continue operating even when other processes in the line have broken down. This is possible

FIGURE 6.4 WORK MINUTES PER SHIFT	
Total Shift Minutes	510
- [Lunch]	30
- [Breaks]	30
- [Process Improvement]	18
- [Startup/Cleanup]	12
Total Available Per Shift	420
Number of Shifts	1
Work Minutes Per Day	420

FIGURE 6.5 PROCESS IMPROVEMENT BOARD

Priority	What	How	Who	When
1	Conveyor on Workstation 1 has a sharp corner.	Buy and install caps.	Bill Doe – Process Engineer	June 3rd.
⋮	⋮	⋮	⋮	⋮
N	Workstation 5 needs light with magnifying glass.	Not necessary. Product must be inspected with naked eye.	N/A	N/A

TAKT TIME

CHECKLIST FOR PROCESS IMPROVEMENT MEETINGS

There is no one right way to conduct Continuous Process Improvement Meetings. There are, however, many wrong ways to handle them. Just a few suggestions:

1. **Keep the meeting short.**
2. **Keep the team members focused on process improvements.**
3. **Make sure that everybody knows that we are NOT in a break.**
4. **Do not piggyback on breaks or lunch,**
5. **Do not have them right before the end of the day.**
6. **Ask for suggestions, not solutions.**
7. **Do not criticize suggestions.**
8. **If there are no suggestions, we go back to building product.**
9. **Ensure that all suggestions are documented, prioritized, and have an answer.**
10. **Make the suggestions and the plan for their implementation public.**
11. **Take a look at the display board in Figure 6.5.**

in a batch environment, since accumulation of unnecessary units is normal. In a multi-product flow environment, all excess inventories are removed, making the resources dependent on each other to continue operating. If the line stops anywhere it will eventually, and usually quickly, stop everywhere.

The most effective way to prevent costly line stoppages is to enlist the help of the people who know the line and its resources better than anybody else: the line operators. Continuous process improvement meetings have been used for quite some time in both manufacturing and administrative environments. These meetings, as the authors recommend, have the objective of soliciting suggestions for improvement to the processes in the flow line. These suggestions can include preventive maintenance and equipment issues, safety and ergonomic matters, materials presentation, or lighting and fixture design.

There are many excellent books and articles written around the topic of Continuous Process Improvement, Kaizen, and other improvement techniques, and we don't need to repeat them here. The main point we want to make is that there are certain deductions we want to make to the number of working hours/minutes per shift per resource, that allow time for these process improvement activities. Those deductions must be clearly documented, so they can be periodically reviewed. The final result should be real and believable.

The number of contribution minutes per resource must be a reflection of the reality of the shop floor.

- Is the total lunch time *really* 30 minutes, or is the time *in* the lunchroom 30 minutes?
- Are the breaks *really* 15 minutes each?
- Are we the poster children for work ethic?
- How many minutes per day are attributable to machine breakdown?

TAKT TIME

Many times, a line is under-resourced because we chose to ignore the reality of the factory floor. If the number of minutes per day we can expect is not the 420 minutes/shift you see in Figure 6.4, it is unlikely that you will be able to change that overnight or by the time you bring the flow line live. Management mandates that take *time* to implement, unless followed up by policies, will not result in magic improvement to the number of contribution hours/minutes of people or machines. We are by no means suggesting that you should accept inefficiencies or unacceptable behaviors, but expecting to change those simply because you announced that "we are going to flow" is a bit naive. If the number of minutes you are using to design the line is a lower number than it should be, make sure that you let supervisors and operators on the floor know that. Then enlist their help to solve the problem.

CALCULATING TAKT TIME

We are now ready to calculate the line's designed production rate, which is commonly known as takt time. Takt time is a time-volume relationship that describes the rate of production both at the end of the line and also for a specific process. Takt time will be used to calculate resources as well as to establish the amount of work content per workstation in a process.

The takt time formula itself is very simple:

Available Work Minutes Per Day
Throughput Volume By Process

Figure 6.6 is a further extension of our process flow map. We expanded the matrix by adding two rows at the bottom, one for available work minutes and another one for calculated takt time. Takt time is usually expressed in minutes per unit, but it can also be expressed in other units of measure: seconds, hours or days. Very low volume environments may even express

CASE STUDY

The determination of the number of available work minutes per shift is sometimes a contentious issue. What we always recommend is to make sure that it reflects the reality of the shop floor as accurately as possible. If we are too optimistic and overestimate the number of contribution minutes a resource makes in a shift, we will create an invalid line design. That happened to a manufacturer of communication equipment where the workers were accustomed to working less than the official number of hours, by stopping early, coming back from lunch late, etc. The simple truth is that this company had a serious problem with work ethic in the shop floor, and it would be nearly impossible to get close to the 420 minutes per shift that they used in their calculations. When the line was brought live, it could not deal with the production volumes it was designed for, because it was under-resourced. It is certainly necessary to fix the problem of work ethic, but if we wait to fix every problem before putting flow manufacturing in place, we may never get there.

USES FOR TAKT TIME

Takt time is a characteristic of a process, not of a product. Processes have takt times, products have standard times. Takt time is used for:

♦ Calculation of resources per process.

♦ Determining the completion rate of the line, and of each process in minutes per unit.

♦ Establish the amount of work content per work station.

TAKT TIME

takt time in weeks or months, although its usefulness begins to fade when the cycle for each product is very long.

It is important to remember that takt time is calculated *by process*, and that it is likely to be different for each process. The factors that influence takt time include:

♦ Differences in shifts
♦ Differences in available work time
♦ Scrap
♦ Rework
♦ Options
♦ Quantity consumed per end-item

TAKT TIME TRAVEL

How did a German word travel from Germany to Japan, and then to the United States? During the military build-up in Germany in the 1930's, German aircraft manufacturers used the work *takt* to describe the time planned for a fuselage at each workstation. Japan's Mitsubishi adapted this progressive aircraft production method (and the word) in its aircraft plants, building over 3,700 Zeros alone before and during World War II.

After the war the word was adapted by Toyota, and then brought to the U.S. during the 1980's as part of the introduction of Just-In-Time concepts. Today the word *takt* is in common usage in all three countries, and around the world.

Let's use a an automobile assembly plant as an easy to understand example, to drive home the concept of takt time. If the plant works one shift, and the total time per shift is adjusted down to accommodate lunch, breaks and meetings, there are probably around 400 minutes available to do work. If the goal of the plant is to produce 400 cars per day, then what is the takt time of the final assembly process? Divide 400 by 400, resulting in a takt time of 1 minute per car. What about some of the other processes? Each car needs 4 wheels and a spare, a total of five wheels per car. To produce 400 cars a day, we will have to produce 2,000 wheels. The takt time of the wheel assembly process will then be 400 divided by 2000, or 0.2 minutes per wheel. If defects occur and some of the cars need to run through the assembly line twice, that will affect the total volume that needs to be processed. Not every car requires a sunroof, so the volume for the sunroof line will be less than 400 units per day, and the takt time for the sunroof line will be greater than one minute. This example illustrates the fact there although there is a takt time at the end of the line, takt time must be calculated for every process.

Armed with the calculation of takt time per process, we just need one more element to calculate resources per

TAKT TIME

FIGURE 6.6 TAKT TIME CALCULATIONS

Part Number	Description	Forecast Daily Volume	Mold	Grind	Motor Assy	Wiring Harness Assy	E Test	Mandrel Assy	Final Assy	Test	Pack
16445DR	Drill	56.0	X		X	X	X		X	X	X
16456DR	Drill	84.0	X		X	X	X		X	X	X
16467DR	Drill	65.0	X		X	X	X		X	X	X
16878SD	Sander	3.2	X	X	X	X	X		X	X	X
16865CS	Circular Saw	64.0						X	X	X	X
16227OS	Orbital Sander	76.0	X		X	X	X		X	X	X
16238OV	Orbital Sander	8.0	X		X	X	X		X	X	X
16144CS	Chain Saw	54.0						X	X	X	X
16155CS	Chain Saw	46.0						X	X	X	X
Process Throughput (Units/Day)			292.2	3.2	292.2	292.2	292.2	164.0	456.2	456.2	456.2
Total Work Minutes			420	420	420	420	420	420	420	420	420
TAKT Time (Time/Throughput)			1.44	131.25	1.44	1.44	1.44	2.56	.92	.92	.92

process, the work content per process, in the form of a standard time. Standard work and standard time will be discussed in the next chapter.

The total work minutes by process, divided by the throughput volume by process, yields the takt time by process. Note that although the work minutes can differ by process, differences in the work times between processes will drive the need for additional inventory, and are thus discouraged. Due to capital and capacity constraints, however, it is sometimes necessary to incur that inventory penalty rather than purchase an additional machine.

GERMAN PHRASES THAT USE THE WORD TAKT

To beat time: den Takt schlagen
To dance in step: im Takt tanzen
Clock pulse: der Takt
Musical beat: der Takt
Engine intake stroke: der Ansang Takt
He beats time with his foot: Er schlug mit dem Fuss den Takt

TAKT TIME

LAW OF RELATIVITY

Relative resource location means relative to the other production resources, not to the actual factory layout.

FIGURE 6.7 MULTI-PRODUCT PFD

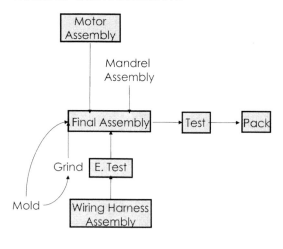

THE MULTI PRODUCT PFD

We have grouped products into families based on their process commonality. When multiple products belong to the same family, we can say with a high degree of confidence that these products will be built on the same line or set of resources. We now need to ensure that commonality of processes also means commonality of flow paths. Two products may have an "X" under the same process column but they could require the use of that process at completely different locations. We must now, review the Process Flow Map with the family definitions and the Process Flow Diagrams to create one master Process Flow Diagram that displays *all* the potential flow paths all the products follow. We will refer to this diagram as the *Multi Product Process Flow Diagram*. This can be a pretty involved task, but its result is essential to our ability to create a viable line design. The multi product PFD provides us with an overall look the *relative* resource locations. This valuable tool also displays us with one of the most important pieces of information in the design of a flow line: *the path of highest volume*. An example of a multi-product PFD for our power tool factory is shown in Figure 6.7.

To create a multi-product PFD, we take the most complex PFDs as a base. From that starting point we will add, one product at a time, all the additional processes and flow paths that apply to that specific family. We may need to rearrange process locations in the diagram to ensure that we get a clear view of all flow paths with special attention to crossing paths, as they will pose a challenge when setting up actual manufacturing resources in the plant layout. Once all the processes and paths have been laid out on the multi-product PFD, the next step is to highlight the paths of highest volume, as documented in Figure 6.7 as the shaded processes.

TAKT TIME

The multi-product PFD for our power tools factory provides us with some very useful information:

There is a main path that every product follows: final assembly → test → pack. The resources associated with these processes are the ones that will determine the basic shape of the line. The most likely scenario is that the location of the other resources will be established after the three central processes have been placed on the layout.

There are several processing paths in second order of volume: motor assembly → final assembly; wiring harness assembly → electrical test → final assembly. These paths will be the first feeding resources to be located in the closest proximity to central processes.

The processing path mandrel assembly → final assembly is of much lower volume than the others, then a compromise on its physical location would be less taxing. The very low volumes in this process makes it also a candidate for becoming an independent process, controlled via an inventory pull signal (materials Kanban)

The processing path mold → final assembly has as much volume going through as motor assembly and wiring harness, but the setup times associated with the injection molding machine in this process makes it a candidate for material Kanban in an independent process.

In Chapter 8, we will create a preliminary layout, based on the data gathered and the resource calculations per process. We will then used the multi-product PFD as our basis for determining resource locations in the factory or office layout so as to optimize product flow.

LESSONS LEARNED

Let's make sure that we keep track of our basic information needs. So far, in Chapters 4 through 6, we have gathered:

1. A product list – 80/20 rule plus products with unique processes
2. Process flow diagrams for all of the models
3. A process flow map, documenting in a matrix the relationship of products and processes
4. Calculation of throughput volume, the number of units that will need to be built in a process to meet a target volume
5. Calculation of available work minutes, excluding meals, breaks and other activities
6. Calculation of takt time by process
7. Creation of a multi-product process flow diagram.

AEROSPACE LESSONS LEARNED

1. The concept of Takt time is less applicable in a high mix environment with highly differing work content times.
2. It is possible and necessary to deal with differing products, but two factors are critical: a flexible, cross-trained workforce and available capacity.

TAKT TIME

AEROSPACE TAKT TIME

Is the concept of takt time applicable in a high-mix, low-volume environment like aerospace? The answer is both yes and no. In Flow Manufacturing takt time is used for several purposes:

♦ Calculate resources
♦ Balance work
♦ Set the rhythm or pace of the line

Takt time is calculated, as discussed in this chapter, by dividing available daily work time by the throughput volume (number of units per day). Takt time is calculated by process, not by individual product. The throughput volume is the sum of the all of the different products that we want to include in our line/cell design process, and the takt time is therefore based on an *average* mix and volume. The challenges for aerospace companies to apply the takt time concept include the following points:

♦ Work is typically done in batches related to a customer order. If the customer orders 20 units, these units are usually built together as a group, as opposed to being staggered throughout the day or mixed with other products. Some products will always take longer than takt time to complete the work, and other products will always take less time. If products are not mixed, it will be difficult to balance the work to a takt time.

♦ It is preferable to group products in a line or cell with similar work content times. This may be difficult or impossible in an aerospace environment with hundreds or thousands of products. The result is difficulty in balancing the work load.

So what is the correct approach? In general, aerospace manufacturers will need to maintain a higher level of flexibility in both machine resources and people. Setup reduction is extremely important. *Line balance* may be done on a product by product basis, without reference to an average takt time.

CHAPTER

8

STANDARD WORK

Standard work definition is a foundation concept for flow manufacturing, creating the basis for resource calculations, line balancing, continuous improvement, training, variability reduction and world-class quality.

STANDARD WORK

It is difficult to appreciate fully the impact of Frederick Winslow Taylor on our modern way of life, since his ideas have become so completely absorbed into our everyday culture. The pursuit of efficiency and the *one best way* seem, to most of us, to be normal and sensible.

Eliminating waste has become the guiding principal in most organizations, and documenting and standardizing work is regarded as world-class behavior. When first introduced, however, "Taylorism" was vehemently opposed by many labor and management groups, and Taylor was forced to defend his ideas before a hostile U.S. Congress.

For better or for worse, Taylor won. By the 1920's in the United States and abroad, both labor and management groups had largely embraced the concept. His works had been translated into over 20 languages, including Japanese, and the Taylor approach to manufacturing became quickly known around the world. Today, the analysis and documentation of work steps and work times is also a foundation discipline of flow manufacturing, known as *standard work*. This chapter describes the process of creating standard work definitions and how they are used.

In flow manufacturing, the creation of a standard work document begins with the desire to establish the best practice for doing a job. The standard work definition is created with the goal of minimizing human effort and time, ensuring safety and ergonomic concerns, reducing ancillary waste like scrap and energy, and achieving zero defects. Workers are expected to follow the standard work documents, and are trained in their use. Descriptions of the standard work definitions are posted in the work areas, preferably in an easy-to-use

STANDARD WORK DEFINITION (SWD)

A definition of the required work and identified quality criteria to build a product in the specific production process.

STANDARDIZATION

"To standardize a method is to choose out of many methods the best one, and use it. Standardization means nothing unless it means standardizing upward. What is the best way to do a thing? It is the sum of all the good ways we have discovered up to the present. Today's best, which superseded yesterday's, will be superseded by tomorrow's best. If you think of 'standardization' as the best that you know today, but which is to be improved tomorrow, you get somewhere. But if you think of standards as confining, then progress stops."

- Henry Ford
***Today and Tomorrow* (1926)**

DETAIL ORIENTED

The excellence is in the details.

- *Gregory L. Sullivan*

STANDARD WORK

MURPHY'S LAW

Murphy somehow managed to unravel the very fabric of the cosmos itself and lay bare the relentless perversity with which it is woven. *"If anything simply cannot go wrong, it will anyway."*, he said. It was a defining moment in history and Murphy's accomplishments provided the foundation for a host of others who would follow in his giant footsteps. There will only ever be one Murphy but his successors have, nonetheless, made significant contributions to his work.

♦ If anything can go wrong, it will.

♦ If there is a possibility of several things going wrong, the one that will cause the most damage will be the one to go wrong.
Corollary: If there is a worse time for something to go wrong, it will happen then.

♦ If anything just cannot go wrong, it will anyway.

♦ If you perceive that there are four possible ways in which something can go wrong, and circumvent these, then a fifth way, unprepared for, will promptly develop.

♦ Left to themselves, things tend to go from bad to worse.

♦ If everything seems to be going well, you have obviously overlooked something.

♦ Nature always sides with the hidden flaw.

♦ Mother nature is a bitch.

- www.filoday.com

graphical format, emphasizing the key work steps and quality checks that may be required. Standardization of work creates a baseline from which improvements can be made over time, and helps to eliminate process variability that has a highly negative effect on flow manufacturing lines.

The standard work definitions should not simply come down from management; the people doing the work itself should have a hand in their creation, and have ownership of them. This approach has several advantages, not the least of which being that the operators know the work best, and are closest to it. Buy-in of any process changes and improvements will be clearly better if the workers themselves originated the ideas. An environment in which new ideas can be introduced and implemented by the workers can help evolve the standard work definitions to a continually improving level. Workers will need to receive the necessary training to be able to analyze work steps and document standard work correctly. Management must also be willing to allow this level of participation from the workforce.

The method for documenting standard work is fundamentally simple: go out on the factory floor or office, observe the work within a process, and document it as a series of tasks or work steps. Take a sampling of work and time by observing a number of different operators doing the same tasks. The scope of a standard work definition covers both a *process*, i.e. a logical grouping of work steps that flow, and a *product* or family of products. If a family of products share the same work steps and times, it can share the same standard work definition.

The standard work definition form, as seen in Figure 7.1, can be tailored to the needs of different work environments, depending on the need for specific types of information. A labor-intensive environment with few machines, will be focused on the balance of labor work

STANDARD WORK

FIGURE 7.1   STANDARD WORK DEFINITION FORM

Standard Work Definition

Process	Final Assembly		Page 1 of 4
Product	HR55		
Multi Product Flow Line	Air Moving		
SWD Name	FA-HR55/57		Motors "R" Us

Work Elements				Material Content			Work Content								Total Quality Management
							Machine Setup		Machine Run		Labor				
Order	Overlap	Description	Code	Part Number	Qty		Attended	Unattended	Attended	Unattended	Setup	Conversion	Transportation	TQM Check	Self Check
10		Retrieve fixture from under the conveyor	DS								0.2				Fixture matches motor series number
20		Retrieve stator and place in fixture	DS								0.8				Check shell for exposed metal, presence of all notches, and all wires tucked in.
30		Insert wire-exit grommet	W									0.5			
40		Attach mounting bracket with one screw	W	6672—bracket 2042—screw	1 1							0.3			Install on wire exit side. Screw gun set to "3"
50		Repeat step 40 once	W	2042—screw	1							0.1			Screw gun set to "3"
60		Retrieve top shield and install with one screw	W	1068—screw	1							0.6			Bearing is greased and grease fitting is tight.
70		Repeat step 60 once	W	1068—screw	1							0.1			Screw gun set to "5"
80		Insert rotor guide into stator	DS								0.2				Do not scratch coils
90		Retrieve rotor and install in stator	W									0.6			Long side of shaft first. Check for free turn.
100		Retrieve bottom shield and install with one screw	W	1068—screw	1							0.6			Bearing is greased and grease fitting is tight. Set screw gun to "5"
Totals											1.2	2.8			

SWD for Manufacturing

STANDARD WORK

TQM SELF-CHECK

A quality check that is performed at any point on the Standard Work Definition where an element of work contains process variability. The self-check is the responsibility of the employee who has had to perform any work steps that could be done incorrectly when only one way is the correct way.

steps, error-proofing the process, and a reasonable estimate of work times. Machine intensive environments need to look at setup times, internal and external work steps, and other machine related data. The columns that are needed on the standard work definition form can vary. In all cases, however, it is important to document the detailed work steps, the work times, the order of work and the quality aspects of the work. Machine and labor times are measured independently, since they can be different.

Some care needs to be applied when observing and documenting work steps and times. The most important point is to let the operators know what is taking place, and the reason for capturing this information. Having workers document their own work helps reduce the concern that the work steps will not be documented correctly. Depending on the company environment and culture, operators may tend to either slow down (thinking that you're out to cut their standard time) or speed up (thinking that you are measuring their individual performance). Individuals naturally work at different speeds, so gathering a sample of work times is necessary.

Simply using preexisting process documentation and standard times is *not* recommended, although we might use this documentation as a starting point. The flow manufacturing implementation is an opportunity to gather fresh information, and to get close to the work. Preexisting work documentation may have been adjusted by various factors that cause it to be very different from the actual base work time. The work steps themselves may have changed over time, and the level of detail in existing documentation may be inadequate. There almost certainly will be data elements missing that will need to be gathered. For all of these reasons, it is a good idea to take a fresh look at the work being done, and not simply rely on existing data.

An important rationale for reviewing the standard work has to do with an evaluation of quality, with an eye to

STANDARD WORK

error-proofing the work steps. In a perfect world a work step can be performed only one way, the right way, with no possibility for error. If this is not the case and a mistake can be made, Murphy's Law will rule and ways must be found to eliminate the possibility of defects, or at least catch the mistake at the place where it occurs. Mistake proofing the process, sometimes called *poka-yoke*, is always the first choice, and often simple tools or fixtures can go a long way to prevent errors at a work step. Worker inspection is a requirement in cases where a possibility of error remains. This technique is called a *TQM self-check* step. If necessary, this self inspection step can be supplemented by having another co-worker check the same work step; this is called a *TQM check point*. By applying both a TQM self-check and a TQM check point, each work step subject to variability will have been looked at by two sets of eyes. Applying these simple and usually inexpensive remedies often has an immediate and powerful beneficial effect on quality.

The final recommendation in documenting standard work is to be realistic with the task times. Flow manufacturing is not intended to be a labor reduction or labor efficiency program per se; productivity gains will come as a result of a focus on flow and balance, and with the elimination of non-value-added steps. The big costs for most products are material and overhead, not labor. There is a tendency in manufacturing to be obsessed with labor reduction, if for no other reason than it is seemingly a controllable cost element. While we are not suggesting that direct labor costs be ignored, it is important to keep a proper focus on the overall strategic goals of customer response and quality.

What level of detail is appropriate for the work steps on the standard work form? How far should we subdivide the process? If we get too detailed, with only seconds per task, we will end up with a large number of work steps and we may never even finish the documentation work. Five hours of total work content documented in 10

STANDARD TASK DEFINITIONS

An entire niche industry exists to address the desire for standardized tasks and times. It should not be necessary, for example, to reinvent the wheel every time you document the work steps for a new product. The time required to inset and tighten a screw may be pretty much the same for every one of your models, including the quality aspects of the work. We could then reuse this task definition where required in our process documentation.

Companies that are mature in the implementation of flow manufacturing are doing exactly that. Even though they may have a large number of different products and models, the creation of a new standard work definition is significantly easier since they are able to draw on a library of standard tasks.

STANDARD WORK

USING TIME ESTIMATES

There is no doubt that the development of standard work documentation can take a substantial amount of time. What happened to the idea of *Rapid Improvement* if we're spending all our time documenting standard work?

There really isn't a good shortcut for understanding your processes in detail, but flow can be introduced more quickly by using educated estimates of process times. Using an estimate of work time, rough-cut resources can be calculated and a flow line put in place. The standard work detail would be completed at a later time. In this way the benefits of flow can be enjoyed more quickly. Also be prepared for more adjustments and more redoing of the line using this approach.

second increments will result in 1,800 tasks and a book the size of *War and Peace*. Not enough detail, on the other hand, will make it difficult to balance the work, and will not give us sufficient visibility of the quality aspects of the work. The right level of detail is driven by the expected target volume of the line, and the total work content of the product. It can take over 500 work hours to build a railcar, for example, and much of this work is welding. Individual work steps in this low-volume environment can be several hours in length. High volume electronic assembly lines, by contrast, may need to complete a product every 10 seconds. In this environment the standard work definition will need to be extremely detailed if we are to have any hope of balancing the work well. For many office or manufacturing environments, tasks measured in minutes is sufficient and the right level of detail. Applying intelligence to the level of process documentation detail needed can be an importance success factor in the implementation process, and in being able to complete it in a timely fashion.

DESCRIPTION OF SWD FIELDS

Following below is a short description of the various data elements we might want to document on a standard work form. Some of these data fields may not be important in some environments, and may not be included in Figure 7.1. We need to understand the right level at which to document work, and the right amount of detail to include in this documentation. Too much detail can be as bad as too little. The main point is that the standard work document should be useful and practical, and provide information that can actually be used.

Header Information
Standard work is documented at the product and process level, so both of these data elements should be included at the top of the form. The date that the SWD was created is necessary, as well as the documenter's name.

STANDARD WORK

Task Description

The most basic element of the standard work definition is the description of the work step itself. How much detail is needed? The task description should be sufficiently detailed to clearly describe the work step, while at the same time keeping the wording concise.

Order

The sequence in which the tasks should be done. The work steps within a process are normally performed one after the other in a sequential manner, but there may be exceptions, especially when documenting a process with more than one labor resource working at the same time and location.

Previous Work Step

If all of the work steps are sequential, one after the other with no exceptions, then this data element is not needed. It is not uncommon, however, to need to document concurrent or overlapping work tasks. For example, on a large product it may be possible to have two or more people working on the unit at the same time. The *previous work element* can be used to correctly document overlapping or out of sequence steps.

Parts Consumed

The product Bill of Material is not normally structured to a specific task or work element. Traditional multi-level Bills of Material are normally structured by subassembly part number, not at the more detailed work step level. When the flow line is set up, however, our material delivery strategy will be to store all of the material required at each workstation using material kanban methods. As work steps are grouped to *takt time*, the required material that goes with the work will need to be identified. It is important to capture this detailed material information at the same time that the standard work elements are being documented. Otherwise you'll just have to do it later. Tooling and fixtures can also be documented here.

USING VIDEO

A video camera can be useful to document the work steps, since the tape can be reviewed as often as necessary and steps can be timed easily from the tape. There is something a bit intimidating about standing next to a worker with a stop watch in your hand, although having a video camera running also is distracting.

Video cameras are also very useful in documenting and understanding setup work steps.

STANDARD WORK

FIGURE 7.2 SAMPLE TASK CODES

Code	Description
DS	Dynamic Setup
SS	Static Setup
DT	Dynamic Transport
ST	Static Transport
W	Work
I	Inspection
T	Test

Quantity

The quantity of each component part consumed when performing the related task needs to be known. This quantity may be less than the Bill of Material quantity, since the same component may be consumed at some other workstation as well. The quantity required at the task level is also communicated on the *graphical work instructions*, to be discussed later in a later chapter.

Work Content Time

Time estimates will need to be measured and documented for each task. This is normally accomplished by observing the work being performed, and timing a sample of this work with different operators. It is not recommended to simply use the company's existing time standards, but rather to gather fresh information through direct observation.

It is important also to document the kind of work being done. Is this task a setup step, a value-added work step, a move or transportation step? This information can be used for process improvement purposes, cost reduction, and line balancing. The standard work definition form in Figure 7.1 demonstrates the use of different columns to capture different types of work. Another technique used by some companies, also shown on Figure 7.1, is to create a *task code* to identify the type of work performed. Sample task codes are displayed in Figure 7.2.

TQM Self Check

A quality check that is performed at any point on the standard work definition when an element of work contains process variability, i.e. it is possible for the work to be performed incorrectly. The self-check is the responsibility of the employee who has actually done the work. Part of the operator training process is to ensure that any required quality checks are clearly understood and are able to be performed correctly. The quality criteria, what is being inspected, is described here.

STANDARD WORK

TQM Check Point

This is a second quality check that is performed to validate that an element of work with variability has been completed correctly. The TQM Check Point is the responsibility of the *next* employee downstream in the flow process. If the product is found to be defective, failing the TQM Check, the piece is passed back to the person upstream who originally performed the work step. That person must remedy the problem. This quality technique is also known as *check-do-check*.

Value Added

A value added work step is a step that advances the product closer to completion, or adds value in the eyes of the customer. Non-value-added work is work that does not advance the product closer to completion, or does not add value in the eyes of the customer. Common examples of non-value-added work steps include setup and move work.

Formally classifying tasks as valued added can serve several purposes. First, it gives you some idea of the size of the opportunity for improvement. Calculate the amount of non-value-added work as a percentage of the total. You may be surprised! Second, it gives you a checklist of continuous improvement activities that can be prioritized and worked on. Non-value-added work steps typically don't require the approval of design engineering, since they don't involve work that physically changes the product itself. Process improvement teams will typically be working on the elimination of non-value-added work steps. Of course, if the NVA work step is easy to eliminate, just do it!

Distance

If the product must be moved from one location to another, this data element is used to document the

PRODUCT TESTING

Questions often arise about how to classify functional tests. There is no doubt that if the customer is willing to pay for a test, or maybe even insists upon it, then that test adds value in the eyes of the customer. What about functional tests that the customer did not pay for directly, or probably doesn't even know about?

One argument is that by testing the product we are finding defects, and that this is valuable in the customer's eyes. After all, the customer doesn't want to receive defective products!

There is no doubt that the end-user wants a quality product, but how we get there is up to us. If we could improve our processes so that defects were essentially eliminated, the test could be eliminated and the customer would be equally happy (or maybe happier). Functional tests not directed by the customer therefore are generally classified as non-value-added. Even so, we may need to continue to do them.

STANDARD WORK

actual distance, in feet, yards or meters. Movement from one workstation to another may or may not be documented as a separate task, depending on the overall takt time. In a high volume environment, the movement of product can be a significant percentage of the total work time, and should be documented separately.

Internal/External

These terms are used in reference to setup or changeover work steps performed with machines. An internal step must be performed while the machine is stopped, while an external step can be performed outside of the machine while it is still running on the previous job. A basic technique of setup reduction is to investigate ways to convert internal steps to external ones. Although an external work step still needs to be done, and is still non-value-added, it does not occupy the machine directly and is therefore is preferred.

Dynamic/Static

A dynamic work step is done for every piece or every product, while a static work step can be done once for a batch. Setting up a press, for example, is a static step since it is done one time before running many pieces. Placing the part in the die manually, or removing a piece from the same press, would be classified as a dynamic work step since it must be done for *every* piece.

Static Quantity

For static work steps (see above) it is useful to know the average static quantity. For the press example above, how many pieces are typically run once the setup is complete? This number, of course, is subject to change as processes improve.

STANDARD TIME MAP

Once we have understood the work content time by documenting the standard work, we can then populate

LEADERSHIP

"The productivity of work is not the responsibility of the worker but of the manager."

Peter F. Drucker

STANDARD WORK

FIGURE 7.3 STANDARD TIME

Part Number	Description	Forecast Daily Volume	Mold		Grind		Motor Assy	Wiring Harness Assy	E Test		Mandrel Assy	Final Assy	Test		Pack	
			L	M	L	M	L	L	L	M	L	L	L	M	L	M
16445DR	Drill	56.0	.3	.7			1.7	4.2	1.3	1.3		3.3	1.5	3.2	2.2	.9
16456DR	Drill	84.0	.3	.7			2.3	4.5	1.3	1.3		12.2	1.5	6.5	2.3	.9
16467DR	Drill	65.0	.3	.7			2.7	5.3	1.3	1.3		4.1	1.5	3.3	2.5	.8
16878SD	Sander	3.2	.3	.9	2.1	2.1	1.7	4.6	1.3	1.3		3.5	1.5	3.4	3.1	.8
16865CS	Circular Saw	64.0									2.8	10.5	1.5	5.9	2.1	.8
16227OS	Orbital Sander	76.0	.3	1.0			3.7	4.6	1.3	1.3		4.5	1.5	3.1	2.5	.8
16238OV	Orbital Sander	8.0	.3	1.4			2.3	4.5	1.3	1.3		4.2	1.5	3.3	2.4	.9
16144CS	Chain Saw	54.0									2.8	11.3	1.5	6.2	2.3	.8
16155CS	Chain Saw	46.0									2.8	9.8	1.5	6.6	3.2	.9
Process Throughput (Units/Day)			292.2	292.2	3.2	3.2	292.2	292.2	292.2	292.2	164.0	456.2	456.2	456.2.	456.2	456.2
Total Work Minutes			420	420	420	420	420	420	420	420	420	420	420	420	420	420
TAKT Time (Time/Throughput)			1.44	1.44	131.2	131.2	1.44	1.44	1.44	1.44	2.56	.92	.92	.92	.92	.92

L= LABOR M=MACHINE

a process flow map matrix format with the total times for each product and process. We can use the same matrix format we used earlier, but instead of an "X", we will enter the sum of the times from our standard work document for both machine and labor. Figure 7.3 shows the process flow map with work times for our power tool products. We should not include any static times in our summation, since static work is done for a batch, and not for every piece. Note that we have documented two times for each product/process, one for the labor time and one for the machine time. This is necessary because the times for machine and labor can be

PRODUCT FAMILIES

In Chapter 5 we talked about a second criteria to refine our family definition. A good example of family definition based on work content time is the Test process in Figure 7.3 above. It shows that 4 products have high work content times, and the other 5 products have low work content times. We would have a hard time making all nine products flow through the same set of resources, working to the same takt time. Instead, think about separating the products into Test 1 and Test 2.

STANDARD WORK

different for the same task. Our resource calculations will also be done independently for machine and labor.

It is important at this point to reassess our original determination of product families, since large differences in work content time between one product and another will pose a challenge to good work flow, and may cause us to reevaluate our original groupings.

Once we have completed our standard work documentation (and this is no small job!) we will be ready to proceed to the next steps in our flow manufacturing implementation: the calculation of required resources, the creation of our physical line layout, and the distribution of work among our calculated work stations.

SOFTWARE TOOLS

The question often comes up regarding which software tools to use, if any, to capture standard work information. While a pencil is the most reliable data collection tool, a spreadsheet is the most common choice and available on almost every desktop. Adding up columns of work times is a breeze, and simple analysis, sorting and printing is also easy. Learning curve issues are non-existent.

We'd also like to suggest the use of project management software (PERT). The advantages of this are several:

1. The software will automatically calculate the "critical path" time, i.e. the elapsed time through the process.
2. The software will allow you to perform "workstation definition" easily, and automatically calculate the time for each workstation.
3. Columns are user-definable so that any standard work form can be created.
4. Project management tools are especially useful for balancing work in the case where more than one person can work on the product at the same time (overlapping work).

LESSONS LEARNED

1. Flow manufacturing requires us to document the details of our work processes, using a tool called *standard work definition*.
2. The standard work definition is used for a variety of purposes: to establish consistency and reduce variability in the work, to identify and eliminate non-value-added steps, to balance work between workstations, to improve quality and to document estimated work time.
3. We can tailor the standard work definition to fit our environment.
4. We can populate a process flow map with work content times. This is used to validate our initial product family assumptions.

STANDARD WORK

AEROSPACE PROCESS DOCUMENTATION

Aerospace companies usually have taken pains to document work steps and create standard procedures for their products. Customers usually require a high level of conformance to standards and specifications as well. What might be missing from our pre-existing process documentation from a Flow Manufacturing perspective?

- ◆ **Work Content Times.** It's not unusual to find work documentation with no time standards defined. An estimate of reasonable work times is an input into our resource formula, discussed in the next chapter. Separate times are required for machines and labor.

- ◆ **Mistake-Proofing Steps.** If there is more than one way to do the work step, this potential variability needs to be addressed and resolved on the Standard Work documentation. If possible, mistake-proof the work step. At a minimum, implement an operator self-check at this step, including a "second set of eyes" by the subsequent operator if the risk of error is high.

- ◆ **Value Added Work classification.** From the point of view of the end-user, does this work step add value? Typical non-value-added work steps include setup, material movement and inspection. Don't be too quick to reduce inspection steps until you've achieved a high level of process capability.

- ◆ **Required tooling, tools and fixtures.** Any required equipment or tooling should be documented on this form. This will make the workstation design step much easier.

- ◆ **Material consumed at the work step level.** Any material to be delivered to the line using the kanban methodology will need to be assigned to specific workstations. Your Bill of Material does not normally show this level of information. This data requirement can easily become an administrative nightmare, however, so careful planning needs to be done regarding this requirement.

One more tip. In an aerospace environment with high product mix, it is possible and desirable to create standard work documentation that can be applied to many different products (assuming that the work itself is the same). Don't reinvent the wheel for every product if you can avoid it.

NOTES

CHAPTER

9

RESOURCE CALCULATIONS AND WORKSTATION DEFINITION

The end result of our data collection and analysis is a detailed line design that we can implement in our factory or office.

RESOURCES

As we progress through the steps of data gathering, analysis, refinement and calculations, we are moving closer and closer to a detailed understanding of our eventual physical line design.

Let's summarize the information available to us so far that will be used to achieve our final objective, a balanced flow line:

- ♦ Product family definition. We understand which products we intend to include in our design, and we have validated this family definition from the perspective of common processes and common work content times.
- ♦ We have documented all of the required processes by creating a process flow diagram (PFD) for each product, and summarized this information on a process flow map.
- ♦ For each product and process we have created a standard work definition, listing the work steps, work times, and other important process data. This gives us estimated work content times for each product and process.
- ♦ We have established a target volume for each of the products in our family, and calculated throughput volume for each process, i.e. the number of units that would need to be completed to meet the target volume goals, including scrap, rework, options and quantity consumed, for each process.
- ♦ We have used the takt time formula, workday time available divided by throughput volume, to calculate a production rate by process.

RESOURCE CALCULATIONS

Wow! That's quite an accomplishment so far, and quite a bit of work. We're not done yet, however. Since we now know how long it takes to do the work, the

RESOURCE CALCULATIONS

The calculation of resources (people, workstations, and machines) is performed one process at a time.

RESOURCES

standard work content time, and we know how frequently we need to complete a unit to meet target demand, takt time, we can then easily proceed to the next step in our design process, the calculation of required resources. The formula for required resources is:

$$\text{Resources} = \frac{\text{Standard Time}}{\text{Takt}}$$

There are some subtleties to this calculation, as simple as it is. The result will tell us the number of resources required, but what *kind* of resources are they? That will depend on the type of resources we have documented in our standard work definition, and which we are using as the numerator of our formula. If our labor time is 3.4 minutes per piece, and our takt time is 1.5 minutes per piece, then the number of labor resources will be calculated as:

$$\frac{3.4}{1.5} = 2.26 \text{ labor resources}$$

Similarly, if the machine time in a process adds up to 12.7 minutes, and the takt time is 3.5 minutes, then the number of machines required would be:

$$\frac{12.7}{3.5} = 3.63 \text{ machine resources}$$

What kind of machine, or what type of labor resources? That is documented on the standard work definition; the formula by itself does not need to know. If more than one type of machine or labor classification is included in a single process, which can certainly happen, then the resource calculation would need to be done independently for each unique resource and resource work time.

In a multi-product line it is *likely* that different models will have different standard work times. We discussed in the previous chapter the need to reassess our product

SEPARATE PEOPLE AND WORKSTATIONS

When we calculate the number of labor resources in our line design, we are not referring to the number of people we will need on a day-to-day basis, but rather to the number of people we would need at full capacity. The actual number of people needed can vary on a daily basis, depending on the number of products that we need to build that day.

We are also referring to is the number of physical *workstations* where work can be performed. That number does *not* change on a day-to-day basis. We would normally expect to have fewer workers than workstations.

RESOURCES

family definitions in the light of differences in standard work content times, but even within a well-defined family there can be differences. How are these handled in order to calculate required resources? We'll calculate an average time using a 8th grade arithmetic concept called a *weighted average,* using throughput volume per product as the weighting factor. We'll simply multiply each work time by its corresponding throughput volume for that product, add up all of these values, and divide by the total volume. The corresponding formula for the weighted work time is:

$$STw = \frac{\Sigma \ (VOL * ST)}{\Sigma \ VOL}$$

FIGURE 8.1, STANDARD TIME MAP WITH RESOURCE CALCULATIONS

Part Number	Description	Forecast Daily Volume	Mold		Grind		Motor Assy	Wiring Harness Assy	E Test		Mandrel Assy	Final Assy	Test		Pack	
			L	M	L	M	L	L	L	M	L	L	L	M	L	M
16445DR	Drill	56.0	.3	.7			1.7	4.2	1.3	1.3		3.3	1.5	3.2	2.2	.9
16456DR	Drill	84.0	.3	.7			2.3	4.5	1.3	1.3		12.2	1.5	6.5	2.3	.9
16467DR	Drill	65.0	.3	.7			2.7	5.3	1.3	1.3		4.1	1.5	3.3	2.5	.8
16878SD	Sander	3.2	.3	.9	2.1	2.1	1.7	4.6	1.3	1.3		3.5	1.5	3.4	3.1	.8
16865CS	Circular Saw	64.0									2.8	10.5	1.5	5.9	2.1	.8
16227OS	Orbital Sander	76.0	.3	1.0			3.7	4.6	1.3	1.3		4.5	1.5	3.1	2.5	.8
16238OV	Orbital Sander	8.0	.3	1.4			2.3	4.5	1.3	1.3		4.2	1.5	3.3	2.4	.9
16144CS	Chain Saw	54.0									2.8	11.3	1.5	6.2	2.3	.8
16155CS	Chain Saw	46.0									2.8	9.8	1.5	6.6	3.2	.9
Process Throughput (Units/Day)			292.2	292.2	3.2	3.2	292.2	292.2	292.2	292.2	164.0	456.2	456.2	456.2.	456.2	456.2
Total Work Minutes			420	420	420	420	420	420	420	420	420	420	420	420	420	420
TAKT Time (Time/Throughput)			1.44	1.44	131.2	131.2	1.44	1.44	1.44	1.44	2.56	.92	.92	.92	.92	.92
Weighted Work Time			.3	.8	2.1	2.1	2.63	4.65	1.3	1.3	2.8	7.88	1.5	4.89	2.42	.84
Required Resources			.21	.56	.02	.02	1.83	3.23	.9	.9	1.09	8.56	1.63	5.31	2.63	.92
Locations				1		1	2	4		1	1	9		6	3	

L= LABOR M=MACHINE

RESOURCES

The Σ symbol means "sum", VOL is throughput volume and ST stands for standard work time. The weighted average work time would then be used in the resource formula presented above. Of course, the weighted average work time would only need to be used when there are work time differences in the product family; if the times are all the same, no weighted time calculations are needed.

In Figure 8.1 we have added three new rows at the bottom of our standard time map, for weighted work time, calculated resources, and number of physical locations. As we indicated earlier, the calculation of resources will need to be done independently for machine and labor work.

Chances are excellent that your resource calculation will not be a whole number, as we saw in our examples above. Most likely the number will include a fraction of a resource. Many companies make the mistake of simply rounding up to the next highest integer, so that 2.26 would become 3, and 3.63 becomes 4. Before we do that, however, efforts should be made to improve the process by eliminating non-value-added work steps, and streamlining the remaining steps in order to reduce the calculated number of resources. A rule of thumb that we could apply is shown in Figure 8.2, showing guidelines for when to round down or up. Remember that we expect to gain productivity and process improvements, and simply adding an additional resource could short-circuit some of our expected benefits. Even if we decide to round up the number of resources, we would not round up the number of actual workers. With a cross-trained workforce we could have fewer workers than workstations, and the workers would be required to move to the empty workstation to do work as required.

The second to the last row of our standard time map in Figure 8.1 shows the results of our resource calculations. These are the number of resources, machines and

FIGURE 8.2 WHEN TO ROUND

Percent Over	Strategy
< 30%	Consider improving the process and rounding down
> 30% and < 50%	Consider rounding down, evaluate performance before adding a workstation
Over 50%	Round up but staff correctly

RESOURCES

workstations, that we will include in our line design. We may find that adjustments are necessary once we evaluate line balance and line flow; these topics are discussed in Chapter 9.

The last row of Figure 8.1 is used to establish the number of physical locations in our line. For labor-only processes, the locations represent physical workstations or places where an operator will do work. Machine locations represent the machine itself, separate from the human operators. The total number of locations defined on the standard time map is 28. Adding up the exact number of labor resources, including the fractions of a resource, we get 20 people. Simply putting a person at each physical location, as we might traditionally tend to do, would result in serious overstaffing and low productivity. The 20 workers would need to manage 28 locations by moving to where the work needs to be done.

We now have the two tools required to create an initial line design. The *process flow diagrams* show us what the required processes are and how the processes are connected, and one of our line design goals will be to physically connect the processes as closely as possible. The *resource calculations* tell us how many and what kind of resources are required in our line design: workstations and machines.

PRELIMINARY LINE LAYOUT

At this stage in our implementation process we are very close to understanding what our final factory or process design will look like. We are now ready to create a preliminary picture of our proposed flow environment, arranging the calculated resources into a flow relationship on paper. The preliminary line design should look very much like our original process flow diagrams, but with two important differences:

HOW MANY HELPERS?

Ms. Christensen, the 4th grade English teacher, normally takes about 20 minutes at the end of the day to clean up her classroom. Today she has an important meeting to attend, and she only has 5 minutes to get the cleanup done. She has decided to ask for volunteers to do the cleanup for her, but how many students does she need to have to get the work done in 5 minutes? Let's apply the resource calculation formula:

Work Content = 20 minutes
Time Goal (takt) = 5 minutes
Number of Resources = 20/5 = 4 students

If the students haven't done the cleanup before, it will probably take a bit longer than 20 minutes. What could Ms. Christensen do if it *had* to get done in 5 minutes?

1. Do some training ahead of time, so students understand clearly what is expected.
2. Add an additional student. The actual work per student would then be 4 minutes instead of 5.
3. Give the students Graphical Work Instructions, i.e. a picture of the work to be done by each student.

RESOURCES

- The preliminary line layout is done at the detail resource level instead of the *process* level. While on our PFDs we may have a generic process called assembly, we could now need 10 assembly workstations
- The preliminary line layout includes *all* of the processes required for our product family. We need to include all processes on the layout, arranging them logically and in close proximity, even though not all products may require all processes. We will attempt to optimize the flow for the highest volume.

The goal in the preliminary line layout is to connect all of the various resources, workstations and machines, in order to accomplish *single piece flow*. The ability to build products one at a time in a flow process is the key to many of the benefits of flow manufacturing: fastest response time through the plant, minimum WIP inventory, quick feedback on quality issues, reduced floor space and improved productivity. Although it may not always be possible, getting to single piece flow is an important objective.

Is it always possible to connect all processes directly? Although this is the ideal, the answer is clearly no. Any time that a resource is shared it will be more difficult (although not impossible) to connect the resource directly to a downstream process. It will also be difficult to physically link machines with lengthy setup times; while the machine is being set up it is not producing, and we would need to have some inventory available to supply the downstream processes while the setup is taking place. We may have processes that cannot be connected for other reasons: clean rooms, dangerous equipment or processes, special environmental or physical requirements. You may even have *monuments*: large pieces of equipment that are too big to move, or would be damaged if you tried to do so. Paint booths in many plants tend to be monuments: even if they're not well located, they are difficult and expensive to move

LINE LAYOUT CONSIDERATIONS

1. Pay attention to the relative volumes, and optimize the layout for the highest volumes.
2. Setups and shared resources will usually prevent single piece flow. Know where your supermarkets will be needed.
3. Can the work be done sequentially, or does all of the work need to take place at a single location? Product test is usually not moved from one test machine to another, for example, while assembly work can normally be divided sequentially.
4. Do you have any *monuments* (machines) that cannot be moved easily?
5. Material delivery requirements will need to be considered. Pallet jacks, forklifts, aisles and material containers need to be accommodated.
6. Don't create barriers to movement. Allow flexible movement of workers.
7. Consider the amount of space allowed. Too much room will increase move time, and allow room for unnecessary things.

RESOURCES

and usually stay where they are. The method we will use to connect these independent processes that cannot be directly connected is called a kanban *supermarket*. The supermarket is an intermediate inventory location adjacent to the consuming line that allows a connection and pull signal to the upstream independent resource to refill the supermarket quantity of material, which will certainly be more than one piece. While single piece flow is not achieved using supermarkets, they do have the benefit of eliminating the need for scheduling the upstream resource, and tying it to actual consumption.

The difficulty in connecting shared resources, and hence the difficulty of achieving single piece flow, is one reason why flow manufacturers prefer smaller, simpler and less expensive machines that *can* be physically connected, even if the machine utilization is less. The strong incentive for a highly expensive piece of equipment is to attempt to use it as much as possible, most likely by sharing it. This can lead to the waste of over-production: keeping the machine running without actual demand, and a management focus on machine utilization. Machine utilization is not ignored in a flow manufacturing environment, but the goal is to produce what is needed when it is needed, not to produce material in order to keep people busy or machines running to "earn hours".

Using our original process flow diagrams, shown in Chapter 4, and the multi-product PFD in Chapter 6 (also depicted as Figure 8.3), along with our resource calculations, we are now ready to create a preliminary line layout. We are calling this a preliminary or conceptual line layout because we are not yet ready to commit to a final, dimensionally correct CAD-level drawing. At this stage we are interested in knowing how the products will flow from workstation to workstation, whether we will organize the work in parallel or sequentially, and where we might need to use the

IDENTIFYING FAKE FLOW

1. Do operators wait while machines cycle?
2. Is there more than one piece of material between stations?
3. Do operators ever wait for work from the preceding station? Do some operators finish their work ahead of takt time?
4. Is any part of the cell more than five feet apart? Are the first and the last workstations close together or at opposite ends of the cell?
5. Does the output of the cell vary from hour to hour, or from one shift to another?
6. Is there an operator assigned to each workstation?

- Rick Harris
Fake Flow, IIE Magazine

RESOURCES

FIGURE 8.3, MULTI-PRODUCT PFD

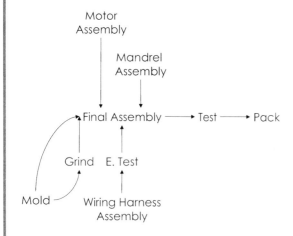

WORKSTATION QUESTIONS

1. Can the work defined at a workstation be performed by a single labor category?
2. Is there enough space for all of the material that will need to be presented at the workstation?
3. How much variability is expected in the work? How consistent will the work time be?
4. Is there a setup or changeover between models?
5. Are there any ergonomic concerns? How much weight must be lifted?
6. How many models will the operator be required to know?

supermarket technique to connect processes. The way in which we organize the flow of work can have a big impact on throughput and quality. We will try to organize work sequentially, in order to allow multiple operators to perform quality checks as a part of the flow process. Too many sequential workstations, however, can add more opportunities for imbalances and can have a negative impact on both productivity and throughput.

Figure 8.4, shown on the following page, is an example of a preliminary line layout for our power tool factory.

WORKSTATION DEFINITION

It is not enough to know that we need a certain number of assembly workstations or machines. We must also understand and formally define the specific work steps that will be performed at each location. We have already documented the detailed work steps as part of our standard work definition, including the tasks that may have a quality risk due to process variability. What needs to happen now in our implementation process is to divide up or *balance* the work among the number of calculated workstations, a step called *workstation definition*.

We are referring here mainly to labor resources, or work performed by human beings. It is difficult and illogical to stop a machine in the middle of a processing cycle, and then transfer the material to a second machine of the same type to continue on with the same work. Human beings are more flexible, however, and can perform many different types of tasks. Breaking up labor work into sequential workstations is possible, common and recommended. Machines will usually be organized

PRELIMINARY LINE LAYOUT

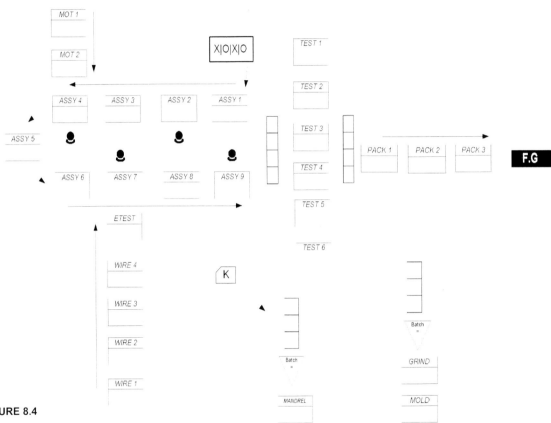

FIGURE 8.4

NOTES:

1. Mold and grind have been linked in a one-piece flow, since the grinding is required for the pieces coming out of the mold. Mold/grind cannot be connected directly to the assembly process due to setup times and multiple molded pieces required; material will go to a supermarket.

2. The work in the test process cannot be broken down into sequential increments, and hence, Test is done in parallel, with a high expected level of variability. A number of IPKs (pieces) have been allowed on either side to help overcome this variability.

3. The low volume mandrel process will build to a supermarket pull signal.

4. The nine assembly workstations have been placed in a U shape to allow workers inside the U to move easily from one workstation to another. Access to the feeder lines must also be created.

5. These are consumer products will a very short response time to the customer required, essentially same-day shipment for any model. Some finished goods will be required, and a finished goods Kanban has been established.

6. Two subassemblies, cables and motors, are now connected directly to the line as feeders.

7. In-process kanbans will be placed later.

RESOURCES

BENEFITS OF MOVING

If we organize the work sequentially, and we have fewer workers than work stations, then the workers will need to move. Here are some reasons why this is a good idea:

1. **Reduced stress and boredom. The same job is not repeated over and over.**
2. **Reduced repetitive motion injuries, by performing different tasks during the day.**
3. **Higher productivity. Partial positions are handled through worker movement.**
4. **High level of cross-training reduces the impact of vacationing and absent workers.**
5. **Moving in a flow line follows a simple set of rules.**

RULES FOR MOVING

1. **If you have an open workstation, and material to work on, then WORK at your workstation.**
2. **If you have an open workstation but no material to work on, then move UPSTREAM.**
3. **If you have a full workstation, then move DOWNSTREAM.**

These rules will be affected by the configuration and the type of work signals used on the line.

to work in parallel with other machines of the same type, and once started the work will be completed on the same machine. There are several reasons why we normally choose to organize labor work in a sequential rather than parallel fashion:

♦ By organizing the work sequentially it is only necessary to present the required materials to one workstation, the workstation where the material is consumed. Otherwise the same material would need to be replicated across a number of parallel workstations.

♦ The operator learning curve at a workstation can be reduced significantly if the operator is only required to learn a portion of the work. For example, two hours of work content divided among six workers reduces the amount of work per workstation to 20 minutes of unique work per operator.

♦ By dividing the work sequentially among a number of different operators, each piece is worked on by more than one person. This can be extremely beneficial for the detection of defects and errors, and for the implementation of the *TQM Check Point* technique (also known as the *check-do-check* method) where each work step that is subject to quality risk or variability is checked by at least two operators before being allowed to continue down the line.

If the work content in a process has been recorded on the standard work definition in sufficient detail, the formal step of defining and balancing the work to be performed at a workstation is relatively easy. It is not as simple as dividing the work equally by the number of workstations, however. The following items need to be considered when creating workstation definition:

♦ The workstation definition in a multiple product line must be done product by product, since the work content and time can be different. Start by dividing the total work content equally by the number of workstations. This gives you a time target to group the work to. Note that this time target may be equal to, less than or greater than the takt time for the process, depending on the work time for the model in question. The time target will not be significantly different from takt time unless we have a wide range of work times in the family.

◆ Do the work steps included at the workstation make sense? It may be physically impossible to break the work sequence between certain tasks, or impossible to move the material. Fixtures or tooling may be required for certain steps that cannot be moved.

◆ Are the operator skills logical and consistent at the workstation? It would not make sense to include certain tasks that are performed by a different labor category.

◆ Is there physical space for the material that will be consumed? Space limitations may put limits on the work steps that can be performed at a workstation.

Where work is to be divided into sequential groupings, *workstation definition* is a highly important implementation step. After all, we are now defining the exact work that will be performed at a workstation, and we have left our high-level calculations far behind. Input from the operators themselves is highly useful and recommended. Otherwise, you may find yourself going back to the drawing table at a later date!

GRAPHIC WORK INSTRUCTIONS

Many companies have already spent a huge amount of time and effort documenting manufacturing and business processes. The ISO certification process, for example, requires companies to document all of their key processes, and to train workers in those procedures. The ISO procedures are also subject to periodic audit, and re-certification also occurs on a regular basis. All of this is good.

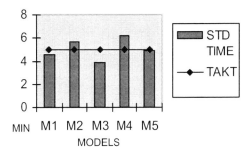

FIGURE 8.5 WORK CONTENT TIME BY MODEL

In a multiple product line, the work to be performed for a model may be equal to, greater than or less than takt time. Sequencing, or establishing a specific order in which to build the various models, can become an important factor for good line balance.

GRAPHIC WORK INSTRUCTIONS

A set of graphical representations depicting the work to be performed at a workstation including TQM checkpoints and self-checks. The identified work elements are derived from the Standard Work Definition and are equal to approximately one takt time.

RESOURCES

FIGURE 8.6 GRAPHIC WORK INSTRUCTIONS

MODEL: 19283CS			
WORKSTATION **FINAL ASSY**	**SEQUENCE #** **90**		
● CHECK DO ■ CHECK	REV. A	PAGE # 1 OF 4	
FIND	PART #	DESCRIPTION	QTY
1		ASSEMBLY	1
2	12345	INNER BIT HOLDER	1
3	53948	SPIRAL PIN	1
4	93283	OUTER BIT HOLDER	1
5	19028	SET SCREW	1

● **TQM CHECK**

VERIFY THAT 6 AND 0
LINE UP ON SCALE.

■ **SELF CHECK**

INSTALL SPIRAL PIN FLUSH
WITH OUTSIDE DIAMETER
OF BIT HOLDER USING
FIXTURE AND BALL PEEN
HAMMER.

Graphic Work Instruction provided by The Flow Center, www.theflowcenter.com

GRAPHIC WORK INSTRUCTIONS

A set of graphical representations depicting the work to be performed at a workstation including TQM checkpoints and self-checks. Part numbers are identified using *find numbers*, and the quality checks are clearly identify with color codes. In this example, the operator will first check the work done at a prior workstation (colored red), then complete the work content (colored yellow), and finally perform a self-inspection step (colored blue).

RESOURCES

The disappointing fact is this: unless workers are forced to study and read procedures, they won't. *We* probably don't read our own procedures either. It may be necessary to look at a written procedure once in a while, but in general we avoid them like the plague. It requires too much effort, they are too hard to understand, it takes too much time. The challenge to get workers to use written procedures is even tougher in a production environment, a fast-paced world where workers are rewarded for producing products, not reading manuals. Try the white glove test. Put on a white glove and run your finger across the cover of a work instruction binder, if you can find one, out on the factory floor. Chances are it hasn't been opened in quite some time.

You may notice, however, that workers will sometimes use "cheat sheets" to help them in their work. These may take the form of hand drawings, sketches, or brief notes. The cheat sheets are sometimes hidden away in tool chests or drawers, away from the prying eyes of management. They document the *real* way to build the product. Wouldn't it be better to give workers useful cheat sheets that agree with the standard work documentation? We call these *graphic work instructions*.

The graphic work instruction is a line drawing or photographic representation of the work that needs to be performed at a workstation or machine. As much as possible, the work is displayed and communicated without text. Words are kept to a minimum, although they sometimes are needed. Standard work steps can be communicated through simple icons, as shown in Figure 8.7. Graphic work instructions are also valuable as training materials, to demonstrate visually to new employees the work steps and quality checks.

Part numbers for the material consumed are also shown on the graphic work instruction. While the exact part

DIGITAL CAMERAS

Digital cameras have become increasingly popular as a way to quickly develop graphic work instructions. The quality of digital photographs has been steadily improving. For some applications a photograph is the perfect medium. Showing a specific label on a box, for example, could be captured and shown nicely. For other types of work, however, the photograph may be hard to understand, and may show too many extraneous details. It is also difficult to show a hardware exploded view using a digital photo without a lot of manual editing. In this case a line drawing is easier to understand and use. Unneeded details can be omitted.

The main point is not to be closed-minded about one or the other, photo or line drawing, but to apply intelligence in their use. The bottom line is this: if the graphic work instructions are not good, people will not use them and your effort will be wasted. It would be better not to create graphic work instructions at all rather than to do them poorly, and it's much less trouble.

FIGURE 8.7, ICONS

 Time the process

 Caution! Piece is hot!

 Write down process results in log

RESOURCES

LESSONS LEARNED

1. The detailed step of assigning specific work steps to specific locations is called *workstation definition*.
2. In a multi-product line it is necessary to group the work product by product, because the total work time can vary by product.
3. The work that is assigned to a workstation needs to make sense, from a time, materials and job skills point of view.
4. Graphic work instructions take the place of written procedures wherever possible.

number is printed on the sheet, a *find number* is often used on the drawing or photograph itself. Actual part numbers can be quite long and hard to read, so the find number is a simple identifier, cross-referenced to the actual part number, used in the graphic image.

Electronic graphic work instructions have been implemented in some manufacturing environments. Instead of a printed copy of the graphic work instruction, the image is displayed on a computer monitor. The operator can zoom in for more detailed views, enter process related data, track quality issues, all from a computer at the workstation. Central control of the graphic work instructions on a network server helps to ensure that the latest revision is used and is immediately available. The computer monitors and equipment do take up valuable workbench space, however, and the maintenance of the computer hardware and network is an additional and not insignificant expense. The relative costs and benefits of using paper graphic work instructions versus going to an electronic format will need to be evaluated, weighed by factors such as frequency of engineering changes, the suitability of the work environment, the need for data collection, and the space available.

Our line design at this stage is quite mature. Although we do not yet have a dimensionally correct factory layout that considers utilities, aisles, building columns and so forth, creating this next level of detail can be easily accomplished. Before we finalize our preliminary design, however, we need to assess the potential performance of the line from the point of view of balance. That is the topic of Chapter 10.

RESOURCES

AEROSPACE LINE DESIGN

In an environment with many different products and many different routes that these products can travel, the concept of a "line design" as presented in this chapter may be difficult to envision for some aerospace companies. At first blush there might seem to be too many different routings for the products to follow, with work center scheduling appearing to be the only option. Keep in mind the following observations:

- Once you've gone through the Process Flow Diagram and Process Flow Mapping steps described previously in this book, you may find that you have more process commonality than you originally thought. In that case, maybe a line dedicated to a family of products actually *is* possible.

- A "line" can include optional paths. Don't think that all products need to share exactly the same routing in order to be included in the design. In our example in this chapter, we did include optional processes. Of course the products in a family *do* need to share a large percentage of processes in common in order for the family definition to make sense.

- The key strategy for reducing cycle time is the technique of linking processes together into lines or cells, and reducing hand-offs and queue time. If you can't link *all* of the processes together in a flow due to an excessive number of different process paths, consider putting sub-sets of the work into a flow. The concept is called *Overlapping Cells*. In this method we create family cells for a portion of the flow process, using the method and criteria previously described. These cells will then link to other cells via a pull signal such as a Kanban card or IPK signal. While some queue time penalty will be incurred, the performance results of overlapping cells is a great improvement over traditional batch and queue techniques.

NOTES

CHAPTER

10 ACHIEVING BALANCE

Physically linking manufacturing processes together, so the completed output of one process can be directly consumed into the next, dramatically reduces inventories and cycle times.

ACHIEVING BALANCE

Traditional departments and work centers are created by grouping together similar types of work and machines. This grouping of work and machines helps with organizational control and the collection of performance, routing, and inventory reporting data.

Similar work and machines are physically placed together in one area of the facility, and in most cases this grouping of work or machines provides little consideration for the equal distribution of capacity. The unequal distribution of capacity creates imbalances between manufacturing processes or work centers. These imbalances manifest as pools of excess inventory between these work centers.

Flow lines overcome this imbalance problem. Flow lines are progressive lines established with a facility layout in which standard work tasks are done in a sequential and progressive manner. Where possible, all the processes necessary to build a product are physically linked together. The physical arrangement of the resources is important because it allows work tasks to be distributed, accumulated, and balanced evenly throughout the entire manufacturing cycle.

Balancing to takt and physically linking manufacturing processes together so the completed output of one process can be directly consumed by another process dramatically reduces inventories and cycle times. Because manufacturing processes are divided into equal elements of work, grouping of similar labor and machines into independent departments is no longer necessary. Only the resources necessary to build the products are placed on the line.

By eliminating imbalanced departments, pools of work-in-process inventory cannot accumulate. By balancing and linking of all processes, products are built in their

DEFINITION OF BALANCE

A balanced line is able to flow products at the designed rate (takt time) at the same time that workers do not have to wait.

ACHIEVING BALANCE

work content time only, since the normal wait and queue times for products that are routed in batches through the different manufacturing departments is eliminated.

Work is not *naturally* balanced, and in order to achieve a smooth flow with minimum queue time and inventory, it is usually necessary to make some adjustments. The six methods used to adjust work balance are the following:

- ◆ Eliminating waste
- ◆ Relocation of work
- ◆ Adding resources
- ◆ In Process Kanbans
- ◆ Inventory and Time
- ◆ Sequencing

ELIMINATING WASTE

The recommended starting point for balancing work is by reducing or eliminating waste in the form of non-value-added (NVA) work steps. Not all of the work that is performed actually adds value to the product. Moving material from one place to another, for example, may be a task that must be done today, but that can be eliminated in the future through an improved factory layout. Setting up a machine for the next production order must also be done, but while we are setting up we are not actually working on the product. These examples of non-value-added work steps become our first area of focus in attempting to balance work flow.

The reason is simple: we can achieve multiple benefits by focusing on non-value-added tasks. First, our objective of improving work balance can be accomplished by reducing the time spent on NVA tasks. Second, we are reducing product cost by removing work time from the product. Third, our manufacturing

IDENTIFYING WASTE

Identifying waste, especially at the start of our flow manufacturing journey, should be fairly easy. While the traditional definition of waste usually says something about *not adding value in the eyes of our customer,* we can paint with a broader brush to start. Waste can largely be classified in two categories:

1. **Time spend preparing to do work. This is also called setup or changeover time.**
2. **Time spent moving to and from the work, but not actually working.**

Examples of the former are easy to identify in machine intensive environments, but even pure assembly lines often have a significant amount of changeover or setup time. Move time sometimes involves moving material, or sometimes it is simply unnecessary operator motion. Start with these two categories, and when you're done, you will have done well.

ACHIEVING BALANCE

response time will be reduced, with a corresponding reduction in work-in-process inventory. Finally, since more worker time will be spent on value-adding work, productivity will increase. A focus on reduction of NVA work is clearly too good an opportunity to overlook.

Do we always find opportunities to eliminate NVA tasks? No, of course not, but we certainly want to assess that opportunity first. We use our source document, the standard work definition, which includes both value-added and non-value-added work steps, and provides documentation on the tasks that may be targets for elimination.

RELOCATING WORK

The second balancing tool in our tool chest is a simple one: do a better job of balancing the work by moving tasks from one workstation to another. There are a variety of reasons why the original work balance was not satisfactory. Perhaps our work content times needed some adjustment, or maybe lack of balance only became apparent once the line was up and running. The relocate work technique simply involves transferring tasks from one workplace or worker to another in order to better balance the flow.

Experienced flow practitioners don't jump too quickly to apply this technique in a new flow line. Some time should be allowed for the line to "settle down", and for the learning curve effect to take place, before applying this balancing tool.

Moving work is most easily done for labor-based work steps. Taking work from John and giving it to Peter is a simple process, providing that Peter agrees! Machine-based work, however, is more challenging. To actually stop a machine and move a semi-completed product to the next machine would not make much sense;

GETTING BUY-IN

Watch out when you start redefining the work that people do, especially in plants that have some history. Work in union environments, for example, tends to be highly pre-defined. Everyone knows which workstations or "splits" are the easy ones, and which workstations are assigned to the new guys. Relocating work can be a major political battle. Recommendation: solicit the involvement and input of the people that do the work when you make changes. And don't be too quick to relocate the work unless you're really sure it's needed.

ACHIEVING BALANCE

typically we would complete the required work on a single machine before moving the product on. For this reason, we normally use the *relocating work* tool to balance labor tasks only.

ADD MORE RESOURCES

A third balancing tool commonly used is to add additional resources, i.e. additional workstations or machines. Because there is a cost associated with additional resources, this balancing tool is not the first choice, but it may be necessary. It may be impossible to distribute assembly work evenly, and in order to avoid a *bottleneck* workstation an additional bench is added. An additional workstation occupies some floor space, and requires duplication of materials and tools.

A more subtle reason for needing to add resources is related to process variability. The initial resource calculations do not take into consideration the impact of variability in work time, or the impact of setup time. The average work time may be 12 minutes, but in actuality the time may vary between 10 and 14 minutes for the same product. Time variability can have a dramatic impact on product flow, and drive a need for additional resources. For this reason, static resource calculations without considering process variability can only be considered "rough-cut".

IN-PROCESS KANBANS (IPK)

The addition of inventory between machines or workstations is a powerful but often misunderstood technique. It is usually the case that actual work content time is variable and statistically distributed around a takt time, i.e. depending on the model being built, sometimes the work takes longer than takt, sometimes it is equal to takt and sometimes it is less than takt. Even for an individual model, the time required to

WHEN DO WE CALCULATE IPKs?

New practitioners of flow manufacturing often wonder when they will need to calculate the number of IPKs or pieces that should be placed between machines or workstations, in order to smooth the work flow. The answer is: never! There is no formula to calculate IPKs, unless there is a chronic imbalance of work content that exceeds the takt time of the line. If we could benefit from some buffer inventory, this could be determined either by trial and error or by simulating the line performance using a computer simulation tool. As a rule of thumb we will have few IPKs, or none at all. Overcoming chronic imbalances through the use of inventory is the tool called *Inventory and Time*, discussed on the following page.

ACHIEVING BALANCE

do the work usually has some inherent variability. Not everyone works at the same pace, and times can vary during the day. Although *on average* the line can meet takt time, variability in the work time or between models can cause delays and bottlenecks. Adding additional inventory in the form of a few units can help smooth the flow of work, without having a significant impact on inventory or response time. This technique is called the addition of *In Process Kanbans* or IPKs. If a resource is not able to meet takt time temporarily, the additional pieces allowed on both sides of the resource can help overcome delays and blockages for a short amount of time. The number of takt time cycles that this inventory will cover depends on the number of pieces allowed between workstations. Although adding additional material violates the principal of *single piece flow*, it is often the best and least expensive solution to process variability, and to overcome time differences between models.

How many pieces or IPKs should be added? A common method to establish the number of IPKs is simply trial and error. Add additional pieces and monitor the throughput results. A more scientific method to analyze the impact of variability would be to create a dynamic computer simulation model and conduct simulation experiments with different buffer quantities. The use of computer modeling assumes that the basic parameters of the variability are understood and can be modeled correctly, and a focus on *reducing* process variability is clearly an important key to a smooth flowing line. The number of pieces or units added using the IPK technique is small.

INVENTORY AND TIME

Another type of imbalance can occur, where the average work time *exceeds* takt time, and the resource

THE EXTRA MACHINE VS ADDITIONAL INVENTORY TEST

Should we buy another machine (add resources) or add inventory and time? Either solution could work. Things we need to consider include:

1. How big is the product, and do we have the space available? Extra inventory in the form of big green tractors between every workstation, for example, would be a challenge.
2. Do we have the additional time available? If we're already running 3 shifts, you're out of time.
3. What is the inventory worth? We would like to keep high dollar value material to a minimum.
4. How expensive is the machine? Do we already have the resource in-house? Can we supplement with a less expensive piece of equipment?

In general, we calculate the cost of both alternatives, and choose the lower cost alternative. Brilliant!

ACHIEVING BALANCE

CALCULATING INVENTORY AND TIME

Let's create some numbers to illustrate the tool of using inventory and time to overcome an imbalance at a machine. The machine cell shown in Figure 9.1 has a takt time of 0.44 minutes, but Machine 3 runs at 0.55 minutes per piece. Buying another machine is not an attractive option in this case, so we wish to use some additional time plus a calculated number of pieces before and after Machine 3 to overcome this imbalance. The formula we will use is:

$$INV = \frac{W\ MIN}{TAKT} - \frac{W\ MIN}{ST}$$

The number of addition units is:

$$INV = \frac{420}{.44} - \frac{420}{.55} = 955 - 764 = 191\ units$$

The additional work time is:

$$TIME = INV * ST = 191 * .55 = 105.05\ min$$

Machine 3 will need to work an additional 105.05 minutes per day, and accumulate 191 pieces in order to overcome this imbalance. Machines 1, 2 and 4 work normal working hours.

will *never* be able to meet maximum demand. That resource or workstation is called a *bottleneck*. This chronic case where takt time cannot be met requires a different solution than the IPK method discussed previously. In addition to adding inventory to the line, it will also be necessary to have additional work time available, since the bottleneck resource cannot meet demand during available work minutes. The strategy will therefore be to build up an inventory quantity by working additional time at the bottleneck resource in order to overcome this shortfall in production. During normal working hours the downstream internal customer can draw from this additional inventory and not wait. Additional work time must be available for this method to be applied.

The formula for calculating the number of pieces that will be required to overcome this type of imbalance is as follows:

$$INV = (W\ MIN/TAKT) - (W\ MIN/ST)$$

where

W MIN = Work minutes available during the day.
TAKT = Takt time for the line.
ST   = Standard Time at the pacing resource, the bottleneck

This calculated inventory quantity would be placed on both the upstream and downstream side of the bottleneck resource. The upstream buffer quantity will be used to supply the bottleneck resource during the time when the rest of the line is not running, while the

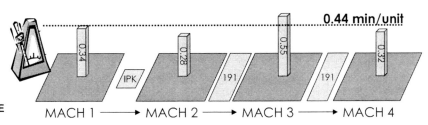

FIGURE 9.1 INVENTORY AND TIME

ACHIEVING BALANCE

downstream buffer will ensure that the next downstream workstation or machine is not starved for material during the normal work time.

This technique violates the *single piece flow* ideal, but it is often preferred over buying a new piece of capital equipment. The recommendation is to evaluate the cost of the additional inventory against the cost of an additional resource, and choose the lower cost alternative.

SEQUENCING

In a multi-product line, where more than one model is produced sequentially on the same line, there may be differences in the work time or setup time for various models that will have an impact on product flow. If the mix and order of production is not managed properly, portions of the line could become *blocked* or *starved* for material, overall capacity could be negatively impacted, and production goals could be missed.

The most common reason for needing to sequence products in a particular order has to do with setup time reduction. If we have setup times between products, and those setup times are always the same, then the actual sequence of products does not matter. More often then not, however, there are differences in the setup times, depending on which product we are going from and to. In the example shown in Figure 9.2, we can reduce the overall setup time by 2.4 hours by sequencing correctly rather than in first-in-first-out fashion.

Another reason why the flow manufacturer may need to pay attention to the order in which products are built has to do with differences in the work content times, shown in Figure 9.3. Conventional logic tells us that we should built all of the same products as a batch, together at the same time. If we need to build Product A, Product B and Product C today, we might be

FIGURE 9.2 FROM/TO SETUP MATRIX

MODEL	A	B	C	D
A	0	4.0	4.5	7.0
B	.5	0	4.0	.2
C	1.2	.2	0	2.0
D	1.9	5.5	.6	0

FIFO ORDER:
AB + BC + CD + DA = 11.9 hours

OPTIMIZED SEQUENCE:
AB + BD + DC + CA = 6.0 hours

SETUP TIME REDUCTION = 5.9 hours

FIGURE 9.3 WORK CONTENT MATRIX

MODEL/ PROCESS	Process 1	Process 2	Process 3	Process 4
A	4.0	12.3	3.5	5.5
B	4.0	6.6	3.5	5.3
C	4.0	4.6	3.7	5.7
D	4.0	10.5	3.4	5.5

CONVENTIONAL SEQUENCE:
AAAAABBBBBCCCCCDDDDD

BALANCED SEQUENCE:
ACDBACDBACDBACDBACDB

ACHIEVING BALANCE

tempted to first build all of the As, then all of the Bs and finally all of the Cs. If Product A requires more work, however, we may find that the more we build, the more the line downstream begins to "dry up", since we are unable to keep up with the designed takt time rate. Similarly, if we attempt to build Product C in a batch and this product contains *less* work content than takt time, we might find ourselves blocked since the downstream resource will not be able to consume fast enough. Sequencing the products and alternating Product A, Product C and Product B can help smooth out the flow and overcome these balancing challenges.

RESOURCE BALANCING

In spite of the seemingly natural flow of work in a machine intensive process environment, it is likely that two or more adjacent resources will not be balanced. This is to be expected since machines normally run at an optimum speed or cycle that is not related to a calculated or desired takt time. These imbalances, unless controlled, have the potential for generating large amounts of semi-processed product. The balancing of resources to a takt time within a line will tie resource utilization to customer requirements. The use of in-process kanbans will therefore control the flow of product between processes, thus keeping inventories of semi-finished product at formulated levels.

The linking together of adjacent processes that are inherently imbalanced may result in underutilization of capital equipment. For example, a machine with a cycle time of 60 seconds per piece will be able to produce approximately 400 pieces per shift. If a second machine, with a cycle time of 30 seconds per piece is linked via In-process kanbans to the first machine, it will also be forced to slow down to run at the 60 second pace. Utilization at best for the second machine will be 50%. The temptation, especially if there is significant

WORK TIME CONSIDERATIONS

Keep this thought in mind: in a flow line, any differences in work minutes between resources will automatically require inventory. Examples:

- **Going from 1 shift to 2 shifts in the same flow line**
- **Scheduling different break times for different processes in the line**
- **Scheduling different meal times in the same flow line**
- **Planning preventive maintenance on a portion of the line**

ACHIEVING BALANCE

capital investment in the second machine, will be to attempt to share the second machine, in order to improve utilization. Management will then need to weigh the cost of the inevitable additional inventory that will result, against the capital investment costs incurred by under-utilizing equipment, and choose the lower cost alternative. It is for this reason that flow manufacturers in a process environment prefer simpler, less-costly capital equipment that can be physically linked and dedicated, without requiring additional inventory or excessive concern about utilization. It is also for this reason that while utilization is a consideration, it is a secondary rather than a primary performance metric in a flow manufacturing environment.

BALANCE AND TPM

The American concept of preventive maintenance (PM) has been around for a long time, and Total Productive Maintenance (TPM) is an extension of this practice. The strategy of PM is to schedule regular intervals for machinery to service and replace worn parts before they fail in operation. TPM extends this practice further to ensure that the equipment is in perfect working order when it is needed.

In a TPM environment, the operator of the machine is expected to have a much higher level of involvement with its maintenance. The analogy that is sometimes made is that of a mother and child. The operator, the mother, cares for her child and makes sure that the child is kept healthy. The machine should not be operated in ways that could cause damage, or when the monitors indicate that there is a problem. The operator can shut the machine down at any time if there is a problem detected. The PM is performed by the operator himself, not by an outside PM specialist. Minor repairs can also be performed by the operator. The maintenance department, on the other hand, plays the role of the

PROCESS INTENSIVE INDUSTRIES

The implementation of flow or lean manufacturing in a process intensive industry is initially focused on five main areas:

1. Housekeeping and organization
2. Reduction of setup or changeover times
3. Total Preventive Maintenance
4. Supply chain and material delivery disciplines
5. Batch size optimization

The manufacturing process itself is often a "black box", machine resources connected by pipes and conveyors and not easily changed.

ACHIEVING BALANCE

LESSONS LEARNED

1. Before finishing our line design, it is important to evaluate the line from the perspective of balance. Without good balance throughput and productivity will suffer.
2. Our toolkit includes six balancing tools: eliminate waste, relocate work, add resources, add IPKs, add inventory and time, and sequencing.
3. Eliminating waste is a great first choice balancing tool since it includes multiple benefits.
4. Balance in a machine intensive environment is more difficult. TPM is a critical tool to ensure machine availability.

doctor, who is called in for more serious issues or more in-depth inspections. A close involvement by the operator can go a long way to resolving machine breakdown issues and operational problems.

TPM also places a great deal of emphasis on diagnosing and resolving root causes of machine problems. The continuous improvement process is implemented vigorously. Visual signals are also used extensively: tools like gauges, labeled parts, control charts, maintenance records, etc. are kept at the machine. In a flow manufacturing environment, preventive maintenance has a higher priority than production, and PM is not skipped due to production demands. The availability, not the utilization, of the equipment is a key performance metric in achieving production volume goals.

AEROSPACE BALANCE

Perfect balance is difficult under the best of circumstances, and even more difficult in a high-mix, low-volume environment. The easiest environment to balance would be a dedicated, single-product line, building the same product over and over. In that circumstance it would be relatively easy to optimize the balance of work, machines and materials to approach perfection. That's not what we're faced with in the aerospace environment!

The difficulties in balancing work loads requires us to be more flexible in a high-mix environment. Specifically:

◆ Cross-training is key to acceptable productivity. Workers need to know how to perform many tasks, and also need to be willing to move to where the work needs to get done. Training and certification of the workforce is essential, and is one of the 3 main tracks of the Supplier Excellence Alliance *Lean Enterprise System*.

◆ Flexibility in machines and equipment is highly desirable. Avoid "monuments", equipment that cannot be easily moved or easily shared. We prefer machines that are smaller, cheaper and slower (maybe) if this will provide us with additional flexibility.

◆ Setup reduction is tied closely to our need for flexibility. The SMED system for setup reduction provides an excellent and easy-to-understand framework for setup reduction, with a goal of reducing all setups to less than 10 minutes.

Finally, we may need to be content with somewhat lower levels of productivity, i.e. units produced per person, if this buys us improved customer response time and the ability to response quickly to changing customer demand.

CHAPTER

11

PULL SYSTEMS

Traditional manufacturing operates on a push philosophy: start dates, work orders, pick lists, ready or not! Flow manufacturing proposes to do work, or consume material, or run a machine, *when needed*. How do we know when it is needed? With a *pull signal*.

PULL SYSTEMS

Simply speaking, only two things are needed to make a product: resources and material. Flow manufacturers balance and link their manufacturing processes together, staffing those resources to customer requirements to build products.

The material required to build product is delivered to the flow lines using a technique called kanban, a Japanese word meaning *sign* or *signal*. The kanban method utilizes a series of signals to indicate when parts are needed for production.

The kanban method is a material delivery technique designed to simplify material handling and inventory management. Instead of picking purchased materials into *kits* tied to production work orders and schedules, materials are instead delivered based on a *pull signal*. This signal, sometimes called a trigger, can take the form of an empty container, a card, or even just an empty spot on a workbench or floor that needs to be refilled.

We all use kanban in our daily lives, although we probably don't call it such. An empty plate could be the signal to serve food at the dinner table. We could say that food is "pulled" to the plate by virtue of it being empty. Unless we have a very insistent mother-in-law, food is not "pushed" onto a plate that is not yet empty. Modern supermarkets also use the pull method, replenishing the shelves with only the product that was sold. Trying to "push" cans of food into the supermarket shelves would be, pun intended, a recipe for disaster. It has, in fact, been noted that the American supermarket actually provided the original inspiration for the use of material kanban at Toyota.

The benefits are many. Kanban systems require fewer inventory transactions, and reduce the amount of system maintenance activities normally required to keep

EVERYDAY USE OF KANBAN

Let's set up a kanban system with our milk delivery person. I have 2 kids, who drink a pint of milk per day each. When they pour their own milk, they tend to miss the glass and waste 10% of the milk on average. I buy milk only in gallon containers. How much milk do I need, if the milk delivery person comes once a week?

2 pints per day = 1 quart per day
1 quart times 7 days = 7 quarts/week
7 quarts plus spill factor = 8 quarts/week
Two gallons per week, right?

So, here is the kanban strategy:

I will always have two one-gallon containers of milk in the fridge. When one is empty, I will place it in the milk box outside my front door. When the delivery person comes around, he/she will exchange any empty one-gallon containers for a full one. In case you are thinking that I need at least three one-gallon containers at the onset of my kanban program, you are absolutely right.

PULL SYSTEMS

EVERYDAY USE NUMBER TWO

On a flow manufacturing implementation in Ireland (nice gig!), we were staying at a small owner-run hotel and pub. As I walked out the door the first morning, I noticed a small tag hanging on a nail on the outside of the door, with the number 3 printed on it.

Later that evening, I confirmed my suspicions with the hotel owner: the tags were milk kanban signals. The milk person (dare we say milkman?) would deliver the number of gallons indicated on a card, which would vary depending on the number of guests staying at the hotel. A little box of cards was kept inside the front door on a shelf.

Why not use empty bottles as a signal instead of cards? Because, as in most places these days, they didn't use bottles. Milk today is normally sold in cardboard or plastic containers.

BACKFLUSH

An electronic inventory transaction that accounts for the completion of a unit of product, by increasing the inventory balance of the finished unit while deducting the inventory balances of all its components.

up with the real-time environment on the shop floor. Materials from suppliers are transacted into stores or directly into a floor inventory location, reducing material handling. Total control over inventory turnover is achieved by establishing fixed kanban replenishment quantities, and delivering material in those quantities. Once it is consumed in the manufacturing process, material is relieved from in-process inventory locations using the *backflush* technique. The backflush transaction reduces the on-hand balance of consumed material by deducting the consumed quantities from the in-process inventory location, based on the product's Bill of Material, and at the same time increases the on-hand balance of the finished product.

Backflush simplifies inventory transactions. The final backflush transaction occurs after all work to build the product is finished, and all required purchased materials are consumed into the end item. Simplifying the material input and output transactions allows the flow manufacturer to maintain highly accurate inventory records. Many flow manufacturers have eliminated cycle counting and annual physical inventories, unless mandated by internal or external auditors.

A kanban system that delivers material directly to the flow line where it is needed offers several advantages to the flow manufacturer. All material that is stored on the line is available for use, i.e. the material is *not* allocated to any specific order. Material is available for consumption in any product that requires its use. Since components are not assigned to a specific shop order or work order, and are already physically on the line, any product can be manufactured without delay. In a kanban system, parts do not need to be "de-allocated' from one work order, and re-allocated to another. The capability for all material in the manufacturing inventory pool to be available for any requirement gives the flow manufacturer a huge amount of flexibility in meeting

PULL SYSTEMS

customer needs. Kanban systems provide the flexibility to insure a rapid response time to the customer. The delay in picking and delivering materials is eliminated.

A *supermarket,* or intermediate inventory location on the factory floor, is an important element in the kanban strategy. The amount of material directly on the line is normally quite small, and to replenish line material directly from the warehouse or supplier could result in a large number of non-value-added movements and transactions. Instead, material is usually pulled to the line directly from an inventory of additional material already on the floor. This inventory *supermarket* can then in turn be replenished from an external supplier (preferred) or internal warehouse. The use of supermarkets has four key advantages over traditional kit picking:

♦ It puts a portion of the inventory under visual control. The signal to refill the supermarket container is an empty container, not a computer message. We may use a computer *min-max* signal as a backup warning, but the primary signal for replenishment is manual and visual.

♦ The number of inventory transactions required is greatly reduced. When material is pulled from the supermarket to the line, no transaction is required. Fewer inventory transactions result in fewer inventory errors. The inventory transactions that remain include receipts from suppliers, movements from the warehouse to the supermarket, scrap transactions and the backflush transaction upon product completion.

♦ A supermarket provides rapid replenishment to the line. Since the supermarket material is on the factory floor and not in the warehouse, if necessary it can be retrieved easily.

♦ The productivity of the material handling organization can be much higher than in a kit picking environment.

THE TWO-BIN SYSTEM

Material kanban is often known as a two-bin system. Maintain two containers of material, consume one at a time, and when the first container is empty, go get more. While the first container is being refilled, consume out of the second container. What could be simpler?

How about only *one* container? The reason for having two containers is to avoid delays and stoppages on the line for material replenishment. But what if my takt time is 3 days, and the material can be replenished quickly? Could I get by with only one container?

Yes, but be careful. It may not make sense to take risks of line stoppage if the material is inexpensive. Stocking only just the right quantity of washers, for example, doesn't make sense. Expensive "A" inventory items, however, would be good candidates for this 1 container approach, if the takt time of the line is sufficiently long.

AEROSPACE SUPERMARKET

A large California aerospace company was able to combine a work order/kitting environment with the supermarket concept. A supermarket was set up adjacent to the production floor, as a part of the stockroom. Instead of kitting to small work orders (a job that was requiring about 6 hours a day from the material handler), the material was issued to the supermarket area in larger quantities, and delivered to the line as required from the supermarket. The effort to keep the line stocked dropped to 30 minutes a day, while maintaining full traceability.

PULL SYSTEMS

SAMPLE KANBAN CHAINS

1. CELL ← SUPERMARKET ← SUPPLIER
2. LINE ← SUPERMARKET ← FAB
3. LINE ← SUPERMARKET ← STORES
4. CELL2 ← PRESS3 ← WAREHOUSE
5. ASSY ← SUPERMARKET ← SUPPLIER

CALCULATING QUANTITIES

The formula for calculating line material Kanban quantities is:

$$FDU \times (1 + SSF) \times DF \times LF$$

where

FDU = Forecasted Daily Usage in pieces per day
SSF = Safety Stock Factor %
DF = Delivery Frequency in days
LF = Line Consumption Factor %

Example:
Our forecasted usage for the part is 125 units per day. We anticipate a margin of error of 20%. Component part number 123-456 is a "C" inventory item that we wish to replenish from the supermarket every 3 days. This component is only used at this workstation, so the line consumption factor is 100%. How many pieces should we have in each Kanban container on the line?

Answer:

$$125 \times (1 + .2) \times 3 \times 100\% = 450 \text{ pieces}$$

Although the kanban method is not supernatural, by using supermarket stocking locations, material shortages are virtually eliminated from the shop floor. A kanban signal is clear and visible: a card, bin, basket, pallet, cart, or other designated physical signal that is difficult to ignore, as opposed to an item on a shortage report hidden away on a desk, When a kanban container is empty, it is empty, and no inventory accuracy debate needs to occur.

Material handling productivity invariably improves using a kanban system. Quick count replenishment methods, where parts do not need to be counted exactly when delivered to the line, can reduce replenishment time by orders of magnitude. A manufacturer of high-tech aerospace products reported that the time required to keep their production lines replenished went from six hours a day picking kits to thirty minutes a day after implementing a kanban system.

To design a kanban system, the relationship that identifies where materials are used, and from where they are refilled must be documented. These relationships are known as *Kanban Points, Kanban Links, and Kanban Chains*. When material has been consumed in the manufacturing process, a need to replenish the material arises and a kanban signal is created. This signal can take the form of a card, or the empty container itself. The empty container or card signals the need to refill or replace the materials that were consumed.

A refilling point for material used on the production line will be located near the line, our *supermarket* locations, and empty kanban containers are refilled from supermarket locations. The designated kanban chain for each component identify the "used at" and "refilled from" locations of kanban material. This information is used by the material handler performing the actual replenishment. In turn, supermarket kanbans are refilled either from stores or directly from the external supplier. *Certified* suppliers are authorized to deliver material

PULL SYSTEMS

directly to the supermarket location, by-passing the stockroom and receiving inspection.

A goal of any kanban system is to keep inventory moving through the manufacturing process at a rapid pace. This velocity is intended to improve the turn rate usage of the inventory investment, and to reduce the working capital requirements of the business. The key to this rapid turning of inventory is the frequency of replenishment of the kanbans. Empty kanbans must be refilled using a predetermined *delivery frequency*.

The delivery frequency is established for each kanban chain for each part or component. The inventory investment is proportional to the frequency of material replenishment. The longer the replenishment times the greater the inventory quantity, and the inventory investment. Conversely, more frequent replenishment means less inventory.

Some analysis is required when establishing delivery frequencies and kanban quantities. More frequent replenishment also results in more material handling. While it may be tempting to think only of reduced inventories, kanban systems must establish the optimum strategy to balance inventory investment and material handling costs. A common strategy for setting delivery frequencies involves the use of ABC inventory codes and the 80/20 rule. The 80/20 rules tells us that 20% of our components represent 80% of our inventory investment. It makes sense, therefore, to assign a shorter delivery frequency to the high-value 20% of our inventory. Conversely, we can reduce material handling overhead by assigning longer delivery frequencies to the "C" or low-cost items, without significantly impacting overall inventory turnover or working capital.

Qualifying or certifying suppliers to deliver directly to the supermarket locations is an important strategy of a

MIN/MAX METHODS

We sometimes hear the comment "We're using a kanban system, but it's all on our computer. When we reach a certain inventory level, the computer generates a replenishment signal automatically."

A computer-only method might work great if we could guarantee 100% inventory accuracy on the system. If our goal, however, is zero line stoppages due to lack of material, then even a 98% inventory record accuracy is not good enough. We prefer to base our material pull signals on physical consumption rather than rely on the computer alone.

Kanban methods are not an excuse for neglecting inventory accuracy, however. Inventory accuracy is even more important when you have less of it; you can run out that much faster.

PULL SYSTEMS

KANBAN SIZING EXAMPLE

In this example, let's say that we have two processes (A and B) that are both divided into 4 sequential workstations. There is a specialty titanium bolt that is used at both processes. The bolt is used at workstations 1 and 3 in process A and at workstation 3 in process B, as depicted in Figure 10.1. The kanban formulas we will use are as follows:

$KANBAN_{LINE}$ = FDU x (1 + SSF) x DF x LF
$KANBAN_{SUPERMARKET}$ = FDU x (1 + SSF) x DF
$KANBAN_{STORES}$ = FDU x (1 + SSF) x DF

where

FDU = Forecasted Daily Usage in pieces per day
SSF = Safety Stock Factor %
DF = Delivery Frequency in days
LF = Line Consumption Factor %

Following the calculation formula above, let's work out the data elements one at a time:

1. *Forecasted Daily Usage (FDU):* This is the number of units of this part number that is consumed in an average day. One common source for this data is your ERP system. Your ERP inventory module can usually provide you with the Estimated Annual Usage (EAU) for a specific part. Let's assume that the EAU for our bolt is 32,000 pieces per year. The FDU for the part is calculated by dividing the annual figure for the number of working days, in our case 32,000 / 240 = 134 pieces/day.

2.
$\Rightarrow$ FDU = 134 pieces/day

2. *Safety Stock Factor (SSF):* Yes, this is the "Just In Case" factor. However, we recommend a statistics-based approach to establishing this number. For our example, we will use 10%.

$\Rightarrow$ SSF = 0.1

3. *Delivery Frequency (DF):* This number establishes the amount of inventory that you wish to carry at the kanban point. For our bolt, we have decided that we will carry ½ day of inventory at the line locations and 2 days of inventory at the supermarket locations. The supermarket is directly replenished by the bolt supplier via kanban signal.

$\Rightarrow$ $DF_{LINE-SUPERMARKET}$ = 0.5 day
$\Rightarrow$ $DF_{SUPERMARKET-SUPPLIER}$ = 2 days

4. *Line Factor* (LF): This number is necessary when the same part number is used at multiple locations in a line. It is not necessary for a single supermarket location that serves as a consolidation point of all the kanban points from the line. As we can see in figure 10.1, workstation 1 in process A uses 5 out of a total of 10, workstation 3 in process A uses 2 out of a total of 10, and workstation 3 in process B uses 3 out of the same total of 10.

$\Rightarrow$ LF_{W1-A} = 0.5 (50%)
$\Rightarrow$ LF_{W3-A} = 0.3 (30%)
$\Rightarrow$ LF_{W3-B} = 0.2 (20%)

With these pieces of information, we are ready for the calculations, shown on the following page.

FIGURE 10.1 KANBAN SIZING EXAMPLE

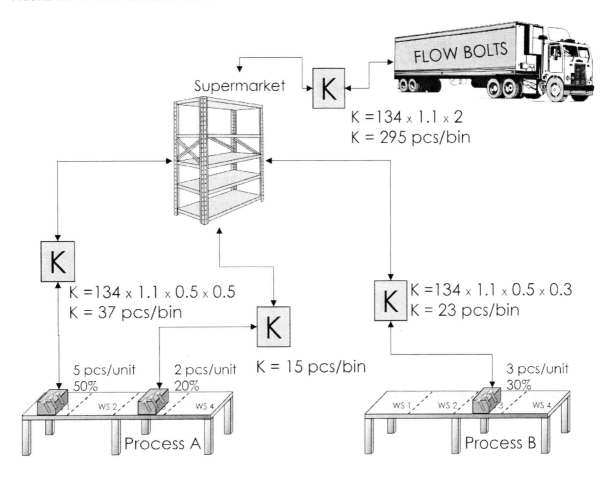

Let's interpret these results:

⇒ At workstation 1 in process A, there must be enough room for 2 containers with 37 bolts each.

⇒ At workstation 3 in process A, there must be enough room for 2 containers with 15 bolts each.

⇒ At workstation 3 in process B, there must be enough room for 2 containers with 23 bolts each.

⇒ At the supermarket, we need enough room for 2 containers with 295 bolts each.

PULL SYSTEMS

complete pull system. The key to dramatically improved inventory turnover, without taking risks of running out of raw material, lies in the vigorous pursuit of this objective. Unless suppliers can be converted to a kanban pull method, and are reliably delivering high quality material in kanban quantities to the supermarket locations, your flow manufacturing journey is not mature.

SCHEDULING PRODUCTION

Scheduling production in a flow factory is significantly simplified once the factory layout and kanban signaling drive the flow of work through the factory. Traditional manufacturing planning methods create production schedules for both end-items and subassemblies, with inevitably long lead times. However, production planning on a flow line can be done only at the finished goods level, since subassemblies are produced on feeder processes linked by kanban signals. There is, therefore, no need to schedule subassembly production, since the output from these feeder processes is consumed directly by downstream processes. Linking subassemblies via kanban signals also opens the door to radically simpler Bills of Material, since many subassembly levels may no longer be needed.

The type of kanban that is used to signal the next unit of production on the flow line is called an *in-process kanban* or IPK, discussed in the previous chapter. The IPK can take the form of a space on a workbench, or a spot on the floor, but the concept is simple. If the spot is empty, fill it up with the next product in the sequence. In-process kanbans therefore generate the communication to the shop floor as to when to begin work on the next product. Products are planned into the flow line one unit at a time in a specific sequence to insure a balanced flow of work through the factory. In a

SCHEDULING DISSAPOINTMENT

Using MRP/ERP scheduling methods can be disappointing if we want to achieve high flexibility and quick response through the factory. MRP normally plans in daily increments, with a minimum planning time of one day. To schedule a product with a multi-level Bill of Material that includes three levels, final assembly plus a subassembly and a fabricated part, the minimum scheduled lead-time through the factory would be three days, one day for each level.

Level 0	1 day
Level 1	1 day
Level 2	<u>1 day</u>
Total	3 days

What a disappointment if the total work content of the product adds up to 15 minutes. Three days to schedule 15 minutes of work! For this reason, and there are others, traditional MRP-based scheduling is not used for shop floor planning in a flow environment. We may, however, continue to use MRP/ ERP for longer-term material planning.

PULL SYSTEMS

multi-product line, or if our product includes options, some additional sales information will need to accompany the unit through the build process indicating the differences.

Because products are manufactured one unit at a time, they can be sequenced to move down the flow line in an optimum order, driven by customer requirements. The planner has only to determine the order of manufacture, or sequence. The person in the first workstation in the flow line, upon seeing an empty in-process kanban as a signal, begins production of the next unit, in the sequence the planner has chosen.

Configure-to-Order custom products may require that a sales order configuration document be sequenced with the product. This *configuration traveler* flows along with the product as it advances through manufacturing. Lead-time through the factory is so significantly reduced that shop floor tracking and expediting can be eliminated.

Manufacturing lead-time is traditionally measured by determining the critical path through the multi-level Bill of Material for a product. However, manufacturing response-time in a flow factory is measured by determining the critical time line through the process relationships required to build the product. This response time can be 1/10 of the original scheduled lead-time.

LESSONS LEARNED

♦ **The kanban technique is a core method that eliminates the need for pick lists and kits**

♦ **The supermarket concept helps speed replenishment of material to the line, reduce inventory transactions, and reduce handling**

♦ **Kanban quantities are calculated based on a sizing formula, and with consideration for material handling costs.**

♦ **Planning in a flow environment is much simpler, primarily because the kanban technique eliminates the need for subassembly scheduling.**

♦ **Inventory accuracy is even more important in a flow environment.**

PULL SYSTEMS

HIGH MIX KANBAN

What we are calling the *Material Kanban* or *Two-Bin System* works best in a multi-product environment, where various products being produced in the line are mixed and not batched. The reason for this is simple: we calculate the amount of material required in each container based on an average daily consumption. If we build in a batch or "run" we are consuming the same material over and over, probably consuming it more rapidly than planned. What we thought was a daily quantity could be consumed in a few minutes or hours, if we don't intermix various other products. For this reason production lines that run in batches, due to the nature of the process, usually don't use the Kanban method but instead are required to set up the line for a run with the materials needed, and clear the line at the end of the production run. The quantities of material consumed during the run can be large, especially for consumer products.

The aerospace environment differs in several regards from the environment discussed above:

◆ The quantities of any one product are low.
◆ Material traceability is required for the raw materials being consumed.
◆ The production quantity is often related to a specific customer order. Breaking apart the order would result in additional setups and inspections.
◆ The number of different components being consumed across all products is high. The number of permanent Kanban containers and Kanban locations for even just the higher-volume materials would be high.
◆ The demand for any one product is sporadic. Relatively few products are built every day or week.

For all of these reasons, the common two-bin Kanban system will be difficult to implement in a high-mix, low-volume environment. We shouldn't give up hope for improving the material delivery system, however; there are several possibilities we should explore. Putting more of your material on a pull system will help reduce delays in the line or cell, reduce material handling costs, and help with 5S organization and housekeeping.

The 80/20 Rule. You may have some products that are built on a frequent basis that would be good candidates for a Kanban pull system. The 80/20 rule says that even in a high-mix environment, 20% of our products represent 80% of our production volume. Focus on those as Kanban candidates.

Supplies and Consumables. Create a two-bin system for consumables and regularly consumed supplies like wipes, alcohol, cotton swabs, latex gloves, etc. Eliminate potential delays that happen when you run out of these items.

PULL SYSTEMS

Hardware Items. Nuts, bolts and screws may be used on a large number of different products, and may be excellent candidates for a Kanban pull strategy. Depending on your traceability requirements, outside suppliers sometimes assume responsibility for keeping these bins restocked.

Kit Racks. If you can't avoid kitting the material, simplify the kitting process for your higher-volume products by designing a kit rack, a dedicated rolling rack with a space for every required piece. A well-designed rack can help reduce picking errors and omissions, provide an error-proofing check for material selection, and help speed the delivery of material to the line.

Material Supermarket. The material supermarket concept described in this chapter can be adapted for use in a lot-control, kitting environment (see Case History *Aerospace Supermarket* in this chapter). The benefit of the supermarket is the ability to replenish the consuming workstations with a minimum of paperwork and delay, and a much higher level of productivity for the material handlers.

Lot Traceability. Print or record the lot number on the Kanban container. When the material is pulled, the lot number would be recorded on a traveler accompanying the product. Medical device companies have been doing this for years, often scanning a bar-code of the lot number. Needless to say, no mixing of lots in the Kanban container!

AEROSPACE LESSONS LEARNED

1. Material Kanban systems *will* be more difficult to implement in a high mix low volume environment, but it's not impossible.
2. Look for opportunities to simplify the material delivery process using pull methods. Supplies, higher volume products and hardware items are all candidates.
3. Also look for opportunities to improve the kitting process. Error proofing through visual methods have been introduced in many companies, with outstanding improvements in productivity, reduction of errors and reduction in line delays.

NOTES

CHAPTER

12

ADMINISTRATIVE FLOW

Do the tools and techniques of flow manufacturing apply to non-manufacturing processes as well? Absolutely! Many companies in need of flow methods are not manufacturing companies at all!

ADMINISTRATIVE FLOW

The same dynamics of flow manufacturing introduced on the shop floor can be applied to administrative processes in the office.

Linking and balancing processes together will yield the same benefits as in manufacturing. Even though the output of office processes are not normally thought of as "products", the work flow used to accomplish tasks is in fact very similar. The products in this case are most often information transfer: a customer order entered into the computer, a paid bill, a financial report, a completed engineering change.

The same functional, departmental organization that is used in traditional manufacturing also exists in the office. Departments are isolated and located independently in most businesses. Work performed in these departments is usually done in batches, in a style similar to traditional manufacturing. Most of the elapsed time required to complete the work is the move time between departments and time the product spends waiting to be processed. The actual work itself is the smallest component of the total lead-time. Administrative batch processing results in the same high levels of inventory as manufacturing batch processing. The only difference between manufacturing and administration inventory is that the administrative work in process inventory can be found on desks or as computer files, instead of on pallets or in containers on the manufacturing floor.

The opportunity is clear: shorten administrative processes by completing the work in its actual work content time, reducing or eliminating the time spent routing the work through multiple departments. *Flow* in administrative processes is a work method that allows administrative tasks to be performed in a successive and progressing manner without wait time, queue time, or other delays. Administrative flow processes are established in office areas that perform repeatable tasks

MODERN EFFICIENCY

"In 1929, those attending meetings of the American Academy of Political and Social Science heard how scientific management was being applied to "the clerical functions." There was now one best way for inserting paper into a typewriter, for pinning pages together, and for secretaries to sit at their desks."

- Robert Kanigel
The One Best Way

ADMINISTRATIVE FLOW

FIGURE 11.1 ADMINISTRATIVE FLOW

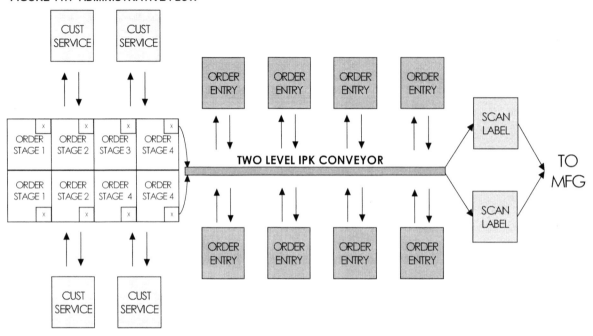

IMPLEMENTING ADMINISTRATIVE FLOW: EXAMPLE

Figure 11.1 shows a preliminary layout of an administrative area dedicated to receipt and entry of customer orders. The work elements related with the Order Staging process (opening the envelope, checking all paperwork, sorting, and placing in containers) can be divided in sequential workstations. The number of required workstations for Order Staging was 8, and we chose to divide them into two mirrored lines of 4 workstations each, as 1/8 of the work content is too little work for each workstation. Any problem with an order is detected at this early stage and transferred to any one of four Customer Service desks, that will place a call to the appropriate customer to clarify the order.

The entry of an order into the computer system cannot be broken down into sequential increments, so the resources in the process Order Entry perform their work in parallel. To move the work from Order Staging to Order Entry, we need to use a gravity roller conveyor. After the order is entered in the system is placed on another conveyor to move the order to the Scan and Label process from where the order will proceed to manufacturing. In this application, the conveyor is the work signal for the Order Entry process; as long as it is not full, the Order Entry operator will remain at the desk. When the conveyor is full, the operator moves toward one of the Scan and Label desks.

The concept of standard work can be applied to administrative processes as well as factory ones. Note the emphasis on the quality aspects of the work, with a goal of zero administrative errors. See Figure 11.2 on the following page for an example.

FIGURE 11.2 ADMINISTRATIVE STANDARD WORK

Standard Work Definition

Process	Order Entry
Product	New Orders
Multi Product Flow Line	Order Receipt
SWD Name	A & B New

Page 1 of 4

Flowall Corp.

		Work Elements				Work Content		Total Quality Management	
Order	Overlap	Description	Code	Divisible?		Machine Time	Person Time	TQM Check	Self Check
10		Open paperwork from EMI box		N			.3		Check account number Cursory review
20		Go to T-905 screen		N			.1		
30		Enter plant location		N			.1		Ensure correct plant code
40		Enter printer number		N			.2		Ensure default to nearest
50		Enter account number		N			.2		Check "ship-to" address If account number is not available, fill out progress notes Route to Customer Service
60		Scan netcode		N			.1		Respond to netcode, if applicable
70		Verify shipping due date		N			.2		If not within 3 days, route order to Customer Service
80		Enter PO number		N			.1		PO—Name If PO number is not available, fill out progress notes Route to Customer Service
90		Enter patient's name		N			.3		Last—First Initial—Check spelling If name is not available, fill out progress notes Route to Customer Service
100		Enter product model		N			.3		Check model If conflicting model, fill out progress notes Route to Customer Service
		Totals for page					1.9		

SWD for the Office

ADMINISTRATIVE FLOW

that can be linked and balanced together in a sequential manner.

The tools required to implement Administrative Flow are remarkably similar to the tools used for factory line design. Understanding the flow of work using the Process Flow Diagram tools is critical, as is the definition of Standard Work. Work content times may be more variable than factory tasks, but reasonable time estimates can be gathered. In-process kanban signals can take the form of in-baskets and out-baskets that are only allowed one piece of paper. Office supplies can be pulled from a central supply supermarket via kanban replenishment signals. Following below are examples of functions or industries that could benefit from the application of flow methods.

FINANCE

What processes might be good candidates for flow in the finance and accounting departments? The principal functions that are performed on a routine basis include A/R collections, the general ledger reconciling and posting process, the infamous monthly closing process, the customer invoicing and billing process, and the capital expenditure process. A good rule-of-thumb way to determine if a process or department could benefit from flow processing is to ask the question: "Is the elapsed time to [fill in the task here] a lot longer than the time it takes actually do it? If the answer is "yes", and it typically is, that process could benefit from the transformation to flow processing methods.

SALES AND MARKETING

There is no doubt that speed-to-market is critical in the sales and marketing functions. Getting a quote back to a customer, for example, usually has a very high level of urgency. Successful sales and marketing people, since

SIMULATION EXERCISE

A simple manual simulation that can be done in a classroom setting demonstrates the remarkable benefits possible by linking processes (read "departments") and by eliminating batching. Select five participants, representing five departments, and begin with a stack of ten post-it notes. Time this exercise. Ask the first participant, department one, to sign each of the ten post-it notes and then pass the pack to the next representative, department two. Continue in this way until the pack has been "processed" by each of the five volunteers. Note the total time required for the first complete post-it note, and the time for the entire batch.

Now repeat the same demonstration, but this time allow the participants to move the post-it notes one piece at a time, instead of batching. The results are predictable, but often surprising. The time required for the first note to be completed will be around 10% of the time that was needed in batch mode, and the entire pack of 10 will be completed in around 25% of the batch mode time. This apparent miracle was achieved not by working any faster than before, but by eliminating queue time from the process, allowing more work to be done in parallel.

ADMINISTRATIVE FLOW

their compensation is tied very directly to their results, tend to be highly motivated and good at pushing forward against obstacles. However, the processes of quote generation, customer requests, prospecting and order booking, are rarely looked at from a flow perspective. Techniques and "secrets to success" tend to be held close to the vest by individual salespeople. The process slows down when help is needed from other organizations like design engineering, technical support, accounting or admin services.

HUMAN RESOURCES

Many of the processes performed by the human resources department are highly repetitive: payroll processing, health plan management, employee pension fund and 401K plans, and the maintenance of accurate employee records. Errors or defects in the completion of this work can be devastating. Imagine errors on health care records, or on your paycheck. Much of this administrative work also involves more than one person, and may require a formal review and approval process. Often the work is performed in batch mode, with stacks of forms and paperwork accumulating in both in and out baskets. Putting this work into a flow will have the expected benefits of a radically reduced response time through the system, improved productivity and a greatly decreased error rate.

ENGINEERING

In many companies the engineering department is regarded as royalty or "artists at work". The design of new products is regarded not so much as a science but as an art. Within that art, however, there are many processes that are strong candidates for flow processing. Maintaining correct documentation and revision control is a highly repeatable process that must be executed error-free. The process of component

THE DEFENSE INDUSTRY

"Although much of the attention that has been paid to productivity improvement has focused on actual production, indirect costs such as overhead and general and administrative (G&A) expenses can also be significant drivers of weapon system costs. Accordingly, a number of lean manufacturing initiatives have been designed to help contain such costs. However, respondents' efforts to reduce overhead and G&A were limited in scope and await systematization before significant savings can be realized."

- Rand Industry Brief
Lean Manufacturing and the Defense Industry, 2001

ADMINISTRATIVE FLOW

PAYROLL KAIZEN

"In the non-manufacturing aspect of business, an administrative kaizen was done on the payroll process, from employees ringing in to paycheck issuance. This process resulted in the elimination of lost and missing checks and a 40 percent reduction in check errors."

- Flow results in a Michigan furniture maker

NON-MANUFACTURING APPLICATIONS

"Perhaps the most remarkable thing about Toyota's new system of production is that the basic concepts have been adapted to a wide range of endeavors, often far beyond the scope of automobile manufacturing. The principles of flow manufacturing have been applied effectively in many service industries, such as hotels and financial institutions. Each of (the flow) principles, I believe, has a parallel in medical care delivery."

- William R. Brody, M.D.
President, The Johns Hopkins University

selection, product development planning, and documentation are all processes that can benefit from a formal flow methodology.

Engineers are often highly independent, and prefer to work alone or in small teams. Flow methods cut across departmental boundaries, and for new product development must include customers, suppliers, sales and marketing, finance, manufacturing and customer service. The challenge for engineering departments is therefore primarily cultural, and improvements will require a paradigm shift from the way this function has been organized in the past.

CUSTOMER SERVICE

Customer service can include a variety of different functions in most companies. Usually the common denominator is the extreme urgency of handling customer orders, dealing with customer problems, and providing information for customer requests. Because this is a very customer-focused area, it often becomes organized around urgency rather than processes. The demand patterns for this function can also be erratic, i.e. sometimes the department is swamped, and sometimes there's nothing to do. In general, customer service is a very fruitful area for process identification and improvement. The principles of flow processing can be applied to eliminate waste and reduce cycle time, which in tern will result in faster response to customers.

HEALTHCARE

All of us are users of healthcare services, and healthcare in the U.S. must change. Waste in the healthcare industry adds up to billions of dollars a year. Healthcare is 12% of our gross national product, and climbing. In hospitals and clinics there are many processes, from the scheduling of expensive operating rooms and

ADMINISTRATIVE FLOW

equipment, to the selection and transport of medications to each floor, to the staffing of nurses, that are targets for improvement through the application of flow processing tools. The first step, as in the factory, is to understand the current work flow, using the tool of process flow diagrams. Standard work definition will follow, along with a detailed look at error-proofing each work step. The simplification of paperwork and non-value-added transactions is a key focus; health care professionals spend far too much time on activities that do not directly benefit the customer, the patient. Undoubtedly there are billions of dollars or waste within the healthcare industry that are suitable targets for flow processing solutions.

SOFTWARE DEVELOPMENT

Software is being used everywhere in today's electronic world, and in the future we can expect to see microprocessors even in our toasters and home appliances. A software capability maturity model, *CMM*, used to measure the maturity of a software development process within a company has been developed by the Carnegie-Mellon Institute for Software Engineering. The Malcolm Baldridge National Award Criteria and the ISO9000 criteria provided a framework for this model, with level 1 being the highest level of maturity and level 5 being the lowest. Large aerospace companies are now requiring their software suppliers to adhere to maturity levels as high as 2 or 3, with level 3 being equivalent to *process standardization* discussed previously in this book. Unfortunately, this criteria is virtually unknown in the commercial software world, and many startup and mature software developers suffer from a high level of defects, non-value-added rework, and poor customer service. Estimates for software development time and cost are notoriously inaccurate, and shipping late is a common occurrence. The flow methodology, combined with the CMM

THE THREE CHALLENGES

There are three main hurdles to overcome when implementing flow manufacturing:

- ♦ **Many people don't understand what the business processes are, and how they are a part of those processes.**
- ♦ **By nature, these processes are comprised of large numbers of interactions between people; therefore, a resource assigned to these types of projects should have very good interpersonal and teaming skills.**
- ♦ **Many of these processes don't have appropriate measurements or metrics that will aid in the direction of the improvement activities, so creating, developing, and evaluating these measurements is a challenge.**

- The AIT Group

ADMINISTRATIVE FLOW

guidelines, provides a framework for implementation of these concepts, and a way to introduce CMM into the commercial software industry.

CONSTRUCTION

It is generally acknowledged that from a flow manufacturing perspective, the construction industry is in the dark ages. Although a few construction companies and organizations are now exploring and implementing flow methods, in general the industry exemplifies a process of huge inefficiency and waste. Since setup and move work are classified as non-value-added, construction involves a large percentage of tasks like moving, storing, delay, preparation and inefficient hand-off from one subcontractor to another. No one would run a factory in this manner, or they would quickly be out of business, but in the construction industry it is considered a normal and inevitable practice. The interest in flow methods for this industry is growing, but a significant commitment from construction managers and owners will be needed.

Since Administrative Flow seems to make sense, why isn't it more widespread? The obstacles are more cultural and psychological than practical or technical. The physical linking of work challenges several time-honored office monuments: the department, the department manager, and the functional specialist. In this new environment the boundaries of "my job" or "my profession" begin to blur, and the need for worker flexibility grows. This can be threatening, or at least disconcerting, to people who tend to see themselves as managers, engineers, accountants or sales professionals, especially if they have a college degree that declares this fact hanging on their wall. A paradigm shift is more needed in the office than any other area of the organization, if the benefits of flow are to be achieved in their entirety.

LESSONS LEARNED

1. The opportunities for the application of flow methods to non-manufacturing processes are many.
2. The same techniques that we applied in the factory can be used in the office or in non-manufacturing industries.
3. Functions or industries that are good candidates for flow methods include finance and accounting, customer service, sales and marketing, engineering, health-care, construction and software development.
4. The biggest challenge is not technical, it is psychological.
5. The job is not done until *all* process flow.

ADMINISTRATIVE FLOW

WHY ADMINISTRATIVE FLOW?

The results of Flow Manufacturing speak for themselves. Volumes of success stories have been written. Flow Manufacturing has raised the performance bar. If you are not building your products in a flow today, your methods may well be considered outdated, putting your organization at a serious competitive disadvantage. So, how do you compete in a market where all the contenders flow their products? The focus must now expand toward "flowing" the entire supply chain. But before we go out running after the "B2B" consultants, let's understand the entire supply chain, and the elements of it that are under our immediate control:

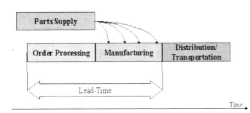

In order to satisfy a customer's demand for our product, we have to do more than manufacture the product. After the product is ready for customer use, we have to reach the customer through the distribution channels. Before we can manufacture the product we have to know what the customer wants and have the materials available for the conversion process. Of the chain of events described above, the typical implementation of flow manufacturing addresses only the factory processes. The manufacturing lead-time of the flow manufacturer is likely to be as short as it can be, barring any continuous improvement activities. Additionally, materials are likely to be available in Kanban containers, ready to be consumed by any product at any time.

The traditional understanding of a process as "*people and machines making something*" can lead you and your company down a path of sub-optimal performance. A process does not necessarily have a physical result. In some cases the result of a process is information. Take the time to look at the number of resources (people, computers, printers, etc.) dedicated to all the administrative processes within your company. Physically follow a particular document from beginning to end and ask yourself:

- Did I have to wait a lot?
- Was my document buried in a batch?
- Was my document processed in minutes, hours, or days? How does that total time compare to the actual work applied to the document?
- Did the document ever fall into a "black hole"?
- How many times did I go back to the same department/desk/place?
- Did the document flow smoothly or was it stop-and-go?
- How many documents are waiting for someone to work on them at any point in time?
- Did I see room for improvement, like I saw in manufacturing before Flow?

Do not let the misconception of "these flow concepts work only in the factory" mislead you. Nothing is farther from truth. The set of steps presented in this book is a proven path for flow-based process design. In many cases, we find that all the forward thinking that made manufacturing efficient and productive has not yet been applied to the rest of the organization.

Leone, Gerard and DiFraia, Paul. *Flow Processing in Administrative Processes*. Advanced Manufacturing Magazine, Canada. February, 2001.

ADMINISTRATIVE FLOW

AEROSPACE ADMINISTRATIVE FLOW

The application of flow methods to administrative and non-manufacturing work remains today, after many years of discussion, a neglected opportunity. Especially in an aerospace environment, non-manufacturing work represents a large percentage of the total response time. It can take several weeks to process a customer order for a product that only takes a few days to make! The following points need to be emphasized:

♦ Most top managers have only a simple and inaccurate idea of the process steps required for many administrative processes, including engineering change management, order processing, new product design, and procurement.

♦ Most aerospace companies are focused on direct labor, which they are using to apply a much larger overhead pool of costs.

♦ Lead-time measurements in the office environment are not tracked and in fact do not exist.

♦ There is a general lack of understanding regarding the benefits of lead-time reduction in the office.

♦ There is a functional mind-set that pervades many administrative organizations, leading to the "response time spiral" of long lead-times.

The solution, which is admittedly more difficult than in a manufacturing environment, is to design administrative cells that allow work to be performed in a flow instead of being handed off from department to department. The cell design tools are similar to those used in a manufacturing environment, but the office politics may be different. One of the key ingredients for success in the implementation of office cells is a strong upper-management champion!

CHAPTER

13

**PEOPLE
ISSUES**

The flow manufacturing company regards its employees as its most important asset. Employees are also expected to take an active role in continually improving the company. In this way, the flow manufacturing company becomes a *learning organization*.

PEOPLE ISSUES

At a recent flow manufacturing conference, attendees were asked to share their biggest challenges in implementing flow manufacturing. Almost to a person, the biggest challenges were *people issues*, and not the techniques of flow manufacturing.

The methodology is the easy part, it was universally agreed. The hard part is getting people to change, and maintaining the change over time. One of the most notable aspects of a mature flow manufacturing company, and a huge benefit, is a high level of employee involvement. Employees are encouraged and expected to be involved in the never-ending effort to improve business processes, and at the same time the company provides a secure environment in which employee brainpower can be developed and applied.

TRAINING

A company implementing flow manufacturing is applying *best practices* in an attempt to be number one at what they do. Not second-best or eighth-best. One of the requirements in order to achieve this lofty goal is excellent employee training.

On the factory floor as well as the office, we train based on the standard work definitions (see Chapter 7). People are trained to do standard work. Don't misunderstand. We don't expect people to become ant-people or zombies, mindlessly performing repetitive tasks. The truth is that *more* creativity and involvement is required of the workforce in this new environment. Unless we are moving in the same direction, following the same processes, there's little opportunity for continuous improvement or the chance to become a world-class organization. The popular term *lean manufacturing* is unfortunate from the point of view that many people

FLOW LEADERSHIP

"Management means, in the last analysis, the substitution of thought for brawn and muscle, of knowledge for folkways and superstition, and of cooperation for force. It means the substitution of responsibility for obedience to rank, and of authority of performance for the authority of rank."

- Peter Drucker

PEOPLE ISSUES

THE LEARNING ORGANIZATION

"I believe our fundamental challenge is tapping the intellectual capacity of people at all levels, both as individuals and as groups. To truly engage everyone-that's the untapped potential in modern corporations. This leads me to the notion of an organization as a learning organism."

- Ray Stataa
President, Analog Devices, Inc.

associate the word *lean* with headcount reductions or layoffs. Flow manufacturers sincerely view their workers as their most important assets. The work environment should fully support worker safety, security and human values, rather than viewing workers simply as another production input.

The relationship is not one-sided. In exchange for a secure work environment and a realistic career path, workers are expected to participate in process improvement activities in the interest of both themselves and their employer. Ideas and suggestions are implemented vigorously. The costs of establishing such a workplace are considerable, since they include high wages and a high degree of job security. The benefits, however, far outweigh the costs.

A trained and *certified* employee has achieved three skills related to the standard work definition for a product and workstation. First, the worker can demonstrate an understanding of the work steps required, as documented on the standard work definition. These skills include not just one product, but in a multi-product line they include knowledge of *every* product that is to be built on that line. Second, the worker can demonstrate an understanding of the quality aspects of the work, including the use of any error-proofing fixtures or tools, and the ability to perform both self-inspection and checks of the work performed at a prior workstation. Third, the worker must be able to demonstrate sufficient proficiency so that work and any additional inspection steps can be completed within the standard time for the workstation. The certification process is normally done under the tutelage of a supervisor or *master* of that workstation, and a record of the certification is made and kept in the employee file. There may or may not be a direct compensation benefit associated with gaining additional certifications, a *pay for skills* component of the total compensation package for the worker.

PEOPLE ISSUES

TEAM LEADERS

As much as possible, decision-making and autonomy is driven to the lowest level in the organization. At Toyota, for example, the rule for rapid improvement events is *one person, one vote*. Workers on the production line have the authority to stop the line if necessary, without waiting for approval from their supervisor. In a flow manufacturing plant, much of the day-to-day responsibility lies with a position called the *team leader*. The team leader, an elected member of the production team, is the first point of contact for production and quality issues. He/she is responsible for communicating the daily production plan to the team, and to monitor production progress during the shift. Visual tools are used to communicate actual units completed against the plan, and the team leader will ensure that this information is up to date. Although the team leader is elected by the production team, and not appointed by management, the term of office expires after a reasonable period to allow other workers a chance to assume this role.

THE FLOW CHAMPION

No implementation as far-reaching as a flow initiative can hope to be successful without a strong champion. The title "C-I Guy" hasn't quite caught on yet, but the idea has. C-I stands for continuous improvement, and the C-I Guy, man or woman, leads the conversion to a new company culture. As we, the authors, look back on the 50+ flow projects that we have worked on, we observe that while all projects were successful, some were more successful than others. What made the difference? The key to long-term gains, especially after senior management has lost interest and the consultants have gone home, was an internal C-I Guy that refused to let things return to their previous state of equilibrium, as they tend to do.

THE CONTINUOUS IMPROVEMENT GUY

One "C-I Guy" implemented flow manufacturing in his plant in 1995. Through a series of promotions (another benefit of flow!) he stayed the course with the plant and refused to let things backslide. His comment in 2002: "Our people would not go back to the old ways even if we wanted them to."

PEOPLE ISSUES

THE OTHER 98%

"**W. Edwards Deming, perhaps the best-known figure worldwide in quality management and a statistician himself, often referred to statistics as 'two percent of the work'. The other 98 percent, Deming believed, involved basic changes in the ways people are recognized and rewarded and fundamental shifts in management-from setting goals and driving people toward achievement to focusing on the continual improvement of "the systems" that govern how the organization works."**

- Peter Senge
The Fifth Discipline

What are the characteristics of the flow champion? First, he/she must be passionate about continuous improvement, and impatient with the status quo. Second, the champion has the attention and respect of both management and the troops. When the champion says that process improvements will not result in layoffs, the champion is believed. Third, the champion has authority or "clout" to make changes happen.

PRODUCTIVITY IMPROVEMENT

One of the expected benefits of flow manufacturing is improved productivity. This comes as no surprise since we are training and certifying workers to perform standard work in a balance flow, we are actively eliminating non-value-added work steps, we are error-proofing the process and reducing scrap and rework. Improved productivity is inevitable. This benefit may also lead us to a quandary: unless we are growing and can absorb this improved productivity, we may end up with more workers than we need for today's demand. As a reference point, we have never seen less than a 15% productivity improvement, and often it is much greater.

The strong word of caution: don't let productivity improvements be used as an excuse for a headcount reduction or layoff. While this might be tempting from a short-term and narrow perspective, the long-term effects on your flow initiative will be devastating. It is important to remember that a large portion of your gains come from the active and enthusiastic participation of the workforce in the never-ending effort of continuous improvement. If your workforce is not on board, flow doesn't work, simple as that. A layoff coinciding with a flow manufacturing implementation (related or not) communicates exactly the wrong message: if you improve the process, you could lose your job.

PEOPLE ISSUES

The fact remains, however, that for a time you may have more people than you need. The recommended response includes several options. If your business is growing, the excess labor will be needed in the near future. In this case it makes sense to carry the extra people for a period of time. Two, examine your use of temporary workers. Releasing temporary workers, while certainly not an attractive alternative for them, is not the same as laying off permanent workers. Third, allow any necessary headcount adjustments to take place over a longer period of time through normal attrition. A normal turnover takes place over time, and the total number of workers can be adjusted. The bottom line: it needs to be strongly communicated to the workforce, before you start, that the improvements related to flow manufacturing implementation will not result in layoffs.

DESIGNING PROCESSES WITH PEOPLE IN MIND

F. W. Taylor, you may recall from a previous chapter, was forced to testify before Congress, to defend himself against the charge that his *one best way* approach to work was actually damaging to the worker, adding stress to the workplace, and weeding out workers who couldn't keep up. These same charges continue to be raised today (see sidebar). The accusation is that flow or lean manufacturing reduces worker freedom and control, in service to a takt time driven pace. Inventory that had previously been used to buffer the ups and downs of the line has been removed, as well as informal breaks. When work cannot be performed at the workstation, the worker is supposed to move to another station and continue working.

The debate has been going on for over 100 years, and we can't hope to resolve it here. While there is no final solution, we offer some suggestions. The challenge for flow manufacturing companies is to look beyond platitudes about employee involvement, and design

ANOTHER OPINION

"Workers are suffering so much from the intense control and exploitation the company imposes upon them under the Toyota Production System. I would like to report how Japanese workers have waged their struggle against the lean production system."

- Takao Kimura
Assistant Professor, Nagoya Economics Institute

PEOPLE ISSUES

manufacturing environments with human beings in mind. There are several possible solutions to high volume, short takt time lines:

1) Subdivide the work content into multiple cells. The warning signs are a sub one-minute cycle time. By taking a one minute line, for example, and creating 4 cells, the work content time on each cell increases to four minutes, with the same overall output. The impact to quality, with a single worker being responsible for more of the work content, is minimal. While the *single station build* approach is often disparaged by flow manufacturing proponents, there is no question that this method is preferred by the workers themselves.

2) Automation. Short cycle time work is a prime candidate for automation, less for cost reasons than people reasons. Certainly any process with less than a ten second cycle should be a high priority to automate.

3) Rapid job rotation. If the work cannot be automated, a policy of rapid job rotation should be implemented. Workers will not remain at any given workstation for long. The rotation positions are predefined, to avoid chaos during transitions. The added advantage of rapid job rotation is the cross-training that becomes necessary. Workers are required to become familiar with many of the positions, instead of a few.

4) Frequent breaks. The modus operandi in traditional batch environments is for workers to build up a small stock of parts and then take a break. When the inventory reached a certain level, they would again pick up the pace to build it back up. In that way the work day was not continuous, but varied in intensity. One of the impacts of flow manufacturing is to remove excess inventory and level the workload. From the employee point of view, they are now

PEOPLE ISSUES

working hard all the time, since the informal breaks have essentially been taken away. More frequent formal breaks may then be needed.

The results of a worker-engaged company speak for themselves. Companies that receive, and are then able to act on, hundreds or thousands of employee suggestions find themselves leading their industries, from a multitude of measurements. The effort requires continual renewal, however, and there are no guarantees. As Peter Senge says in *The Dance of Change*: "Sustaining any profound change requires a fundamental shift in thinking."

LESSONS LEARNED

1. The hard issues are the people issues. The technology is the easy part.
2. Leadership in the form of a C.I. Guy is necessary.
3. Don't let productivity improvements be an excuse for a layoff.
4. The biggest gains will come over time from an engaged workforce and continuous improvement.

A FEW FLOW STORIES

Bud, the most talkative employee on a residential HVAC line, approached us to complain that he was working harder in the flow line than he was before. When asked why, he replied: "Those 9 to 10 part shortages that we used to have every day were the perfect time to take a break. That doesn't happen anymore in this flow line." We've heard similar comments many times: informal breaks tend to disappear as the work flow evens out and material delivery improves. These people concerns need to be acknowledged and a reasonable solution developed.

During the day that we went live on a line that makes PBX cabinets, the line came to a sudden and unexpected halt. Why? Our star wirer didn't know that the 40 minute informal breaks that he used to take prior to flow were no longer ok. He had been accustomed to using his wiring skills to outrun the rest of the line and take long breaks while everyone else would catch up to him. With the introduction of IPKs, workers could no longer out-run the line by more than the IPK quantity.

The machine had been used to manufacture artillery shells during World War II, and had no safety devices. In order to keep operators from injuring themselves on this draw press, the operator would wear a set of wrist straps that would physically pull the operator's hands away from the machine during the downward cycle. The operator was literally and physically tied to the machine. No moving here!

NOTES

CHAPTER

14

THE 10 MAIN CHARACTERISTICS

When you walk into a flow manufacturing environment for the first time, you notice that things are different. Some things are visible and obvious, others more subtle. This chapter identifies the main characteristics of flow manufacturing.

10 MAIN CHARACTERISTICS

Creating lists is a useful way to organize and retain information. The Ten Commandments, the Seven Wastes, the Six Balancing Tools. Are there only ten characteristics of flow manufacturing? Yes, exactly ten!

I. HIGH LEVEL OF HOUSEKEEPING

In the flow factory, orderliness and neatness are critical in everyone's working environment. All material locations are clearly marked. Only the necessary tools, fixtures, gauges, and other resources are present at the workstations. No clutter or mess is noticeable or accepted.

When you enter a flow manufacturing facility, you immediately notice how organized the factory is. You will also notice that most operators are building product, not moving it around. Cleaning and organizing the work environment is often the first step in the implementation of flow manufacturing, and it alone can yield large benefits. Removing from the factory floor everything that is not needed to support current production can free up a shockingly large amount of space. Cleaning machines, improving lighting, creating shadow boards for tools, and repainting walls and floors are a few of the housekeeping activities that need to be done. Housekeeping discipline is sometimes referred to as the 5Ss: Sort, Set In Order, Shine, Standardize, Sustain.

II. LINKED RESOURCES

The essence of flow manufacturing lies in the *flowing* of work and material by physically connecting the required resources. In stark contrast with the discrete batch manufacturer, the manufacturing resources in the flow factory are not arranged into functional departments or work centers. The flow factory layout instead follows the sequence of manufacturing processes required to make a product family. Regulating the flow are signals between resources

THE FIVE S's

Sort (Seiri)
Separate what is truly needed from what is not. Get rid of what is not needed.

Set In Order (Seiton)
Organize what remains, logically for ease of use.

Shine (Seiso)
Clean everything up. Sweep the floor and clean up those machines.

Standardize (Seiketsu)
Develop a process or procedure to maintain a high level of housekeeping.

Sustain (Shitsuke)
Formalize and make housekeeping a discipline and practice, not a one-time event.

10 MAIN CHARACTERISTICS

called In-Process Kanbans (IPKs). These signals regulate the product flow as downstream workstations pull the semi-finished unit from the In-Process Kanbans. Resources within a production line are balanced, and products move at a relatively constant pace. In a flow factory, you can tell how a product is made by simply looking at the production line that makes it.

III. PRODUCTS MOVE

In a flow factory, products are manufactured in a progressive fashion, accumulating work as they are moved from workstation to workstation. The most likely unit of material transfer is one unit of product at a time. However, there are cases in which it might make sense to transfer more than one unit of product at a time (one customer order could be for two units). In a flow operation, accumulation of semi-finished product in between workstations is eliminated. The only valid accumulation of inventory would be for balancing a resource whose work cannot be broken down in takt time increments. Even in such cases, the amount of inventory is calculated and kept constant. It is also very likely that you will see a variety of products being built at any point in time in a manufacturing process.

IV. PEOPLE MOVE

The flow process does not chain the person to the workstation or the machine. In order to throttle the line up or down in response to customer requirements, people are placed into or removed from the flow line. As the multi-product flow line operates with less than the full compliment of people each day, the people building product will *move* from workstation to workstation to overcome any understaffing. Highly flexible and cross-trained employees are a key source of productivity in flow processing.

V. MATERIAL MOVES

Supplied materials consumed by the various resources involved in making a family of products are available at the line in material Kanbans for the operators to

JUST IN TIME PRODUCTION

"We have found in buying materials that it is not worth while to buy for other than immediate needs. We buy only enough to fit into the plan of production, taking into consideration the state of transportation at the time. If transportation were perfect and an even flow of materials could be assured, it would not be necessary to carry any stock whatsoever. The carloads of raw materials would arrive on schedule and in the planned order and amounts, and go from the railway cars into production. That would save a great deal of money, for it would give a very rapid turnover and thus decrease the amount of money tied up in materials. With bad transportation one has to carry larger stocks."

- Henry Ford
My Life and Work (1922)

consume. The majority of parts are within the operator's reach or very close by. As materials are consumed, the on-hand inventory at the line is depleted and a visual signal is generated for replenishment. Once the container, gaylord, or pallet is removed from the workstation, the operator is left with a secondary quantity of material. This extra inventory will allow the operator to continue working while the kanban is replenished. The use of kanban in the flow factory has resulted in the virtual elimination of material shortages on the line.

VI. WORKER INSPECTIONS

Production employees in a flow factory frequently use a series of graphic work instructions. These graphical renderings are color coded to emphasize any quality checks that may be needed at that workstation. Employees do not rush through their work; they take the appropriate time to ensure that the units transferred to the next downstream workstation are of perfect quality. Since quality is built into every product along the way, the need for final inspection is greatly reduced, unless regulations require it.

VII. HIGH EMPLOYEE SATISFACTION

Because of the requirement to move with the flow of the product, operators receive extensive training in a variety of jobs. Operators also participate in Kaizen (Rapid Improvement) activities resulting from their daily feedback to production management. The line supervision required is significantly decreased because of the line design. The product flow indicates what to do and when to do it. The operators in a flow factory are highly motivated and nearly self-managed.

VII. VISUAL SIGNALS

By simply taking a walk through the factory floor in a flow facility, you can easily tell what is going on. *Sequencing boards* at the head of each line clearly communicate the product mix to be built that day. At the end of each

INCENTIVES

Flow manufacturers use a variety of incentives to motivate their employees. Accomplishment of the daily production plan is a very high priority, and a system is sometimes put in place to reward the team accomplishment of this goal. Needless to say, defective units don't count as completed units. The production teams must focus on both *quantity* and *quality*.

10 MAIN CHARACTERISTICS

line, the output rate variation is posted along with the *line flow rate*, indicating how the line is doing so far that day. The kanban boards indicate how fast material is turning and highlight any potential shortages. At the end of the day, the In-Process Kanbans and workstations will tell us if the line was under or over-staffed. Furthermore, the operators performing work will provide key information on the line's balance.

IX. EASIER PLANNING
Because the line can build a family of products with a minimum elapsed time, the planning methodology revolves around sequencing customer orders to the line on a daily basis. Gone are the games played with forecasts and non-firm orders. Once an order hits the manufacturing floor, it will be completed within the product's flow-based response time.

X. SUPPLIER INVOLVEMENT
A flow manufacturing company is not an isolated island, but has developed a powerful network of supplier relationships. Suppliers are able to respond to kanban pull signals for the delivery of raw materials, are actively involved in the management of the kanban system, and in some cases even provide product design input. The certified supplier can deliver high-quality components directly to the supermarket locations in kanban quantities. The flow supplier applies flow manufacturing methods within their own facilities as well.

THE STREAM FLOWS

Until the *entire* value stream is flowing, the journey of flow manufacturing cannot be considered mature. Most of the total customer response time, in fact, lies outside of the factory walls, in processes like procurement, receiving, planning and logistics.

CHAPTER

15

**FLOW
SYSTEMS**

We need to use software to help run our businesses efficiently. Manual systems can be a major source of *waste*. At the same time, software is a difficult issue for most companies, and a huge cost of running the business.

FLOW SYSTEMS

Any company that has decided to implement flow manufacturing or is trying to manage an existing flow environment will have some very specific system software functionality needs.

Software is a difficult issue for most companies. You need software to run your business efficiently. Acquiring off the shelf products is the best choice, but the application may not do what you want, or it may force you to change the way you want to do business. Custom software, while tailored specifically to your needs, can be incredibly expensive and time-consuming to develop and maintain. Updating software to continually meet a changing business environment can be next to impossible.

Most manufacturing companies today are using integrated ERP/MRP manufacturing systems to run their factories and businesses. ERP consists of a large number of integrated modules, and is intended to provide software functionality to virtually all aspects of the manufacturing business, across physical locations. There are hundreds of different ERP software systems available on the market today; the largest vendors include SAP, Oracle, JD Edwards, SSA GT and Baan. There are few manufacturing companies in the U.S. today that are not using some form of MRP/ERP software. The methodology inherent in MRP/ERP is what we call *traditional* or *scheduled* manufacturing, and virtually all of the ERP packages are designed using these methods.

The global conversion to flow manufacturing is prompting a fresh look at these software tools and systems. ERP/MRP systems were not designed to support specific flow manufacturing requirements, although many functions remain the same. The biggest differences between flow and scheduled manufacturing are in the way that ERP/MRP handles production planning and shop floor functions. ERP tends

STANDARD ERP?

"That was why we chose not to implement a standard enterprise information system. The systems in the market could not support our business model. We built something like 45,000 lots of 1, which was what the Dell direct business model was all about. But standard systems didn't support that number of unique transactions."

-Jerry Gregoire, CIO
Dell Computers

FLOW SYSTEMS

to be batch-driven, scheduling in daily or weekly buckets, and assumes infinite capacity. The work order and pick list methods are examples of *push* methods. The ERP logic attempts to push process and planning information through the Bill of Material, scheduling start or release dates for both final and subassembly levels. Process-oriented line designs and *pull* methods are not used. While ERP/MRP software vendors are certainly aware of these differences between flow and traditional manufacturing, flow methods represent major changes to their software, and so improvements have been slow in coming.

A further concern for companies needing to use software tools is the accelerating rate of change in our economy and world. Traditional application development normally takes a long time. The typical estimate from the IS department for any software change, however minor, is "six months and sixty thousand dollars". By the time the enhancements are implemented, the business requirements might have changed. Traditional software development takes too long to create, and it is too hard to modify.

What are the new system requirements in a flow manufacturing environment? Flow-based manufacturing software must support three main functional requirements: initial factory process design, material and supply chain pull methods, and daily production planning and execution. The list of requirements includes the following capabilities:

- ◆ Kanban sizing database
- ◆ Process relationship documentation
- ◆ Process flow maps
- ◆ Standard work definitions
- ◆ Standard time maps
- ◆ Process-based throughput volume and takt time calculations
- ◆ Rework, scrap, and options maps

THE FLOW IMPROVEMENT RATIO

When we implement flow manufacturing in the factory, we expect improvements in response time to be up to 10 to 1. Might the same ratio and benefit apply when we take a lean approach to software application development?

Experience has shown that in some cases, with the right software platform, the ratio holds: software applications developed in 1/10 the time and 1/10 the cost.

FLOW SYSTEMS

- ◆ Workstation definition
- ◆ Graphic work instructions
- ◆ Finite capacity planning
- ◆ Sequencing tools
- ◆ Flow metrics tracking and reporting

If commercially available software to provide this kind of functionality is not available (yet), the alternative is to develop custom tools. How can we do this efficiently? Custom software is notoriously expensive, buggy and takes a long time to develop. While there is no magic solution, methods and tools have been offered for years to shorten the application development time. The most widely distributed and used development tool is Microsoft's Visual Basic™ software environment. VB applications abound, and certainly compared to the application development environments of the past, progress has been made. For some types of applications, VB is a good development platform, especially when integrated with a strong database server. For other types of applications, however, even VB is too slow and inflexible. Enhancements and modifications can still be painfully time-consuming. In general, custom (and commercial) application development is expensive, slow, inflexible, high maintenance, buggy and often out of date before the development is even completed, and that fact has not changed.

Flow manufacturing companies and small software development companies have struggled with these issues for many years. If developers want to provide highly customized, high performing tools to their internal or external clients, they will have to find a new way. They need to be able to deliver the functionality their clients require, and respond to changes as the world changes, without requiring months of time and effort. The best alternatives being applied today are to use PC-based tools.

AEROSPACE SYSTEMS

It is not unusual to find, even today in the year 2003, aerospace suppliers that are not using formal manufacturing systems common in other industries. The computer systems in place are often *home-grown* and highly customized, and represent lifetime job security for the programmers that keep them running. It was felt, no doubt, that off the shelf software would not meet the specialized requirements of the aerospace environment and that a internally developed system was necessary.

The authors have recently encountered (2003) several U.S. aerospace companies that are in the process of implementing MRP/ERP systems for the first time.

FLOW SYSTEMS

THE GLOBAL EXPERIMENT

"Spreadsheet software enabled organizations to ask themselves questions they had never been able to answer before. And the same spreadsheets could be used to help answer those questions.

This ongoing global experiment affirms the hypothesis that the proliferation of cheap prototyping tools can dramatically transform how an industry manages itself and the value it creates for others."

- Michael Schrage
Serious Play

It needs to be acknowledged up-front that not all applications are good candidates for this type of application development approach. Accounting information, for example, needs to be in a highly controlled environment, backed up, and protected from unauthorized access. If the information needs to be accessed on a real-time basis, is shared by many users, or the users are dispersed geographically, an ERP system is often the best solution. The types of information that is best suited for a shared and distributed MRP/ERP environment include:

- ◆ Accounting and Finance
- ◆ Purchasing
- ◆ Engineering and Bills of Material
- ◆ Inventory
- ◆ Order Entry
- ◆ MRP/Long range planning and forecasting

ERP/MRP REVIEW

One of the more obvious opportunities for flow manufacturing companies is to make sure that they are using their existing systems to their full capability in support of flow manufacturing. A survey of existing ERP capability will show that *most* of the functionality of an existing ERP system will still be used in a flow manufacturing environment, albeit in different ways. For example, inventory transactions to receive, move, scrap and relieve inventory quantities will still be done in a flow environment, but we expect the transactions to be simplified and reduced significantly. The software itself is probably already adequate.

Before gaps can be identified in the existing software, a good understanding of the "to be" flow requirements needs to be developed, and a complete review of the legacy software capabilities needs to take place. The outcome of this analysis will identify areas where policies

FLOW SYSTEMS

and procedures need to be updated, areas when the legacy system itself needs to be enhanced, and areas when missing functionality will be addressed via stand-alone or third-party solutions.

FLOW APPLICATIONS

Flow-related applications can often either be more loosely integrated with MRP/ERP, or run independently. *Loose integration* suggests that flow manufacturing data can be shared with an MRP/ERP system, but with a simple data transfer method and normally not on a real-time basis. The criteria for determining whether the information needs to be stored in a central ERP-type database or not depends on several factors: sensitivity, criticality, frequency of change, difficulty of integration, need for real-time access. The more tightly the information needs to be integrated within a large MRP/ERP system to be useful, the greater the development risk and the longer the development time. The types of flow manufacturing information that we can consider for stand-alone or loose integration include:

♦ Kanban sizing
♦ Flow line design
♦ Daily production planning
♦ Line design simulation modeling
♦ Supply chain tools

Loose integration can take the form of a flat file transfer between the application and the MRP/ERP system, possibly done overnight on a daily basis. Real-time integration, while theoretically possible, is not a realistic goal or need for the types of flow applications discussed here.

Actual applications have been developed and are being used successfully by flow practitioners for all of the functions presented in this chapter.

CUSTOMER SPECIFICATIONS

"It is really impossible for clients, even those working with software engineers, to specify completely, precisely and correctly the exact requirements of a modern software product before having built and tried some versions of the software they are specifying....

The truth is the clients do not *know* what they want. They usually do not know what questions must be answered, and they almost *never* have thought of the problem in the detail that must be specified."

-Fred Brooks
The Mythical Man-Month

FLOW SYSTEMS

The advantages of this *lean* approach to application development include:

- Proven technology. The application can use proven methods and planning algorithms, with no loss of actual planning functionality.
- Team based development. Since flow manufacturing solutions are often customized in order to work well, user input is critical. Consistent with flow manufacturing principles, a simplified and flexible development environment can become a *team* solution; not a solution that is owned and operated by a centralized corporate IT department. The manufacturing team owns all the application, algorithm options and the data. In addition, a familiar interface like Excel is easy to use by non-engineers.
- Fast. The simplification that the PC environment provides in architecture lowers the implementation time literally from months to weeks.
- Flexible. It is much easier to make changes in the application as the environment changes than a typical multi-tiered application. The changes to the algorithm and data structures, which typically take a formidable effort to implement, can be implemented even during on-site testing visits.
- Short Learning Curve. Most people are already familiar with the PC environment.
- Easy Support/Installation and Distribution. The installation of Excel or Access-based tools is as easy as copying a file.
- Cost effective. PC-based tools cost a fraction of a comparable system that has the same functionality, without sacrificing the performance. Consequently, the payback is typically in a few months or even weeks.
- Integration. PC applications like Excel can be integrated to most databases. As a part of the implementation, the integration can also be automated.

FLOW SYSTEMS

◆ Buy-in. The application shell is developed with user involvement. His/her feedback is always welcomed, and is incorporated into the solution within hours. As a result, the users will feel application ownership. During use, they can further customize the look and feel of the interface, add additional data/drawing/ comments/objects, and create charts and reports that are incorporated into the solution.

FLOW-BASED LINE DESIGN

A large portion of this book has been focused on the methodology of designing processes in a flow, with information like customer demand and work content times, and calculations like throughput volume, takt time and calculated resources. This type of information and related calculations are relatively simple and eminently well-suited for automation in a relational database environment. Do the line design calculations need to be an integrated part of our MRP/ERP environment?

In reality, the overlap of flow manufacturing line design data and methods with traditional MRP/ERP data is small. Some necessary information does reside in traditional manufacturing systems: part numbers, some process data, demand and forecast information. Much of the required information is new: product routings, for example, do not translate smoothly to the flow manufacturing definition of a process flow diagram or PFD. Throughput volume, takt time and resource calculations are new.

In addition, the line design calculation process is not something that is done on a daily basis. One of our goals is to design a robust process that does not have to be redesigned or adjusted often. The line design process is something that we do infrequently. Our recommendation, then, is to supplement your legacy

NOT A SOFTWARE PROJECT

Implementing flow manufacturing is not a software implementation. You can achieve great benefits with very simple software tools. Don't get off the track with excessive concerns about which software package you will use.

FLOW SYSTEMS

ERP functionality with a *stand-alone* flow line design application. Extract required information from existing sources, but do your line design calculations in a simple PC environment.

MATERIAL KANBAN MANAGEMENT

The case for integration is much stronger, however, when we look at the data requirements to manage a material kanban system. The management of the kanban pull system is something we do frequently, and in fact it requires daily management to perform well. We are also drawing on more of the data that resides in a traditional ERP system: part numbers, inventory balances, Bills of Material, supplier and inventory transactions. One of the key inputs to our kanban sizing formula, the *Forecasted Daily Usage* would normally come from our existing MRP/ERP system. While an initial kanban sizing calculation would be done up-front, we are willing to recalculate our kanban sizing database much more often than we are willing to redesign our entire line, and it is much easier to do so. Periodic adjustment of the kanban sizing to match changes in customer demand is expected and prudent.

Where should we store our kanban information? Since we are drawing on legacy data with more frequency, a strong case can be made for making kanban an integrated function to your MRP/ERP system. It is interesting to note that ERP vendors typically add kanban as one of the first flow/lean enhancement to their systems, and that many ERP systems already have some kanban capability. On the other hand, there are large companies today that are managing their Kanban systems quite well in an off-line environment, using loose integration like flat-file transfers to keep their information up to date. An off-line kanban application is quite simple to create, and can be an interim strategy while the cost and effort of creating an integrated solution can be assessed.

WHAT'S YOUR SOFTWARE DOING FOR YOU?

Some software providers claim to have a magic kanban formula that will solve all your problems. We proposed a kanban calculation formula in Chapter 10, but that is not the most important aspect of the kanban management system. The discipline is far more important than any calculation you could perform.

FLOW SYSTEMS

SUPPLY CHAIN TOOLS

One of the ten characteristics of a flow manufacturing environment is a tight relationship and integration with suppliers. One of the fundamental requirements is the communication of changing requirements with suppliers so that material delivery surprises don't happen often. It is important to remember that the elimination of inventory from both the shop floor and from the supply chain brings with it an element of risk: if the supply is not consistent and of high quality, the benefit of reduced inventory will quickly be wiped out by the inability to build products and deliver them on time. We recommend caution when it comes to raw material reductions. Reducing raw materials without a strong supply chain strategy is an invitation to headaches or disaster.

The new requirements of flow manufacturing and suppliers has to do with an increased need for flexibility and response, and the introduction of pull methods. We do not want to simply push inventory upstream in the supply chain. From a systems perspective, supply chain is a highly integrated function that includes inventory, material planning, demand information and Bills of Material. Companies will continue to use their MRP/ERP system to do material planning, and supply chain capabilities like EDI, auto-fax and material triggers are already a part of many ERP systems. Integration of material planning with the new Kanban system, so that suppliers can do a better job of internal planning, is often the missing piece of functionality.

SIMULATION MODELING

We mention simulation modeling here briefly to raise awareness of the growing importance of this technology, especially as it applies to flow

FLOW SYSTEMS

THE $250,000,000 MISTAKE

A well-known computer company decided to implement an assemble-to-order strategy a few years ago, and dedicated a building to the creation of this new line. One of the concerns was the amount of staging space required for orders awaiting shipment, and the best advise from a number of consulting companies was around 25,000 SF. At the last moment, the company decided to contract with a consulting company to create a simulation model of the proposed line, to test these assumptions. The result of the model: 120,000 SF, a space almost 5 times larger. What did the company do? Ignore the results of the model, of course.

When the line went live a short time later, all was well until the production volumes reached a level predicted by the model. The staging space filled completely up, and blocked the line. The company eventually went back to the old way of building computers. The loss, including lost opportunity, was estimated at $250,000,000.

manufacturing. Flow manufacturing is an ideal application for the use of simulation modeling tools, and in fact most large companies already do so. From General Motors on down, companies today are using modeling tools to test their proposed process changes prior to implementing them. Simulation modeling is highly recommended at the line design process, and models can also be used as a planning tool to validation daily production plans and anticipate production problems ahead of time. The more dynamic a production environment, the more useful simulation modeling is.

There are many simulation software products on the market, but none of them are particularly easy to use. Some large companies are investing in in-house expertise to learn this software, while others prefer to draw on outside expertise on an as-required basis to develop these models.

FLOW PRODUCTION PLANNING

The planning requirements for flow manufacturing should be considerably simpler than in a scheduled, traditional environment; otherwise you're doing something wrong! One of the goals of flow is to replace complex scheduling with *pull signals*, so that ideally only one point in the line needs to be formally planned. Subassemblies and independent processes in a flow environment are connected with *Kanban* signals, and are not scheduled as independent entities. Paperwork should be simplified or eliminated, while work orders and pick lists are no longer used. Even with all of these advantages, many significant planning challenges remain in a flow environment:

- ♦ What is the right sequence of customer orders? It could make a big difference in how the line performs.

FLOW SYSTEMS

- ◆ Do I have the materials I need? Why would I even start work if I don't have all of the material?
- ◆ What do I do about "lumpy" orders? Customer demand is not inherently smooth.
- ◆ How do I give my customer a valid delivery date? With a backlog of orders, the actual completion date is a moving target.
- ◆ How can I optimize setup times? If I don't do a good job of planning for setups, I could be in real trouble from a delivery and capacity viewpoint.
- ◆ What impact does my plan have on my Kanban sizing? Does my Kanban design support what I want to do today?
- ◆ How many people do I need today? I don't want to overstaff or under staff.
- ◆ What happens to my plan if a machine goes down? All of my due dates are now at risk.
- ◆ How can I plan for the future? When will I run out of capacity? Can I perform what-if analysis?
- ◆ What happens when my customer changes priorities? They want it now. What does this do to all of my other orders?

The methodology of choice for shop floor planning in a flow environment is Advanced Planning and Scheduling, or APS. APS is a proven method for the planning and optimizing of manufacturing resources, both labor and machine. It performes finite capacity planning, and considers the impact of setups and changeovers, preventive maintenance, shifts and actual work content. APS will also attempt to optimize customer orders, based on specific optimization goals. In some environments the goal may be setup reduction; in others it could be smoothing the work flow. Companies have found that the APS planning logic and flow manufacturing pull systems work well together, and that APS can support the *pull* philosophy.

There are many software vendors that offer APS solutions, most of which are tightly integrated with MPR/ERP

FLOW SYSTEMS

systems. The integration and implementation effort is typically large for these types of APS systems, and the risk is also high. The percentage of APS systems that are still in use one year after implementation is depressingly low. The fault is not with the APS methodology, but with the difficulty of integrating complex systems and maintain the input data at the necessary very high level of accuracy. Add to this functional risk the fact that these systems are usually very expensive, and Return On Investment (ROI) becomes hard to find.

An alternative to large and expensive integrated APS planning tools is a loosely integrated, PC-based approach, using the same planning algorithms but a much simplified software environment. This approach has been taken with success by several large manufacturing companies, and we expect the trend to continue.

We will not be going back to a world of manual systems and methods, and as we pointed out earlier, the lack of formal tools and the use of manual systems can be a bottleneck in our manufacturing or information flow. The hard fact, though, is this: the return on investment for most large system acquisitions is simply not there, and we often base our systems decisions on emotion rather than hard-dollar payback. The solution, for the right type of application, is to move to a flexible PC-based platform *with* sophisticated algorithms and methods. Many of the flow manufacturing needs discussed in this chapter fit into this category of applications.

LESSONS LEARNED

1. We need to use computers in our business. Doing things manually can be a source of waste. Most companies use a version of MRP/ERP to run their business.
2. Data-driven flow manufacturing methods can be integrated well with computer applications. ERP systems are missing much of this functionality.
3. *Lean applications* developed with standard PC software like Microsoft Excel or Access may be the best solution to provide missing functionality from our ERP systems.
4. Applications that are good candidates for this approach include our line design calculations, Kanban database, shop floor planning, supply chain tools and simulation modeling.

CHAPTER

16

**FLOW-BASED
SUPPLY
CHAIN
MANAGEMENT**

The competition today is not really between companies. Success depends on the strong cooperation of an entire supply chain, so today it's really supply chain vs. supply chain competition.

SUPPLY CHAIN MANAGEMENT

As companies in the 1990's began to introduce flow processing in large numbers into their factories, it quickly became clear that internal manufacturing lead-time is not the longest element of overall customer response time.

This is especially true in mature flow processing environments where products can be built within their work content time or less. Companies like Dell Computer can assemble their products, configured to individual customer order, in a few minutes. Many automotive plants have also reduced WIP to a few hours of production. The key to rapid customer response lies not only in their fast manufacturing process. The key to success lies in the management of the *entire* product delivery process, or what is commonly referred to as the *supply chain*.

To understand the major components of a supply chain, and how they are related, an *extended process flow diagram* is an excellent first step. As opposed to looking only at the line or cell level, the extended process flow diagram documents a bigger picture, linking suppliers, warehousing, information flow, planning, product design, and any process in the critical path. This step is also know as *Value Stream Mapping*. The definition of a "process" still applies: a logical grouping of work steps that flow. Failure to group work at this level will have one of two consequences: either the extended process flow diagram will be too high level and of little use, or it will be too detailed and too complex. The purpose of the extended process flow diagram is to be able to see and understand *all* of the processes that will need to be analyzed and put into a flow. The response time through the factory, after implementing flow manufacturing, may be one of the smallest time elements in delivering products to your customer. Information flow is equally critical, and needs to be included in the extended process flow diagram.

SUPPLY CHAIN COMPETITION

"Today's business environment is no longer company vs. company, but supply chain vs. supply chain. Today's consumer is looking for high quality, high customization, and low price. This cannot be provided by a link of a chain, but rather, is the result of the entire chain working as one. All supply chain partners must reflect honesty and integrity if the supply chain is to be successful. "

- James Tomkins
Dimpled Chads in the Board Room

WHAT IS A PROCESS?

A process is a physical location where a logical grouping of resources performs sequential work tasks.

SUPPLY CHAIN MANAGEMENT

THE DELL PHILOSOPHY

"We currently have less than 30 strategic suppliers, which represent the majority of the materials we use. When an order comes in, these strategic suppliers are alerted. Traditional organizations use the supply-demand management organization or the 'push-philosophy', but at Dell, we use the demand-supply management organization or the 'pull-philosophy' in order to reduce resistance. As a result, the transformation costs, as a percent of revenue, can be driven lower and lower."

- Keith Maxwell, Vice President of America Operations
Dell Computers

The procurement of raw materials and components from external suppliers is typically a major focus in most manufacturing companies, and a major challenge. Over the years many companies have pursued an out-sourcing manufacturing strategy, keeping product design, final assembly, and perhaps a few other core competencies in-house. A large and larger percentage of the product cost comes from purchased material, while the in-house direct labor content of the product shrinks. Quality and delivery of purchased material then becomes a critical link in the supply chain, and supplier management takes on an increasingly important role. The challenge for a flow manufacturing company is to be able to manage this critical link in the supply chain, optimizing the balance between inventory levels and being able to supply the production lines. The challenge is especially delicate because even if the factory itself can build products directly to customer orders, it is unlikely that the end-user will allow enough lead-time to procure the raw material as well. Raw material procurement therefore is typically driven by a sales forecast rather than by direct customer orders, even in a flow environment.

In order to support the high level of flexibility required by a flow manufacturing strategy, there are several phases that a company must go through. They are evolutionary rather than revolutionary, since they normally take time to implement and require a focused and concerted effort to accomplish. The four phases are:

- ♦ Supplier Certification
- ♦ Kanban Release
- ♦ Supplier Partnerships
- ♦ Supplier Alliance

SUPPLY CHAIN MANAGEMENT

SUPPLIER CERTIFICATION

Supplier certification is the formal process of ensuring that suppliers are able to deliver materials with quality, on time, and in the desired quantities. In the perfect flow manufacturing world *all* suppliers are certified, i.e. they provide parts-per-million level quality, the material does not require in-process inspection, and it can be delivered economically in kanban quantities. Unfortunately there is no magic wand that can transform frog-like suppliers into princes overnight. Many flow manufacturing practitioners actively encourage their suppliers to implement flow as well, knowing that the benefits will also flow to them. Of course, the more clout a customer has with a supplier, the easier it is to influence change. Small manufacturers may have a more difficult time convincing a large supplier to go along with the program. Major industry segments like automotive maintain an active involvement in supplier certification, and essentially dictate best practices to many of them.

The need for world-class levels of quality and delivery is easy to understand, but what about the requirement for kanban quantities? Unless the supplier can deliver in supermarket quantities, typically a few days supply, then raw material levels will remain high, even if work-in-process inventory is minimal. A key to overall inventory turnover improvement has to include a supplier pull strategy tied to the kanban system.

KANBAN PULL STRATEGY

A kanban supplier pull strategy is the next evolutionary step in achieving a complete pull system. The prerequisites from the Supplier Certification Stage (quality, quantity and delivery) need to be in place prior to being able to move on to this step. Without a solid foundation of reliable delivery of high quality material, implementing a pull system is an invitation to frustration and disappointment.

CASE HISTORY

The economic downturn of 2001 left many companies with excess inventories, simply because they could not turn off the "faucet" quickly enough to prevent the receipt of large quantities of now unneeded materials. The existing contracts, scheduled deliveries and material pipeline continued to flow for a period of time even after demand dropped.

With a supplier pull system in place, as demand drops the in-house material is consumed more slowly and the release signal to the supplier arrives less frequently. The supplier only ships upon receipt of a pull signal, and therefore slows down the frequency of delivery. While this method is not a panacea for all supply chain ills, it does put a visual limit on the amount of material either in the plant or in process from the supplier, regardless of what the ERP system calculates.

The method works the other way as well. As demand grows, the pull signal to the supplier is sent more frequently and deliveries are received more often. All of this activity should take place within negotiated limits of flexibility and capacity, and suppliers do continue to receive a long-range projection of material requirements.

SUPPLY CHAIN MANAGEMENT

The purchasing department will play an instrumental role in setting up and managing the supplier pull strategy. Suppliers will continue to receive a long-range forecast of material requirements, presumably as they have in the past. The specific terms of the supplier relationship will need to be negotiated beforehand. The many details will be clearly spelled out regarding quality and quantity expectations, delivery requirements, payment terms, unit price and other non-recurring costs. Risk-sharing will need to be agreed upon if the supplier is expected to procure raw material, and possibly maintain a Kanban quantity of finished product ready to ship.

FIGURE 15.1   **Supplier Kanban Pull Strategy**

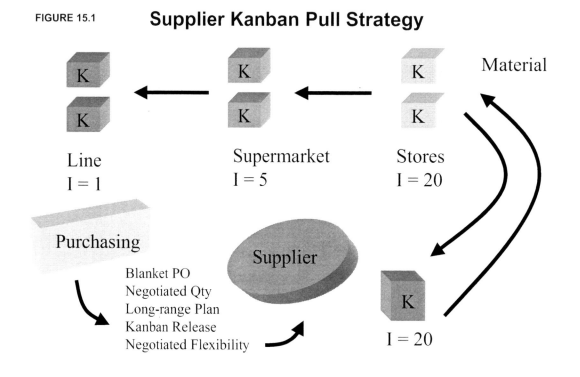

Line
I = 1

Supermarket
I = 5

Stores
I = 20

Material

Purchasing

Blanket PO
Negotiated Qty
Long-range Plan
Kanban Release
Negotiated Flexibility

Supplier

I = 20

SUPPLY CHAIN MANAGEMENT

Figure 15.1 demonstrates the step-by-step pull relationship from the production line to the supplier. The pull signals would occur as follows:

1. Material is used at the final point of consumption, the line or cell. A small amount of material is stocked at this location for use, 1 day of inventory supply in this example. A two-container method is shown, where the material is consumed from one container at a time. When a container is emptied, it then represents the signal for replenishment. While the first container is being refilled, material in the second container is available for use. The first container would need to be refilled within a day to avoid running out on the line altogether. The kanban container is refilled from the *supermarket*.

2. The same two-container method is used in the supermarket, an intermediate inventory location adjacent to the line location. The supermarket inventory quantity is larger than the quantity on the line, and in this example represents a five day supply of the same component. The number of days supply will depend on both the frequency of replenishment and the value of the material. Inexpensive and easy-to-procure items, inventory classification "C", can be stocked in larger quantities without seriously degrading inventory turnover. Expensive components, inventory classification "A", will be controlled much more tightly, with less inventory allowed. The tradeoff lies in the number of replenishment trips and the material handling overhead expense.

3. The two-container method may also be used in the warehouse or stores locations, or suppliers may be permitted to by-pass the warehouse altogether and deliver directly to the supermarket. Direct delivery to the supermarket contains an element of risk, since the inventory quantity will be less, and the frequency of delivery greater. If there is some doubt about the ability of the supplier to deliver on

THE DELL MODEL

Dell Computer is well known as a pioneer in the "configure to order" business model. Customers ordering PCs over the internet or by phone can select from a large number of options, and configure a machine to their specifications. The pricing for this machine is calculated on-line, and the order is placed with a credit card. The order information is then communicated to the factory floor, sequenced into the production plan, and assembled in a few minutes.

Dell does not need to wait for the necessary components: disk drives, chassis, memory, processors, monitors. All of the necessary components are available for immediate consumption, supplied by a local network of supplier hubs. Unlike the automotive industry (that operates in a similar fashion), Dell does not carry finished goods. The result is a business model that can run on "negative working capital". The cash to run the business is provided by customers and suppliers. Raw material and work-in-process is owned by the supplier, while finished goods is owned by the customer.

SUPPLY CHAIN MANAGEMENT

MICHAEL DELL ON VELOCITY

"In this business, it is not about how much inventory you have, but about how fast it's moving through the cycle. I don't want a warehouse of stuff, because it becomes obsolete so quickly. With our model, we start with the customer whose order pulls inventory through the channel. That results in our ability to deliver a desktop computer in 3 days which is configured exactly as the customer wants. That provides a great deal of value."

-Michael Dell
Dell Computers

THE 80/20 RULE

The job of implementing a supplier pull system can be a huge task, especially if there are many suppliers and components that need to be analyzed and planned for. With new products constantly being introduced, and a high level of engineering change, it might seem like the supply chain effort is like Sisyphus pushing a rock up a mountain. The 80/20 rules says, however, that 80% of your inventory dollars are tied up in 20% of your part numbers. Focus on the 20%, and set up simple replenishment methods for the remaining 80% of your inventory.

time, or without defects, the direct-to-supermarket strategy should be postponed, and the supplier should continue to delivery to the warehouse for the time being.

4. Upon emptying a kanban container, either in the supermarket or the stores locations, a replenishment signal is then sent to the external supplier. This signal can be as simple as a fax or phone call, or as sophisticated as an bar-code initiated EDI record. The message to the supplier, however, is to release a kanban quantity of the material that was consumed, in order to refill the empty container. The supplier may have a kanban quantity of this material ready for shipment or, if the supplier's own manufacturing lead-time is sufficiently short, the supplier may produce the material to order. Either way, there is an expectation that a full container will be delivered to the customer within the pre-negotiated delivery frequency.

SUPPLIER/CUSTOMER PARTNERSHIPS

The next evolutionary step in the complete pull relationship with suppliers is to involve the suppliers directly in the day-to-day management of the kanban system. Rather than providing the supplier with a pull signal, the supplier will take an active role in monitoring inventory levels and restocking empty Kanban containers. This practice is already quite common in the replenishment of hardware items like screws, bolts and washers. Common electronic components are often managed directly by external suppliers in many companies.

The replenishment signal in a supplier partnership relationship can take several forms. In some cases the supplier is allowed access to the production floor and supermarket locations, and take full responsibility for refilling empty containers. In other cases the pull signal is initiated by the customer, but the required material is

SUPPLY CHAIN MANAGEMENT

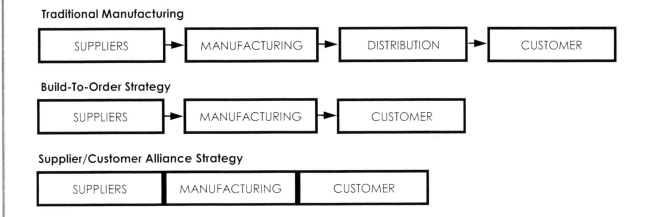

Traditional Manufacturing

SUPPLIERS → MANUFACTURING → DISTRIBUTION → CUSTOMER

Build-To-Order Strategy

SUPPLIERS → MANUFACTURING → CUSTOMER

Supplier/Customer Alliance Strategy

SUPPLIERS | MANUFACTURING | CUSTOMER

SUPPLIER ALLIANCE

Toyota (and more recently Chrysler in the United States) has developed long-term partnerships with suppliers who are given implicit guarantees on future business. In return, suppliers make relation-specific investments to enhance their productivity in the Toyota relationship. Past studies indicate that these relation-specific site, physical and human asset investments reduce inventories, improve quality, and speed product development.

- Dyer, Cho, Wu
Strategic Supplier Segmentation: The Next Best Practice in Supply Chain Management

FOCUS ON TIME

When a fire in the manufacturing plant of a supplier destroyed the main source of brake parts for Toyota in 1997, experts expected Toyota's own manufacturing plants to be down for several days or weeks waiting for a new source for the critical parts. Because Toyota has developed a close-knit family of suppliers over the years, however, it was able to use this large support system of 36 suppliers (including a sewing machine company that had never made car parts) to replace the lost manufacturing capacity within five days, a remarkably fast recovery. Toyota clearly showed that it could avoid the risk of relying on suppliers, as in this case, by building a loyal network of a closely knit family of suppliers that would come to Toyota's aid in a crisis. All the members of the "family" knew how important it was to recover Toyota production as quickly as possible.

"Toyota's Fast Rebound after Fire at Supplier Shows Why It Is Tough,"
The Wall Street Journal, May 8, 1997

SUPPLY CHAIN MANAGEMENT

ARCHITECTURAL INNOVATION

Even though Japanese suppliers, on average, seem to have greater responsibility for more complex systems and a higher percentage of them design parts themselves rather than jointly with their customers, it is found that in general US suppliers have comparable levels of responsibility for design, analysis, prototyping and testing. US suppliers are also found to be just as likely to influence the requirements for the components they design and build, receive specifications that are not more restrictive, have design capabilities comparable to those of their Japanese counterparts, and communicate even more frequently with their customers in the early stages of the design process.

- Bozdogan, Deyst, Hoult, Lucas
Architectural Innovation In Product Development

LESSONS LEARNED

1. **Today the competition is as much between supply chains as it is between companies.**
2. **The development of a strong supply chain is not an overnight effort. It takes significant time and effort (years).**
3. **As the supplier relationship matures in a flow manufacturing environment, the supplier relationship can evolve from scheduled deliveries to a Kanban pull relationship to vendor-managed inventory to a full supplier alliance.**

available for quick replenishment from a near-by supplier depot. Payment for the material consumed can be initiated either at the time of delivery to the line or supermarket, or at the point of backflush once the product is completed. Ownership at the point of backflush means that from a factory viewpoint, the company only owns finished goods; all other material is supplier-owned. While the advantages for the company are obvious in this relationship, the supplier also benefits from a strong customer relationship and perhaps favorable payment and cash flow terms. It clearly needs to be a "win-win" for both sides.

SUPPLIER ALLIANCE

The last stage in the supply chain relationship extends the cooperation beyond the exchange of goods to a partnership in new product design and development. Instead of providing the supplier with engineering drawings and requirements already completed, the customer provides detailed requirement specifications and the supplier will provide the final component or subassembly design. After all, who knows how to build the part better than the supplier? At some automobile manufacturing companies over 50% of the product design is done outside of the company. Japanese manufacturers, with their close networks of "keiretsu" or interlocking business relationships, are seemingly most advanced in this area. Still, in the U.S. there is a strong trend for GM, Ford and others for moving in this direction. The advantages from a quality, functionality and speed-to-market perspective are great.

SUPPLY CHAIN MANAGEMENT

AEROSPACE SUPPLIER STRATEGIES

In the foreword to this book, Michael Beason presented the idea that the challenge for the aerospace industry is essentially a supply-chain challenge. From an industry perspective, it does little good for individual suppliers to improve their internal processes if this does not result in an overall reduction in the response time for the industry as a whole. Clearly a new and higher level of thinking and cooperation will be required to impact an industry who's inventory turnover has not improved after a decade of waste elimination and process improvement efforts.

As a part of the Lean Enterprise System method, the SEA supplier training seminar addresses the following topics:

- ◆ Doing Lean Math: Analysis for Procurement.
- ◆ Measuring Supplier Performance.
- ◆ Building Supplier Pull Systems
- ◆ Use of ERP/MRP and Flow Manufacturing
- ◆ Supplier Flow Audit Process
- ◆ Reducing the "Whiplash Effect" on suppliers
- ◆ Vision of Perfection: The Lean Procurement Model
- ◆ Concurrent Planning
- ◆ Educating and Assisting Suppliers
- ◆ 10 Good Reasons to Buy from a Lean Supplier
- ◆ The Impact of Large Lot Sizes on Procurement

NOTES

CHAPTER

17

SELLING
FLOW

The implementation of flow manufacturing, under its many names, is not an option. There is no other approach to improvement that can deliver these kind of results.

SELLING FLOW

While there is no magic wand or formula that will guarantee success, flow manufacturing methods have been applied successfully in thousands of companies world-wide. To get started requires a company-wide focus and top management commitment. Here are some ideas, suggestions, and recollections of successful implementations to help you "sell" flow manufacturing within your company.

CALCULATING BENEFITS

No matter how good the benefits of flow manufacturing may sound, and in spite of the fact that we intuitively *know* that this is something we need to do, company management continues to insist on a reasonable assurance of quantifiable benefits that can be taken to the bottom line. If management has confidence that the flow manufacturing project will result in real dollar savings, and fairly quickly at that, the approval for a flow manufacturing project should be speedy. If the benefits are small, hard to understand, at substantial risk or delayed, then the flow manufacturing implementation project will have difficulty getting through the approval process.

Fortunately, the hard dollar (euro, peso) benefits are often substantial, especially for companies moving from traditional, functional manufacturing methods to a flow environment. The expected reduction in WIP inventory, for example, can be as much as 90% when implementing flow, along with a 90% reduction in factory response time. Justifying a flow implementation with benefits like that should be easy, and not require too much analysis. Finished goods and WIP inventory reductions alone might sell the program.

It's usually not so easy. Companies have been making improvement efforts for a long time, and often the obvious benefits have already been gained. It may be

A GRASSROOTS EFFORT?

Can a flow manufacturing initiative be driven from lower levels in the organization, rather than from the top? Changes and improvements using flow methods can certainly be applied by anyone, in any process. But what about a company-wide and long-lasting initiative?

We haven't seen that happen. The changes are too extensive and the paradigm shifts too great to expect that a company-wide transformation will occur without strong and continuous top management leadership and pressure.

So, if you're not a top manager (yet) and you're reading this book, it would be a good idea to begin to strategize with some of your revolutionary colleagues about how you're going to get the top management support that you'll need. Otherwise, *you* may personally have fun implementing flow in your area, but don't expect the world to follow your example.

And if you *are* a top manager, what are you waiting for?

SELLING FLOW

INVENTORY CARRYING COST

Attempting to calculate the benefits of inventory reduction is sometimes a controversial subject. Inventory is a balance sheet item, not something that shows up directly on the profit and loss statement. There are costs associated with having inventory, however; it isn't free. An estimate of what the inventory actually costs us is called the *inventory carrying cost*, expressed as a percentage of the inventory value. Reducing inventory by a million dollars, for example, does not result in a million dollar benefit on the P&L, but if we spend 20% of the inventory value per year to maintain or "carry" it, then our legitimate savings or benefit would be $200,000/year.

What sort of P&L costs are incurred by having inventory around? Following is a list of costs that should be considered when calculating a carrying cost percentage:

- Interest Expense or Opportunity Cost
- Obsolescence
- Material Handling
- Scrap
- Warehouse Space
- Inventory Transactions

What is a reasonable cost-to-carry inventory percentage? It really depends on your industry, but 18-25% would not be unreasonable. Anything much less than that needs to be questioned.

necessary to dig a little deeper, but the benefits are there and the improvement process is never complete. Following are some places to look when estimating flow manufacturing benefits:

- WIP Inventory. Work-in-process inventory is directly related to the response time through the factory. If your average response time is expected to go from five days to one day, for example, the WIP inventory should be reduced by 80%.
- Finished Goods Inventory. If the factory response time is reduced, the amount of finished goods required to meet target customer service levels can also be reduced. Be conservative in FGI cuts until the line performance is actually achieved.
- Raw Material. Many companies make the mistake of going after raw material reductions first. We often leave raw material savings out of the analysis, since this is mainly a supply-chain issue not related directly to the line response time. Supplier kanban is a powerful tool to help manage raw material levels.
- It makes perfect sense that by standardizing work, eliminating non-value-added work steps, and reducing waste, that productivity will improve. A 15-20% improvement would not be surprising. Productivity improvements are difficult to qualify initially, however, so you should be conservative in the claimed benefits in this category.
- Scrap and Rework. It is very helpful if this information is available, but often rework is a hidden cost that shows up in the productivity measurement. The amount of improvement possible in the short term in this category is related to the root cause. If high scrap levels are related to workmanship, then we can expect major improvements once we have implemented standard work and check-do-check techniques, coupled with a robust training and certification program. Machine process or design issues are harder to resolve in the short term, but eventually these will need to be addressed as well.

SELLING FLOW

FIGURE 16.1 PROCESS DESIGN ANALYSIS SHEET

CURRENT	BENEFIT	MEASURE	PROPOSED
	Floor Space Used	Total Square Feet	
	Total Part Travel	Linear Feet	
	Number of Operators Required	Headcount	
	Number of Support Personnel	Headcount	
	Work In Process Inventory	Dollars	
	Units per Labor Hour	Units	
	Cost per Piece	Dollars	
	Manufacturing Lead Time	Days	
	Housekeeping Rating	5S Weighting	
	Value Added Ratio	Percentage	

Format suggested in *The Kaizen Event Implementation Manual* by Geoffrey L. Mika, p. 80.

OTHER MEASUREMENTS

Other measurements can be added to the ones listed above, as appropriate to the specific company environment. A reduction in manufacturing response time can also permit a reduction in *Finished Goods Inventory*. Kanban pull methods are used to control *Raw Materials* as well. Simplified planning needs will result in a reduction in *Planning Response Time,* a reduction in *Shop Floor Paperwork*, and a reduction in the number of *Inventory Transactions*. The number of suppliers that are under a *Kanban Pull Relationship* is another useful goal and measurement, which should also lead to fewer *Part Shortages*. Improved processes and operator inspection will lead to reduced *Scrap* and *Rework*.

SELLING FLOW

CREATIVITY

Creativity can solve almost any problem. The creative act, the defeat of habit by originality, overcomes everything.

-- George Lois

♦ Overtime. Many of the tools of flow manufacturing will help control overtime expense. The line will be designed to support a target volume that typically exceeds today's demand. Meeting the daily product plan within normal working hours then becomes a matter of applying the correct number of labor resources. The need for unplanned overtime should be reduced significantly.

♦ Overhead costs. Overhead costs usually represent between 15-25% of your product costs, are largely non-value-adding to the product, and represent the best opportunity for overall cost reduction. Some examples are given in Figure 16.1.

Flow manufacturing is a low-cost implementation strategy, and the main expenses are related to training the workforce and the time to make the necessary transformations. Capital investment can be low. The payback, even with conservative estimates, can be 5-1, 10-1 or greater. Implementation of flow manufacturing is usually the best investment that a company can make; there are few other.opportunities that offer this kind of payback.

PROPOSING A PROVEN SET OF TOOLS

To sell your flow manufacturing implementation internally, it is usually very helpful to propose a proven and low-risk methodology or path. The flow manufacturing tools we have described throughout this book have the advantage of being simple, consistent, repeatable, and proven. They are a way of providing a measure of standardization to the design of business processes in a flow. These tools have been proven many times over with a wide variety of products, product mixes, levels of customization, production volumes, machine or labor-intensive environments, and different cultures. This set of tools is intended to supplement your common sense as well as your knowledge of your

SELLING FLOW

products and your processes. Follow the path and the tools we described throughout the book, carefully document your steps as you move forward, and your chances for success will be greatly enhanced. But do not forget that it is *you* who designs the line, not the tools. The tools are intended to *help* you, not replace you.

FINDING A TOP-MANAGEMENT OWNER

Yes, we know this is needed for success in *every* endeavor, but it becomes critical when it comes to implementing flow manufacturing. In spite of the simplicity of the tools we have explained throughout the book, the magnitude of the wall-to-wall transformation is quite significant. Roles change, performance metrics change, work changes, even the look of the environment changes. What until yesterday (literally) was considered the behavior of a good soldier, today is what is "preventing our company from becoming competitive". Such deep transformation is unlikely to succeed if not driven from an involved leader in a high management position. The ideal situation is a complete and un-compromised top-down approach where the top-management team sees the potential results, and enables a team to carry out the conversion.

UNCOVERING A FLOW CHAMPION

This is something we have seen in *every* successful flow implementation project. There is a need for someone to become the strongest flow believer in the company, regardless of rank, position, gender, education, or any other distinctive feature. This is the person that works the hardest to develop an understanding of the fundamentals of flow manufacturing, their application to the company's specific processes, and visualizes the results. The flow champion wants to be involved in every aspect of the project, from the planning to the execution. Find that person and nurture his/her desire to

LEADERSHIP

"I will move these people into the future willingly, if possible, kicking and screaming, if necessary."

-Peter the Great

COMPANY PRESIDENT INVOLVEMENT

At the kick-off of a flow manufacturing implementation for a large consumer products company with an assembly plant in North Carolina, the company president flew in from the Midwest and over a two day period personally gave a 20-minute talk to small groups of workers on the importance of the project. Did this make an impression about the seriousness of top management? You bet.

SELLING FLOW

STEP BY STEP PROCESS

1. Identify products to be included in the design. This product list will be validated as we go forward.
2. Create a process flow diagram (PFD) for every product that documents the basic processes and their relationships. PFDs can be shared.
3. Document the relationship of products and processes on a process flow map, and validate your product family selection.
4. Record the detailed work steps for each process on a standard work definition, including reasonable time estimates for each work step.
5. Develop an estimate of anticipated production volumes, with sales and management input.
6. Perform calculations of throughput volume, takt time and required machine and labor resources, by process.
7. Based on your PFDs and the required resource calculations, create a preliminary layout of the flow process. Consider cases where the processes cannot be linked directly, and where supermarkets will be needed.
8. Apply the balancing tools to areas when the work cannot flow to takt time.

If you don't drive your business you will be driven out of business.

-- B. C. Forbes

learn and to make a mark in the company's performance. Do not make the mistake of thinking that the flow champion should be found within a specific department, business process, or discipline. We have seen flow champions coming from every discipline within the company. Do not limit yourself and your company to thinking that flow is "that thing they do on the shop floor, with shop floor people" for it will only lead you to a path of sub-optimal performance.

COUNT PEOPLE IN FROM THE BEGINNING

At the center of the success of flow manufacturing are the people that staff the processes, make the processes work, and relentlessly review them to make them better. The old-school approach of looking at the shop-floor employees as arms and legs, rather than contributing team members, will only lead you down a path of partial success. The shop floor can *look* like flow heaven, but if the people staffing it are not involved in making it work, it will perform like flow purgatory.

WATCH OUT FOR FLOW SNAKE OIL

Every time a methodology proves itself to yield great results, "experts" begin to come out from under every rock you turn and every bush you shake. Many of these experts have participated in *a* flow implementation at their prior place of employment, and one flow implementation is clearly better than none. However, the unique processes, products, and culture of a specific company are not always transferable to every business and its products and processes. We also recommend you exercise caution when the "flow snake oil" salesman makes claims to amazing new inventions and novelties. With all the different names, all the unique vocabularies, and all the twists and turns, we are all talking about the *elimination of waste through the linking and balancing of resources*. It may have been renamed or repackaged, but nothing about flow manufacturing has been invented in modern times

SELLING FLOW

IT'S NOT A SOFTWARE PROJECT

Please, do not interpret this as "we are against software". Nothing could be farther from the truth. We strongly believe in the use of software tools to assist you in documenting, calculating and storing information related to the design of the flow processes. What we do *not* believe is that software can take the place of your common sense, discipline and knowledge of the products and processes that you are putting in a flow. We have seen some flow implementation projects come to a grinding halt because they were being led by software, not by people. Software products cannot make the decisions necessary to succeed in flow manufacturing, people can. Software does not provide discipline. Whatever software product you choose to use or develop, it must reflect the realities of the new flow environment, rather than forcing the flow environment to adapt to a computer system's capabilities, or inadequacies.

LESSONS LEARNED

1. Leadership, from both management and from internal *flow champions*, is a critical success factor.
2. An experienced mentor can help you get up the learning curve quickly. However: you'll have to do it yourself.
3. Don't let software drive the implementation. Software is not a substitute for discipline and understanding. Seriously apply the KISS principle when it comes to the software tools you use.
4. Flow manufacturing is actually really enjoyable. You get results, life is better, chaos is reduced, everyone wins.

One final point from our many years of experience in designing and implementing flow manufacturing in a variety of companies: it is *not* magic, it is *not* that difficult, it is *not* for the selected few. And, it really can be *fun*.

NOTES

APPENDIX

1

TIMELINE OF FLOW MANUFACTURING

FLOW TIMELINE

YEAR	EVENT
1760	First known record of work standards and time studies by Jean Radolphe Perronet for pin manufacturing
1792	Work standards are used to run a production schedule at the Old Derby Ceramic works by Thomas Mason
1878	Frederick W. Taylor joins Midvale Steel Company
1883	Taylor begins time studies at Midvale Steel
1885	Frank B. Gilbreth begins work in time and motion studies
1895	Taylor's "A Piece Rate System" is published
1903	Taylor presents paper "Shop Management". In the same year Henry Ford produces the first Model A, and Gantt develops the "Gantt Chart"
1904	Thorstein Veblen publishes "The Theory of Business Enterprise"
1907	Gilbreth applies time and motion methods to the construction industry
1908	Ford produces the first Model T with interchangeable parts
1911	Taylor publishes "The Principles of Scientific Management"
1912	Harrington Emerson publishes "The Twelve Principles of Efficiency"
1912	Gilbreth publishes concept of "therbligs". Taylor's work is translated into Japanese.
1914	Clarence B. Thompson edits "Scientific Management", a collection of Taylor's works
1915	Robert Hoxie publishes "Scientific Management and Labor" 1921 Gilbreth introduces the tools of process analysis symbols to the ASME
1916	Lillian Gilbreth publishes "The Psychology of Manufacturing". The F. W. Taylor society is established in the U.S.
1919	Gantt publishes "Organization For Work"
1921	Gilbreth introduces the tools of process analysis symbols to the ASME

FLOW TIMELINE

YEAR	EVENT
1922	G. S. Radford publishes "The Control of Quality in Manufacturing". Toyoda invents the automatic loom.
1923	Alfred P. Sloan becomes president of General Motors
1930	Shewhart develops the SPC control chart. Hathaway publishes "Machining and Standard Times"
1932	Taiichi Ohno joins Toyoda
1934	General Electric performs micro motion studies
1937	Ralph H. Barnes publishes "Motion and Time Study". Toyota Motor Company is founded.
1941	Fritz J. Roethlisberger publishes "Management and Morale"
1945	Shigeo Shingo presents paper "Production as a Network of Processes" to the Japanese Manufacturing Association
1946	Peter Drucker publishes "The Concept of the Corporation"
1948	H. B. Maynard publishes "MTM-Motion Time Measurement". Larry T. Miles develops VA-value analysis at General Electric. Shigeo Shingo publishes "Process Based Machine Layout"
1950	Mundel publishes "Motion and Time Study, Improving Productivity". Shigeo Shingo develops SMED (Single Minute Exchange of Dies).
1951	W. Edwards Deming and J. M. Duran begin training programs in Japan. Juran publishes "The Quality Control Handbook" and has it translated into Japanese.
1955	Shigeo Shingo begins Totoya Motor Group lectures on "Separation of Workers and Machines"

FLOW TIMELINE

YEAR	EVENT
1956	Industrial Engineering discipline redefined by the American Institute of Industrial Engineering
1957	R. L. Morrow publishes "Motion and Time Study"
1960	Nissan Motors wins the Deming Prize.
1961	Shigeo Shingo publishes work on Poke-Yoke, ZQC and Source Inspection.
1962	Quality Circles launched at Toyota Motor Company
1963	H. B. Mayard publishes the Industrial Engineering Handbook
1964	Abraham Maslow publishes "Motivation and Personality"
1968	Roethlisberger publishes "Man In Organization"
1971	Taiichi Ohno completes the Toyota Manufacturing System
1975	Shigeo Shingo promotes NSP-S: Non-Stock Production System.
1977	Yoshiya and Nakane publish "MRP Systems: New Production Control in the Computer Age"
1978	Takano publishes "Complete Information on the Toyota Production System"
1979	Ford Motor Company buys 25% of Mazda
1980	Shigeo Shingo publishes "Study of the Toyota Production System from the Industrial Engineering Viewpoint"
1982	F. Aona publishes "Toyota's Strategy"
1984	Shigeo Shingo publishes "A Revolution in Manufacturing: the SMED System"

FLOW TIMELINE

YEAR	EVENT
1985	Shigeo Shingo publishes "Zero Quality Control: Source Inspection and the Poke-Yoke System"
1986	Eli Goldratt publishes "The Goal"
1990	Womack, Jones and Roos publish "The Machine That Changed the World : The Story of Lean Production"
1996	Womack and Jones publish "Lean Thinking"
2002	Leone and Rahn publish "Fundamentals of Flow Manufacturing"

APPENDIX

2

GLOSSARY
OF
TERMS

GLOSSARY OF TERMS

Activity Based Costing
A system where the costs of specific cost centers are accumulated and subsequently allocated as a percentage of overhead costs assigned to each product through the standard cost build-up process.

Backflush
The process of performing inventory transactions to update inventory balances upon completion of one finished unit. At the point of completion at the end of the line of one complete unit, a transaction occurs incrementing the inventory quantity in finished goods by one unit while simultaneously reducing component inventories by item and quantity listed on the bill of material.

Bill of Material
A listing of all the sub-assemblies, parts, and raw materials that go into a parent assembly showing the quantity of each required to make that assembly. For an MRP system to perform time-phased and shop floor control routing, the bill of material must be indented to simulate the manufacturing process and establish start and due dates for each department of the manufacturing process.

Certification
The acknowledgment of competency for a manufacturing operator recognizing the ability to perform the standard work definition identified at a primary workstation plus one upstream and one downstream within a takt time while performing the defined quality criteria.

Configuration Traveler
A document that physically accompanies each unit of production to indicate the unique configuration of that particular unit.

Continuous Flow Batch Machine
A machine that has an output that is determined by the rate or speed through the machine. Examples include automated conveyance drying ovens, automated paint lines, SMT lines, multi-workstation robotic welding processes.

GLOSSARY OF TERMS

Continuous Process Improvement / Kaizen
An iterative process of seeking the elimination or reduction of non-value adding work imbedded in a process. Non-value-adding work is described as elements of work that a customer is unwilling to pay for. They include set- ups, moves, scrap, rework, and process variation.

Customer Lead Time
The difference in time between when a customer places an order with a supplier and when delivery is expected, i.e. the due date.

Customer Quoted Lead Time
The sum of time required to move purchased parts and components through all the manufacturing processes and ship the completed product as specified to the customer. In some cases, this time may include the time required to purchase raw material. This is the time reported to the customer as necessary to produce the product to the customer specification.

Daily Customer Requirements
The quantity of products, based on customer orders, planned to be produced in any given day of production. In flow manufacturing, the establishment of customer requirements is performed as a daily routine.

Delivery Frequency (DF)
An interval of time required to replenish supplied materials consumed. Delivery frequency is a time element used to calculate kanban quantities in a flow line.

Designed Workstation Definition
A description of a physical location and a listing of specific work elements to be performed as defined in the standard work definition. Workstation Definition includes work elements, TQM check points, TQM self-checks, and would equal approximately one takt time.

Downstream workstation
The next adjacent workstation that continues the elements of work and TQM check points defined in the standard work definition.

GLOSSARY OF TERMS

Employee Qualification Board
A display designed in a matrix format with the horizontal axis indicating the designated workstations or areas based on flow manufacturing designs and the vertical axis listing an assigned team of employees. The current certification level of each employee is recorded at the junction of the two points.

Extended Process Flow Diagram
A process flow diagram (see definition) that documents the process relationships at an enterprise level, and includes planning, information flow, product design, suppliers, warehousing and other critical-path processes.

External Setup
Elements of setup work that can be performed while the process continues to operate. Setup work done in parallel to run time.

Fail-Safe
A process, individual work element, or component that contains no variability. Because of its design, the process, work element or part cannot be produced any way other than the correct way.

Fixed Quantity Batch Machine
A machine process where the lot size is established by parameters other than actual demand.

Flat Level Bill
A listing of all parts and raw materials that go into a parent assembly showing the quantity of each required to make that assembly. A flat bill of material does not contain sub-assemblies or attempt to define parent assembly product routing.

Flexible Staffing
The ability to assign only the number of trained and certified employees to a flow process necessary to match the actual demand for work on any given day.

GLOSSARY OF TERMS

Flow-based response time
The accumulated work content time along the longest path of the process flow definition (PFD). Because work is performed in parallel, work performed in a Flow Process is always shorter than the total work content time.

Flow Production Planning
The daily process of determining the mix / volume of customer orders and forecasted requirements planned for production. The planning steps include resource time availability verification and kanban material validation.

Graphic Work Instructions
A set of graphical representations depicting the work to be performed at a workstation including TQM checkpoints and self-checks. The identified work elements are derived from the standard work definition and are equal to approximately one takt time.

IPK, In-Process Kanban
A clear and visible signal placed on the downstream side of a workstation to signal the upstream workstation to perform another T AKT time amount of work. An IPK also serves as a signal for an employee to flex to waiting work.

Internal Setup
Elements of setup work that can only be performed while the process is halted. Setup work that cannot be completed in parallel to run time.

Kaizen
See Continuous Process Improvement.

Kanban
A Japanese word that defines a communication signal or card. It is a technique used to pull products and materials through flow manufacturing lines. Kanbans may have several variations based on application; in process, material two bin, one-time use, and multiple signal card.

GLOSSARY OF TERMS

Kanban Point
A place that a material kanban is located by design.

Kanban Link
Any two kanban points that form a "consumed at" and "refilled from" (kanban link) relationship for part or an item.

Kanban Chain
Two or more kanban replenishment links that form the complete replenishment path for a part or an item.

Layout
The physical positioning of balanced resources to optimize the flow of work elements to the customer while minimizing or eliminating the non-value added work times.

Line Balancing
The process of establishing individual workstations approximately equal to a takt time amount of work. The elements of work to be performed at each workstation is determined by the standard work definition divided by the takt time.

Material Two-Bin Kanban
A material replenishment methodology using two equally sized containers containing quantities based on the time required to replenish. As the first container is emptied, it becomes the signal for replenishment while the second continues to supply the point of consumption.

Multiple signal card Kanban
A material replenishment technique that uses multiple material kanban cards as signals to communicate the requirement to replenishment. Multiple signals are typically used in processes or independent cells where long set-ups and replenishment times are present.

Multi-Product Family
A family definition consisting of products grouped together based on similar manufacturing processes and standard times to produce those products.

GLOSSARY OF TERMS

One-time use Kanban
Material that once consumed is not automatically replenished. The one-time use kanban is used for highly configured, customized products, or for materials whose usage is very small and continuous replenishment would not be a cost-effective strategy.

Output Variance
A measurement of the number of units actually produced compared with the planned number of units for that day.

Planned work minutes
A statement of the amount of time available to manufacturing employees to perform work.

Process Flow Map
A matrix showing the manufacturing processes identified from the PFD along the horizontal axis and the products along the vertical axis used to determine multi-product families with common processes and standard work times.

Process
A physical location where a logical grouping of resources performs sequential work tasks. A process in manufacturing is a combination of resources (people and machines) that convert material toward the completion of a product. All resources in a process must have the same takt time.

Process Capacity
The highest output rate that can be achieved at a process with the current product specifications, product mix, labor and equipment.

Process Flow Diagram
A graphic depiction of the time based relationship of resources that perform work tasks. The work tasks these resources perform are required to build a product or complete an administrative activity.

Sequencing Control Board
A scheduling communication tool, usually a board, that prioritizes the order that products are to be built or administrative tasks accomplished.

GLOSSARY OF TERMS

Resource
A person, machine, and/ or office equipment that can carry out work tasks required to produce a product or perform an administrative activity.

Resource Time Available (RTA)
The work minutes available in a day from a series of Flow Processing resources (employees, workstations, and/or machines) to build products or perform administrative activities. A calculated simulation of the resource minutes required to perform work in a day versus the resource minutes available in that day.

Resource Time Required (RTR)
The work minutes required in a day from a series of Flow Processing resources (employees, workstations, and/or machines) to build products or perform administrative activities. A calculated time value derived by multiplying the quantity of products or administrative tasks planned to be performed in that day and their SWD times

Safety Factor
An estimate of the a percentage of over-planning needed to overcome inaccuracies in volume predictions.

Sequencing
The process of selecting the order in which the daily production volume will be produced on the Flow Line or in an administrative activity.

Sequencing Rules
A series of guidelines developed to optimize the sequence of products to be build in the Flow line.

Setup Matrix
A matrix indicating the setup times from one product to the next through a cell or individual machine used to determine the average set-up time for Kanban replenishment quantities.

GLOSSARY OF TERMS

Standard Time Map
A process flow map that documents the work content times from the standard work definitions.

Standard Weighted Time (STw).
The time in the numerator used for resource calculation that is weighted by the volume consumed.

Standard Work Definition (SWD)
A definition of the required work and identified quality criteria to build a product in the specific production process.

Stores
The physical location where raw and purchased materials are stored for consumption into work in process.

Supermarket
An inventory storage area located adjacent to manufacturing processes. Materials stored at this location are used to refill materials that were consumed in built products that are signaled by kanban. These supplied materials consist of purchased and in process materials to support kanban replenishment of material.

Supplier Certification
A recognition process for the successful evaluation of a supplier to: assess their process capability, to consistently deliver product on time, with the specified quality criteria achieved.

TAKT
A time volume relationship calculated as the rhythm, beat or cadence for each process of a flow line. Takt is used to establish resource definition and line balance in flow processing.

TQM Check Point
A secondary quality check that is performed as validation that an element of work that could have contained process variability has been performed correctly. The TQM check point is the responsibility of the next employee in the flow process. If an element of work is found to be defective, failing the TQM check, the unit of work is passed back to the person upstream who originally performed the work steps. That person must remedy the problem.

GLOSSARY OF TERMS

TQM self-check
A quality check that is performed at any point on the standard work definition where an element of work contains process variability. The self-check is the responsibility of the employee who has had to perform any work steps that could be done incorrectly when only one way was the correct way.

Transport time
The amount of time allowed for the physical movement of an item from one workstation, process, or cell to the next.

Upstream Workstation
The previous adjacent workstation where work elements and TQM self- checks defined in the Standard Work Definition were performed.

Value Stream Mapping
See Extended Process Flow Diagram.

Volume Forecast (FV) for line design
A statement of anticipated future demand for products to be manufactured in a flow line. FV is one of the factors in the calculation of takt time.

Waste
Any activity or element of work that does not change the form, fit or function of the product is considered as not adding value to the product.

Working Capital
The amount of funds that must be retained from earnings to support the costs of manufacturing. These costs include raw material, in-process, and finished goods inventories plus accounts receivable minus accounts payable.

Workstation
The physical location and space where work elements approximately equal to the calculated takt time is performed.

APPENDIX

3

SOURCES

SOURCES

RECOMMENDED READING

1. Business Process Consulting Group and J.D. Edwards, white paper *Fundamentals of Flow Manufacturing*, Denver, 1999.
2. Eckes, George. *The Six Sigma Revolution: How General Electric and Others Turned Process into Profits*. New York, New York. John Wiley and Sons, 2001.
3. Henderson, Bruce A. and Larco, Jorge L. *Lean Transformation: How to Change your business into a lean enterprise*. Richmond, Virginia, The Oaklea Press, 1999.
4. Ford, Henry. *Today and Tomorrow*. Portland, Oregon, Productivity Press, 1988.
5. Hirano, Hiroyuki. *5S for Operators: 5 Pillars of the Visual Workplace*. Portland, Oregon, Productivity Press, 1997.
6. Imai, Masaaki. *Kaizen: The Key to Japan's Competitive Success*. New York, New York. McGraw Hill Publishing Company, 1976.
7. Kanigel, Robert. *The One Best Way: Frederick Winslow Taylor and the Enigma of Efficiency*. New York, Viking Press, 1997.
8. Mika, Geoffrey. *Kaizen Event Implementation Manual*. Wake Forest, NC, Kaizen Sensei, 2000.
9. Monden, Yasuhiro. *Toyota Production System: An Integrated Approach to Just-In-Time*. Norcross, Georgia, Engineering and Management Press, 1998.
10. Ohno, Taiichi. *Toyota Production System: Beyond Large Scale Production*. Portland, Productivity Press, 1988.
11. Rahn, Richard and Kiran, Ali. *Fundamentals of Flow Manufacturing*. Boulder, Colorado, Flow Publishing, 2001.
12. Rother, Mike and Shook, John. *Learning To See: Value Stream Mapping*. Brookline, The Lean Enterprise Institute, 1999.
13. Schage, Michael. *Serious Play: How the World's Best Companies Simulate to Innovate*. Boston, Harvard Business School Press, 2000.
14. Schoenberger, Richard J. *Japanese Manufacturing Techniques: Nine Hidden Lessons in Simplicity*. New York, New York, The Free Press, 1982.
15. Senge, Peter M. *The Fifth Discipline*. New York, New York, Bantam, Doubleday Dell, 1990.
16. Senge, Peter M. *The Dance of Change*. New York, New York, Doubleday, 1999.
17. Shingo, Shigeo. *A Study of the Toyota Production System*. Portland, Oregon, Productivity Press, 1989.
18. Suzaki, Kiyoshi. *The New Manufacturing Challenge: Techniques for Continuous Improvement*. New York, New York, The Free Press, 1987.
19. Taylor, Frederick Winslow. *The Principles of Scientific Management*. Mineola, New York, Dover Publications, 1998.
20. Tompkins, James A. *Future Capable Company*. Tompkins Press, 2001.
21. Walton, Mary. *The Deming Management Method*.
22. Womack, James P. and Jones, Daniel T. *Lean Thinking: Banish Waste and Create Wealth in your Corporation*. New York, New York, Simon and Schuster, 1996.

SOURCES

FLOW

"The progressive achievement of tasks along the value stream so that a product proceeds from design to launch, order to delivery, and raw materials into the hands of the customer, with no stoppages, scrap or backflows."
Lean Thinking, p. 306

"A process is a series of individual operations required to create a design, completed order, or product."
Lean Thinking, p. 309

"Physical merger of processes: The third-stage configuration is physical merger of processes. The advantages are elimination of inventory buffers and shop paper as well, resulting in a highly simplified and streamlined operation."
Japanese Manufacturing Techniques, p. 115

"Every link in the just-in-time chain is connected and synchronized. By this, the management work force is also reduced drastically."
The Toyota Production System, p. 5

"Material is always moving, always being worked on, always having value added to it, rather than just standing still, accumulating cost."
APICS Just-In-Time Certification Review, p. 82

"To shorten the production cycle, it is far more effective to reduce process delays than to reduce processing time."
Shingo, A Study of the Toyota Production System, p. 99

"The solution [to good flow] is further refined with the use of a complex *mixed production system* in which the assembled vehicles move along the line in a variety of combinations."
Shingo, A Study of the Toyota Production System, p. 99

TAKT

"The available production time divided by the rate of customer demand."
Lean Thinking, p. 310

"The key to continuous flow manufacturing is what is known as takt time by lean producers."
Lean Transformation, p. 58

"Takt is the drumbeat of consumption, the speed at which products are ordered by customers."
Lean Transformation, p. 107

"In a continuous flow environment, an individual worker will produce only at the takt time of the entire cell or work group, rendering the individual incentive meaningless."
Lean Transformation, p. 217

"[Takt] time is equivalent to total working time divided by production quantity. Don't be fooled into thinking that reducing takt time necessarily has anything to do with productivity improvement."
Shingo, A Study of the Toyota Production System, p. 105

SOURCES

"Dividing the number of bikes by the available hours of production tells the production time per bicycle, the takt time..."
Lean Thinking, p. 55

[Calculation of available work hours]
Japanese Manufacturing Techniques, p. 138

"Takt time calculation = total daily operating time divided by the total daily required quantity."
Kaizen Event Implementation Manual, p. 89

PROCESS FLOW DIAGRAMS

"We've found that there's a logical sequence for the implementation of lean...First map the final assembly process for the areas to be transformed. "
Lean Transformation, p. 99

"When laid out this way, action by action, so it's possible to see every step for a specific product, the value stream for physical production is highly though-provoking."
Lean Thinking, p. 43

"Value stream mapping is identification of all the specific activities occurring along a value stream for a product or product family."
Lean Thinking, p. 311

Mapping the entire stream is too much for getting started!
Learning To See, p. 3

"Value Stream Mapping forms the basis of the implementation plan by allowing the whole manufacturing cycle to be seen and addressed."
Kaizen Event Implementation Manual, p. 103

RESOURCE CALCULATIONS

"To calculate operators needed, add up all the cycle times and divide by the takt time. Total cycle time divided by takt time."
Kaizen Event Implementation Manual, p. 86

"Dividing the work content by the takt time reveals [the number of resources required].
Learning To See, p. 63

HOUSEKEEPING

"Our former colleagues at Toyota and Honda will tell you that 25-30% of all quality defects are directly related to [cleanliness in the workplace]."
Lean Transformation, p. 100

SOURCES

BALANCE

"The objective is to have each operation or group of operations match the takt time of the line (which will match the takt time of the customer demand). each operation must take about the same length of time."
Lean Transformation, p. 115

"Line balancing is a special challenge in mixed-model operations, because different models may have different work contents."
Japanese Manufacturing Techniques, p. 120

"Set the overall cycle time to balance the rate of production with rate of consumption. Adjust the work content to match the work cycle time at each station with the required cycle time."
APICS Just-In-Time Certification Review, p. 147

EMPLOYEE FLEXIBILITY

"Cross training of the operators on the assembly line is crucial to the success of a lean producer, as we will see in 'Flexing the Line'."
Lean Transformation, p. 119

[Example of Production Multi-Skill Chart]
Lean Transformation, p. 120

"You might decide to deploy seven instead of ten [operators], and have these seven "flex" to cover what would be more workstations in a full-capacity situation."
Lean Transformation, p. 121

[Graphic example of Flexing]
Lean Transformation, p. 122

"Production lines: Western vs. Japanese. Western top priority: line balance. Japanese top priority: flexibility."
Japanese Manufacturing Techniques, p. 133

KANBAN

"The order point, that is, the quantity at which parts must be ordered, is determined by the formula: Order Point = Daily quantity consumed x production cycle time + safety valve quantity."
Shingo, A Study of the Toyota Production System, p. 168

"The kanban system works on the simple principle of replenishment…Kanbans are the way a customer's takt time, the factory, and your suppliers all stay in sync.
Lean Transformation, p. 125

[Graphic Example of Supermarket concept]
Lean Transformation, p. 126

SOURCES

"In many cases, certain items are ordered infrequently, say every few months, in unpredictable quantities...This is where a one-time kanban can be used."
Lean Transformation, p. 133

"Kanban literally translated, means "visible record" or "visible plate". More generally, kanban is taken to mean "card"."
Japanese Manufacturing Techniques, p. 219

"Wouldn't it be logical for the earlier process to make only the number of parts withdrawn? We will call this means of indication *kanban* (sign board) and circulate it between each of the processes to control the amount of production, that is, the amount needed."
Toyota Production System, p. 5

VISUAL SIGNALS

"A common method of signaling a downed line is an "andon light"...green means everything is running okay, yellow means that there is a material shortage, and red means that the line is down due to a machine problem, and immediate help is needed."
Lean Transformation, p. 148

"Complete display, so everyone can see where production stands at every moment, is an excellent example of another critical lean technique, *transparency* or *visual controls*."
Lean Thinking, p. 56

"The switches turn on yellow or red lights, which signal a warning or stop the line, respectively...This is a Toyota type of display (called an andon)..."
Japanese Manufacturing Techniques, p. 77

"Visibility systems included posted schedules and results, physical layout, signal lights, charts and logs, limited inventory and color coding."
APICS Just-In-Time Certification Review, p. 34

LINE DESIGN

"It is Process Engineering's responsibility to translate customer takt time into continuous flow processes."
Lean Transformation, p. 199

[Graphic: Creating a flow shop sequence]
APICS Just-In-Time Certification Review, p. 97

ADMINISTRATIVE FLOW

"The reengineering movement has recognized that departmentalized thinking is sub optimal and has tried to shift the focus from organizational categories (departments) to value-creating "processes".
Lean Thinking, p. 23

SOURCES

"The kaizen process in the office melds thinking and doing, planning and acting, just as it does in the plant."
Lean Thinking, p. 122

"Kanban systems are extremely effective in simplifying office work and giving autonomy to the factory floor."
Shingo, A Study of the Toyota Production System, p. 188

QUALITY

"Correcting one's own errors: The worker or work group that made the bad parts performs the rework itself to correct the errors.:
Japanese Manufacturing Techniques, p. 61

"Certification is positive knowledge of total process control, not absence of previous complaints, acceptably low defect rates or a legal document."
APICS Just-In-Time Certification Review, p. 58

"A supplier can be designated as a JIT supplier when predetermined quality, cost, delivery and count objectives are met."
APICS Just-In-Time Certification Review, p. 166

"For a complete elimination of defects, 100 percent inspection must be adapted."
Shingo, A Study of the Toyota Production System, p. 117

PLANNING

"The Kawasaki plant also follows the Japanese TQC pattern of not scheduling at full capacity."
Japanese Manufacturing Techniques, p. 77

[Listing of JIT benefits for material procurement]
Japanese Manufacturing Techniques, p. 160

METRICS

"Obsolete measurements of performance include equipment utilization, worker efficiency, individual incentives and costing based on direct labor hours."
APICS Just-In-Time Certification Review, p. 215

"Linearity is production at a constant quantity, or use of resources at a level rate, typically measured daily or more frequently."
APICS Just-In-Time Certification Review, Glossary

" A 10 to 20 percent improvement in productivity and considerable reductions in finished product stocks are usually achieved [through mixed model production]."
Shingo, A Study of the Toyota Production System, p. 136

SOURCES

HISTORY

"Production lines are certainly not a Japanese innovation."
Shoenberger, Japanese Manufacturing Techniques, p. 131

SYSTEMS

"If this sounds complicated it is because trying to run operations off of MRP systems doesn't work well."
Learning To See, p. 72

APPENDIX

4

**FLOW
FORMULAS**

FLOW MANUFACTURING FORMULAS

TAKT TIME CALCULATION

$$\text{TAKT TIME} = \frac{\text{W MIN}}{\text{VOL}}$$

Where

W MIN = Workday Time Available
VOL = Throughput Volume for the process

RESOURCES REQUIRED

$$\text{RESOURCES} = \frac{\text{ST}}{\text{TAKT}} \quad \text{or} \quad \frac{\text{STw}}{\text{TAKT}}$$

Where

ST = Standard Time for the process
STw = Weighted Average Standard Time for the process
TAKT = Takt time for the process

WEIGHTED AVERAGE STANDARD TIME

$$\text{STw} = \frac{\sum (\text{ST} * \text{VOL})}{\sum \text{VOL}}$$

Where

$\sum$ = Sum symbol
ST = Standard Time for the process, by model
VOL = Throughput volume for the process, by model

KANBAN SIZING FORMULA (2 BIN)

$\text{KANBAN}_{\text{LINE}} = \text{FDU} * (1+\text{SSF}) * \text{DF} * \text{LF}$
$\text{KANBAN}_{\text{SUPERMARKET}} = \text{FDU} * (1+\text{SSF}) * \text{DF}$
$\text{KANBAN}_{\text{STORES}} = \text{FDU} * (1+\text{SSF}) * \text{DF}$

Where

FDU = Forecasted Daily Usage
SSF = Safety Stock Factor
DF = Delivery Frequency
LF = Line Consumption Factor

ADDITIONAL INVENTORY

$$\text{INV} = \frac{\text{W MIN}}{\text{TAKT}} - \frac{\text{W MIN}}{\text{ST}}$$

Where

INV = Additional Inventory
W MIN = Workday Time Available
TAKT = Takt time of the line or cell
ST = Standard Time of the imbalanced workstation

ADDITIONAL TIME REQUIRED

$$\text{TIME} = \text{INV} * \text{ST}$$

Where

INV = The additional inventory required to overcome a chronic imbalance
ST = Standard Time of the imbalanced workstation

INDEX

INDEX

INDEX

INDEX

INDEX

INDEX

INDEX

ABOUT
THE
AUTHORS

AUTHORS

Gerard Leone, MS IE - MBA

During Mr. Leone's nearly 20-year career in manufacturing management and consulting he had the opportunity to work with a broad range of manufacturing enterprises. Originally from Buenos Aires, Argentina, his multilingual skills have been a very valuable tool in spreading the word of Flow Manufacturing around the world. He taught statistics at the University of Buenos Aires and Production Management at Colorado State University, his two Alma Maters.

A widely recognized leader in the fields of productivity improvement and manufacturing systems, Gerard has instructed and implemented Flow Processing techniques in the factory and in the office with companies like GN ReSound, The New Piper Aircraft, Whirlpool, Mobile Tool International, Lucent Technologies, Beltone, AVAYA, Thermo King and Boeing, to name a few.

Today, Mr. Leone is a Senior partner with the **Business Process Consulting Group**, a consulting firm dedicated to training and consulting in Flow Processing for the factory and the office, based in Littleton, Colorado. He can be contacted at:

Business Process Consulting Group
PO Box 270650
Littleton, Colorado 80127-0011
gleone@bpcg.us
Ph 720-981-1111
www.bpcgflow.com

Photo © Judith Philips

AUTHORS

Richard D. Rahn, MBA, CPIM

Richard D. Rahn is the president of **FlowAlliance** a Flow Manufacturing consulting, publishing and software tools firm headquartered in Boulder, Colorado. Formerly a vice-president with both the Kiran Consulting Group and the John Costanza Institute, Richard is a recognized leader in training and implementation of Flow Manufacturing. He has lead over 30 successful implementation programs in the US, Canada, Europe and Mexico, and has trained over 3,000 manufacturing professionals in Flow Manufacturing techniques. He has introduced Flow Manufacturing to some of the world's largest companies, including General Motors, Johnson & Johnson, John Deere, Kodak and Emerson Electric.

FlowAlliance is a pioneer in the development of lean tools for Flow Manufacturing, including the use of computer simulation modeling and Advanced Planning methodologies. This approach is presented in Richard's first book, *Advanced Flow Manufacturing*.

Richard was raised in Manila and Mexico City, and teaches and consults in Spanish and English. He graduated Cum Laude from Middlebury College, Middlebury, Vermont and received his MBA from the University of Colorado. He has 14 years of manufacturing and management experience with Ball Aerospace in Boulder, Colorado and Storage Technology Corporation in Louisville, Colorado. Flow Manufacturing has been his specialty for the past 12 years.

He can be contacted at:

FlowAlliance
7690 Watonga Way
Boulder, Colorado 80303
(303) 494-4693
richard.rahn@flowalliance.com
www.flowalliance.com

Photo © Judith Philips

Also Available From Flow Publishing
www.flowpublishing.com
contact@flowpublishing.com

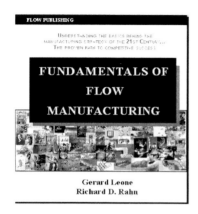

"Finally, a comprehensive yet practical book on flow manufacturing. This book should be required reading for all levels and functions in all manufacturing operations. Leone and Rahn have laid out a straightforward approach you can start applying immediately. Well done!"

John J. Gallo
Vice President of Product Operations
The New Piper Aircraft, Inc.

ISBN 0-9713031-8-5
Paperback
$34.95

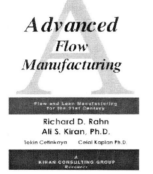

Not every flow/lean manufacturing effort is successful, but the fault is not with the techniques. Company after company has proven that flow/lean manufacturing works. So why do implementations get off track? Discover is this book:

♦ How to eliminate risk and uncertainty from your line design
♦ The two necessary tools: modeling and Advanced Planning
♦ How to debug your design *before* you implement it
♦ The key benefits of flow, and why it is a requirement today

ISBN 0-9713031-9-3
Paperback
$15.95

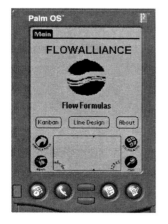

Flow Formulas is a companion tool for Fundamentals of Flow Manufacturing for the Palm Pilot PDA. All of the flow/lean manufacturing formulas are included. Each formula is explained in detail, and a calculation page allows you to enter and calculate actual results for each formula.

ISBN 0-9713031-7-7
Palm Software
$19.95

ORDER FORM

Fundamentals of Flow Manufacturing: $34.95
Advanced Flow Manufacturing: $15.95
Flow Formulas Palm Application: $19.95
Shipping: $4.00
(add $2.00 per additional title)

Title	Quantity	Price
	Shipping	
	Order Total	

☐ Check   ☐ Credit Card   Order online at
www.flowpublishing.com

_____

Card Number   Expiration   Signature

Contact/Shipping Information:

Name	Company	
Address		
City	State	Zip
Telephone	Fax	
Email		

Please fax this form to Flow Publishing: (303) 494-4693 or mail it to:
Flow Publishing, 7690 Watonga Way, Boulder, Colorado 80303.